DOG DAYS

Elspeth Barker

DOG DAYS

Selected Writings

Elspeth Barker

BLACK DOG
BOOKS

for Bill

First published in England 2012
Black Dog Books, 104 Trinity Street, Norwich, Norfolk, NR2 2BJ.
www.blackdogbooks.co.uk

Text © Elspeth Barker

Front cover portrait © Pippa King

All rights reserved. No part of this publication may be reproduced, stored in a retrieval system, or transmitted in any form or by any means, electronic, mechanical, photocopying, recording or otherwise, without the prior permission of the copyright holders.

A CIP record of this book is available from the British Library.

ISBN 978-0-9565672-1-5

Typeset in 11.5/15 point Times.

Printed in Great Britain by HSW Print, South Wales

CONTENTS

WORDS FROM THE HENHOUSE   7

Moving On

BIRDS OF EARTH AND AIR   13
FIFE   18
MOMENT OF TRUTH   24
BY HEART: *Elizabeth Smart: A Life*   29
THE CHAMELEON POET   33
MEMORIES OF GEORGE BARKER   36
THE LONGEST GOODBYE   38
BROKEN HEARTED   41
CHERUBIM   45
A HANDBOOK ON GOOD MANNERS FOR CHILDREN   48
JEALOUSY   50
MOVING ON   53

Literary Lives

ALEXANDER THE GREAT	59
TENNYSON	63
WRITING DANGEROUSLY: *Mary McCarthy and Her World*	65
OTHER PEOPLE: *Diaries 1963-66* FRANCES PARTRIDGE	68
GAVIN MAXWELL	70
IN EXTREMIS: LAURA RIDING	73
PATRICK HAMILTON	76
ROALD DAHL	79
ROBERT LOUIS STEVENSON	84
HENRIETTA MORAES	87
EVELYN WAUGH	89
CHRISTINA ROSSETTI	93
FISHER'S FACE	97
ANGUS WILSON	100
PAUL GAUGUIN	104
LETTERS OF JOHN BETJEMAN *Vol Two 1951-84*	107
THE YEATS SISTERS	110
R D LAING: *A Divided Self*	112
SELECTED LETTERS OF EDITH SITWELL	115
SKATING TO ANTARCTICA: JENNY DISKI	119
THE NINE LIVES OF NAOMI MITCHISON	122
FANNY BURNEY	126
MY FATHER'S PLACES: AERONWY THOMAS	131
JANE'S FAME	134
A JURY OF HER PEERS: *American Women Writers*	137

Thoughts in a Garden

THOUGHTS IN A GARDEN	143
A NATURAL HISTORY OF UNICORNS	146
APRIL	149
AMPHIBIANS	152
PORTIA	155
DOG DAYS	161
HENS I HAVE KNOWN	167
FRIENDLY FIRE	171
SPRING	176
THE DRIVER'S SEAT	179
AUF WIEDERSEHEN PETS	182
EAST ANGLIA: *A Literary Pilgrimage*	184
THREE NORFOLK ARTISTS	187

Telling Tales

CATULLUS *Charles Martin*	197
AMERICAN GHOSTS AND OLD WORLD WONDERS *Angela Carter*	201
THE INFINITE PLAN *Isabel Allende*	204
LOVE AND SUMMER *William Trevor*	206
ELECTRICITY *Victoria Glendinning*	208
THE INFERNO OF DANTE *trs Robert Pinsky*	210
BABEL TOWER *A S Byatt*	214
A BOTTLE IN THE SHADE *Peter Levi*	217
THE WITCH OF EXMOOR *Margaret Drabble*	220

EVERY MAN FOR HIMSELF   *Beryl Bainbridge*   222

THE UNTOUCHABLE   *John Banville*   224

GRACE NOTES   *Bernard MacLaverty*   227

VITA BREVIS   *Jostein Gaarder*   229

CASANOVA   *Andrew Miller*   232

LAVINIA   *Ursula Le Guin*   234

COUNTING THE STARS   *Helen Dunmore*   237

A MERCY   *Toni Morrison*   240

THE GOOD PARENTS   *Joan London*   243

COLLECTED STORIES   *William Trevor*   246

THE ARABIAN NIGHTS   *trs Malcolm C Lyons*   248

WORDS FROM THE HENHOUSE

'Tis pleasant, sure, to see one's name in print!
A book's a book, although there's nothing in't.

I remember these lines of Byron from childhood; and the thrilling image of the dark leather cover, the gold lettering. Imagination ventured no further; the pages remained blank. Later I read of Colette's father's unpublished book, always kept on a high shelf, an object of awe to his children. Whatever his shortcomings, he had *written a book*, and, one day it would be off into the wide, eager world. In stealth and solitude, after many years, his daughter dared to draw it from the shelf. Nothing in't.

There is a yawning abyss between wanting to have written and actually writing. As a child I wrote, variously in the derelict henhouse, the loo, or the glory hole under the stairs, perilously illuminated by candle stubs. It was clear to me that this had to be a secret activity, although my mother, who had always read aloud to us, was fervently encouraging. She said, 'You must go for long walks to gain inspiration.' One of the attractions of writing was that it was an indoor occupation; fresh air and exercise had no part to play. Also I didn't want anyone to see what I had written. Mostly I wrote moody verses about pine trees and winter seashores, or vengeful ballads inspired particularly by 'Binnorie':

> *The eldest cam' and pushed her in. . .*
> *Sister O sister, sink or swim. . .*

Prose works concerned horses and dogs. I had almost finished a novella, 'Buccaneer, the Story of an Exmoor Pony' (influenced more than a little by *Black Beauty, Lorna Doone, My Friend Flicka, Bambi* by Felix Salten, and a host of others), when my mother found it, stole it and lost it. I loved then the physical act of writing, the imprint of the nib on the fresh paper, the pleasurably painful inky bump on my middle finger. I always wrote with my fountain pen; writing was too sacred for the banalities of dip pen and inkwell. My pigtails used to fall forward and drift across the page, leaving a smudgy wake. I knotted them together and held the ends in my teeth. My shoes had to be laced up very tight before I could begin. At horrible girls' boarding school, and at university I continued to write, extremely awful verse supposedly in the manner of Hopkins or Yeats. I stalked the streets of Oxford shrouded in lengths of purple taffeta, hoping to resemble Maud Gonne, or Emily Brontë, who is unlikely to have had a use for purple taffeta. After Oxford I went to London to write my great novel. In fact, all my energies were taken up by waitressing in Lyons Corner Houses and dodging about the underground in flight from a lunatic Nigerian who claimed to have married me by proxy. Back in my freezing, lightless garret I began to realise that I knew nothing and had nothing to say. I lost two stone and wrote not a word.

Then came marriage, and babies, lovely babies, cherubim. I couldn't have enough of them. Writing faded into a dim aspiration, a Maybe one day. Suddenly they were all grown up. There was time; I could stay awake after nine o'clock in the evening. I could even read books. But with the passing years had come self-doubt.

> *If the sun and the moon should doubt,*
> *They would both immediately go out,*

observed William Blake (or something to that effect).

'There are twenty-four hours in the day and twenty-six letters in the alphabet. All you have to do is rearrange them,' urged my husband. Robert Louis Stevenson wrote *Dr Jekyll and Mr Hyde* in three days while ill in bed. None of this helped. My oldest daughter, now working on a glossy magazine, telephoned. 'Mum, you know how you're always going on about your hens. We're doing an Easter feature with hen *things*. Write something.'

'I will, I will,' I cried, but did nothing.

She telephoned again. 'I'm coming home this weekend. Have you done your hen piece?'

'Yes,' said I. Driven by panic I wrote three thousand words overnight on the glories of hens I had known. The glossy wanted a hundred rather different words to thread around photographs of egg-cups and hen tea-cosies. I sent my article to *The Observer*, who took it and printed it, and asked me for another. Then came a magic, dream letter from the fiction editor of a publishing house. She had read my pieces; was I thinking of writing a book? If so, she would be very interested. I could not believe this letter's existence; I stood washing clothes at the sink and kept looking back at it on the kitchen table. At one point, in fact, it disappeared and I thought I had indeed been dreaming; it turned up again among my son's car documents.

I sent two thousand words off to the publishers. A week later, on Robert Burns' night, I came home from work to find a letter waiting. In mortal fear I made beds, brought in firewood, fed animals, put supper on, before I opened it, hoping that God would look kindly on my simple toil and reward me for it. He did. My almost non-existent novel had been accepted. Outside a hurricane was blasting about. What cared I? I drove ten miles through blackness and falling trees and lagoons of ice water to buy celebration drink. In the morning there were six trees down around our house and no way out. There was nothing to do but write.

In a year's time, also, oddly, on Robert Burns' night, the book was finished. My exhilaration then was even greater than it had been on the night of acceptance. I had done what I had set out to do. I knew that it would be published. I had written a book. It seemed as marvellous and metaphysical as calling a bird down from the sky. I expected nothing further; it was enough in itself. Over that year I had discovered one or two things which surprised me, although they may seem obvious. I found that writing came to me in spasms, sometimes for two or three weeks at a time, often for much less. Between those spasms were ghastly periods of the familiar self-doubt and fear. When the book was going well I lost all sense of time and place. Once I wrote for thirteen hours and thought it had been three. I was convinced that I couldn't do dialogue and prevented my characters from speaking for one third of the book. Then I discovered that it wasn't so hard as I had thought. Having only written articles before, and precious few at that, I enjoyed the leisurely pace of a longer form, and the sudden realisation that I could make the characters do anything I liked, moving them back and forth through time. Possibly the barren periods are inscrutably productive; I write in longhand, and do no rewriting. Often I don't know what is going to happen next and the pen surprises me. Moments like these make the hours of solitude and cold, the anti-social nature of one's task, exciting and worthwhile. Just as often I stare at the blank white sky and the blank white paper and wonder why I ever thought writing was a good idea. This is a mystery. I can only explain it as an addiction to words, a constant nagging in the bleak recesses of the skull. At the beginning of the day I will do almost anything to avoid the moment of picking up the pen, even when things have gone well the day before. I'd rather wash the kitchen floor. I'd rather unblock the drains. But then, on a good day, to write gives me more happiness than almost anything I now know. And all you need is an A4 pad and a pen.

MOVING ON

BIRDS OF EARTH AND AIR

With what a commotion of wings and legs and beaks and damp earth do we come thudding into the world. Thank you, friendly stork. As for leaving, we hope to be ushered hence by flights of angels. In the interim the plumed ones weave their mysterious ways through our lives. The Roman armies carried sacred chickens into the battlefield and much was made of the scatter of corn from their beaks as they stamped their excitement at feeding time (*tripudium solistimum*) – literally, the most perfect stamping. The flights and cries and formations of birds informed the augurs of divine censure or approval; birds encountered on journeys were significant too, as indeed they are now. Do we not feel chosen, blessed even, by a heron rowing its way across the heavens, an owl's motionless glare from a pine branch, the harping outstretched flight of swans? Are we not accursed by the single magpie? How hard it is to break the curse by crossing oneself and spitting, while steering one's vehicle along life's motorway.

The crowing of the cock at Gethsemane or indeed in any early morning may betoken disaster one way or another; they crow by day and they crow by night and they just don't care, although some people do, especially those who have left the city for the great enfolding peace of the countryside. Pigeons make a lot of noise too in the country. Londoners are rude and uncaring about these fine birds. Although we do eat them out here in the rural, their great confusion of cooing is one of summer's most divine orchestrations. On an August night in Northumberland I watched shooting stars plunge across the black sky and woke at dawn to massed choirs of pigeons in fugue: 'I mourn, I mourn,' calling and calling over and again 'for my love, my love, my love.' By day I climbed the hill and found myself on Flodden Field where one summer afternoon in 1513 the English hacked to pieces the Scottish king and his nobles, the Flowers of the Forest. It was all over by teatime. Still the birds sob in the woods.

For myself, my first objective memory, outside the dim, cosy, nursery world, is of a bird, a huge white seagull perched, motionless and marmoreal, on top of the drawing room door. We children had been plucked from our beds and brought down to see him; he stared sideways at us from an unwinking angry golden eye.

My father came from a long line of parrot-keeping men. From his infancy, around 1913, he could remember a white cockatoo who had campaigned with Wellington's 'infamous army' in 1815. This bird, almost a century old, spoke, or rather swore, in a version of English long gone from the world, just distinguishable, and as my father put it, fruity. His own parrot, an African Grey called Punlel, did not swear but enjoyed a spot of sarcasm 'very funny, very funny, that's very funny, good night.' He bit female children. My grandfather's African Grey also bit female children and when he first bit me, aged four, I was violently sick into his cage. Punlel, some twenty-five years later, bit my four year old daughter, who reacted identically. A delightful moment of mother and daughter communion. Pun slalomed expertly about the dining table and with his harsh African cries terrorised the gentle Scottish garden birds as he patrolled the lawns. You will have heard of them, mavis, laverock and throstle. When he was nineteen years old, Pun laid an egg. It was too late then for us to recreate him in Eve's image, and he continued his transgender life for a further three decades.

Where I grew up there were jackdaws everywhere, in the trees, in the chimneys, and all too often in the fire. 'Suttee?' quavered my grandmother, who had lived long in India. The bird I have loved most was a jackdaw. I found him in long wet grass, crying most piteously, a tiny pink form almost entirely composed of a gaping cross-billed mouth. Perhaps he had been flung from his tree-top nest because of the crossed bill, or perhaps the fall had caused it. Anyhow, in the way of children of those days, I brought him in and kept him warm in a haybox, and fed him from the back of a silver mustard spoon. Astonishingly, he survived, became fledged, learnt to fly and catch beetles in his crossed bill. I took him back then to become a bird in the pine grove where I found him and he soared up into the dark branches. I sat alone in my bedroom; with a heavy heart I contemplated his empty box and the traces of down caught in the hay; before the first tear had rolled the length of my cheek, he was at the window, tapping. He was always completely free to come and go as he pleased, and he remained with me for eleven years, taking off from my lofty sill into the windy skies or mounting enjoyable raids on the jackdaw colonials in the countless chimney pots; he would march round the edge of the chimney poking his head in and screeching until the inmates lost patience and emerged in a great furious fluster to pursue him back to the triumphant safety of my open window. My room became a guano-ridden cavern and my books to this day bear his mark; some have torn pages, too, for he had no time for reading and would rip the paper impatiently. Henry James and Jane Austen drew particular hostility. Everywhere possible he went with me, perched on my shoulder, or flying ahead and back and round in circles. My horse became resentfully accustomed to his presence on her withers. In the car he was happy to travel on my lap, but there were journeys on which he was unwelcome, like the 80-mile round trip to the dentist. Then, and only then, he was a dreadful nuisance, pursuing the car and trying to settle on the bonnet like a parody of the Rolls-Royce nymph. In the end I removed my little sisters' dolls house and made it into a holding centre for these occasions.

The castle staircase was immense, rising in stately measure from the vaulted entrance hall and gradually narrowing as it spiralled upwards, all grim grey stone. Claws, as I called him, never flew up or downstairs, but hopped his way, step by step, a sight immeasurably poignant, reminding me of Catullus's heartbreaking image of his mistress's dead pet bird on its dark path to the underworld, hopping too. The most marvellous of all his gifts to me was in essence metaphysical. I would see him, a dark speck among the tumbling clouds, and call his name, three times always, and see him swoop from the heavens in an unfaltering ellipse to my shoulder. To call a bird from the air is so extraordinary, rivalled in my experience only by the appearance of one's abstraction of thoughts and images in the tangible form of a book. And even then, the bird wins.

From the beginning, Punlel and Claws chose to ignore each other; one afternoon they ignored each other a little too much and collided on the luncheon table. Pun was executing a daring skiing manoeuvre and Claws as usual was tripping from plate to plate, helping himself with undiscriminating relish from grey mounds of well-cooked cabbage and tremulous orange jelly. A cross-billed jackdaw enjoying orange jelly is a painterly sight; words like shard, stipple, lucent, even chiaroscuro leap to the lip. (A Labrador engaged on a Hobnob is good, too.) The impact was shocking to both birds and resulted in synchronised shrieking, feather loss, broken china and a temporary ban from family meals.

At the sea, my parents had a normal house, which they reached each summer after a migration of insane proportions, involving cars, trains, a carrier lorry, baggage rolls containing blankets and saucepans and supplementary furniture and cooking devices and cages, on the just-in-case principle which makes life so difficult. All the animals, birds, fish and reptiles, came, as well as we five children, Nanny, Nanny's helper, and Nanny's sister. I have horrible memories of the horses escaping from the train and galloping down the railway line, and the scrabble of the tortoises' claws against the floor of their box as the train swung over the perilous Tay Bridge. My jackdaw enjoyed these holidays, cruising low along the beach over picnicking families; how envious they were when he landed on our rug. He slept always on the end of my bed and his still brooding form in the twilight gave me a great desire to teach him to say 'Never more'. Imagine my astonishment when he interrupted my patient repetitions of this phrase and said 'Never mind' in a patronising, manly voice. This was the evildoing of my brother. 'Never mind' was all Claws ever said and as my brother pointed out, it is a more useful phrase than 'Never more.'

One spring he started bringing things, leaves and twigs and feathers and scissors and setting them in my pocket. Then he climbed into my pocket and stared at me sideways and twisted his head about as if beckoning. A quick referral to Lorenz's *King Solomon's Ring* told me that Claws was offering me matrimony. My first ever proposal; my truest lover. O *lacrimae rerum*.

He might have lived for fifty years or more had I not at last betrayed him by leaving home to seek my fortune. My sisters offered love and care but he would have none. For a few weeks he hardly stirred from my empty chamber. Then one bitter winter morning he flew repeatedly into the castle wall and killed himself.

Other birds have shaped my life in other ways. As an indolent and bookish child, I used to hide in the henhouse and read all afternoon while my parents thought I was out in the fresh air building dams. The hens were friendly enough but they died away swiftly in the jaws of the Golden Retriever, and his vigorous assistant, the Irish Terrier. Then the dogs were obliged to wear the hens' corpses slung around their necks to teach them a lesson. They did not learn their lesson, and soon I had the henhouse to myself. I made it into a delightful secret study with cardboard box bookshelves, a torch, exercise books and bottles of Quink. Thus began my literary life.

Years later, and many birds later, a piece I wrote, about hens I have known, for a Sunday newspaper, inspired a publisher to suggest a novel. I could say a great deal about interesting hens, and also about owls; my mother, from time to time, raised baby owls in her tower, untroubled by their disgusting eating habits. But dwelling as one does in time and space, one must call it a day. I shall mention only that in Crete the tiny owl *stryx*, marks the passing of darkness into dawn with a final melodious single yelp; immediately after this comes the first crow of the cock, the first bray of the ass. Here in Norfolk three delightful Indian Runner ducks have joined me. They live in the garden where my American spouse makes busy, fetching bowls of snails for their degustation; they require that he crack the shells. Fortunately he has German blood. I am hoping to persuade them to move occasionally in graceful single file up and down the stairs; they will show to great advantage against the yellow wall. And when Winter begins we plan a pair of Muscovies to warm our laps for Sunday evening television.

FIFE

The Ancient Kingdom of Fife forms a blunt peninsula which shoulders out into the North Sea, bounded on one side by the Firth of Forth. Driving up from Edinburgh, you used to take the ferry across, under the shadow of the mighty railway bridge, where men suspended in little baskets were eternally repainting, eternally and fruitlessly, for as soon as they reached the end they had to start again.

Battleships and submarines gleamed in the shifting sunlight and sometimes a school of porpoises performed acrobatics beyond the ferry's wake. Cars were assisted on and off board by a turntable which pointed them in the right direction, leaving no chance of driver error. This was a relief to me, for the whelming deep washed voraciously on to the end of the pier and was all too visible through the many fissures of the ramps. Sweet and green, the hills of Fife welcomed us like a benison.

So it was in those days. Now traffic goes roaring over the Forth Road Bridge, which takes time off the journey but mars the significance of crossing the water, the sense of entering another land. The coastal villages and small towns, however, have not changed very much. Kirkcaldy, home of linoleum, still smells deliciously of linseed oil; Leven sprawls more than it did, and has an air of loucheness uncharacteristic of cleanly East Fife. Nearby are the caves of Wemyss and their Bronze-Age drawings; here you may see the earliest depictions of a boat to be found in these islands. There used to be boatyards all along this stretch, with seagulls marching proprietorially over the great vaulting wooden ribs which dominated the quaysides.

In Largo, Alexander Selkirk was born; it was he who so enraged his fellow mariners that they dumped him on the island of Juan Fernandez. After four years of solitude he was rescued, and recycled for posterity as Robinson Crusoe. But for me this is all peripheral.

Two places form the heartland of my Fife, and the first of these is Elie. Elie is an old fishing village; its houses, many of them crowstepped and gabled, border a wide, curving bay. At one end of the bay looms the harbour and gaunt stone granary; at the other end Elie has merged into Earlsferry. A dark and rock-strewn headland encloses the pale shore. Round the point lies another bay, then more cliffs, higher and menacing. Here Macduff took to a boat and fled from Macbeth across the water, leaving his family behind:

The Thane of Fife had a wife.
Where is she now?

Macduff evidently knew where he was going. As a child I assumed that the smudge of land you could sometimes see on the far horizon was Abroad. Abroad was only visible when rain was threatening and the light inky and lurid.

I had a great fear of war, and when the occasional plane came droning over from that inscrutable foreign land (in fact, the coastline of North Berwick) I would flatten myself in the dunes, and hold my breath and pray until the danger had passed.

Almost everything that I remember of Elie centres around the beach. It is a perfect place for little children. They play now as I did, as my father did 100 years ago. Sandcastles, digging to Australia, rock pools and shrimping nets. Nothing has changed; there is no promenade, no commercial aid to maritime pleasure. The faded beach huts are still dotted along the shore. One of the excitements of New Year was always the abrupt departure of these huts into the massive

January tides which came lashing over the sea wall, drowning the harbour road and seriously inconveniencing the clientele of the Ship Inn. Once a derelict whale rolled up on the sands. We were not allowed to go near it on the grounds that it might explode. Eventually it was removed on a system of rollers and ropes, dragged by eight Clydesdale cart horses.

On the far side of the harbour is another bay, known as Ruby Bay, where a ship of the Spanish Armada, blown far off course, spilled a cargo of rubies on to the sea bed. To this day, children still find their glowing fragments scattered about the shore among the white cowrie shells and black bladderwrack. A slope of grass, starry with thrift, climbs towards the lighthouse and the Lady's Tower, once a discreet bathing place.

In summer, Mr. Haig's beach ponies used to plod tirelessly up and down the central bay. They wore scarlet or yellow harness and jingling bells; their saddles had horns to hold on to. Sometimes a fluffy foal frisked alongside and one year there was a black baby donkey. To belong to the select band whom Mr. Haig allowed to lead the ponies on their threepenny or sixpenny treks was every child's ambition. It was my first taste of elitism. The other great attraction in the summer months was the Children's Special Service Mission, known as the Cism. Each morning we laboured with buckets and spades and built a great altar and studded it with arabesques of shells and frondy whorls of seaweed. Then we sat behind it on the warm, soft sand and sang:

'I'm H.A.P.P.Y, I'm H.A.P.P.Y
I know I am, I'm sure I am,
I'm H.A.P.P.Y'

Beyond the altar the gulls swooped and cried, the sea glittered and the day dazzled with promise. Life was a sunlit dream where you wore your bathing suit all the time.

As children grow older, they require danger. The cliffs at the end of

West Bay are wild, slippery and lethal. To clamber round them you need nerve and expertise, neither of which I had. Nonetheless I forced myself along tiny ledges above jagged, gurgling gullies, clung to the towering basalt pillars, leapt inelegantly over chasms. It was always terrifying, and it was always thrilling.

Seals play in the waters here, and flocks of cormorants skim through the waves or stand motionless on the rocks. The water is very deep, translucent and green as glass. Behind Elie, there is an old and hallowed golf course, but it never attracted me. My brother, my enemy, used to whirl his driver round his head, let go and send it hurtling like a cruise missile straight at me. Golf balls whistled past my temples. No thanks.

Gradually, too, the beach lost its charms for me. I became a fat sullen teenager who refused to be seen in a bathing suit. I sat scowling on the sand while my little sisters dug and delved with infant absorption. The bright sea wind baked the scowl on to my face; once it stayed there for 36 hours. Although I continued to join in my family's mammoth, thrice-yearly migration from our home in the north to the house by the sea, it was against my will and I remember nothing of those times apart from the insane scale of the operation, which involved five children, nannies, dogs, the chief cat, budgerigars, tortoises, goldfish, a parrot, a jackdaw and for a while two horses, who travelled by train until the day when they escaped and wrought havoc at Elie station. Thereafter they were banned from seaside holidays. Lucky them, I thought. Only when I had children of my own did I realise again what an enchantment I had wilfully lost.

Elie has a southerly aspect. A chain of small fishing villages leads northward, round the point of Fife Ness towards St. Andrews. Each of these villages, St. Monans, Pittenweem, Anstruther, has its own grave charm like Elie; though they have their share of winter's blast, in my recollection they are always sunlit, bright with the impulse of the moment, the gull swooping, a blue boat lifting on the wave, the slap of water on the jetty. They are also pragmatic. Near the tip of the peninsula, Crail has many of the summer delights of those other villages, but is hard going in winter. Robert Louis Stevenson, who took some pleasure in Scotland's desolate places, found Crail too much for him: 'This grey, grim, sea beaten hole,' he wrote.

Once you round the tip you are on to the northern outlook and St. Andrews is another matter altogether. Its shattered towers, gaunt and spectral on their rocky headland, stare unforgivingly northwards to the Arctic. On still days the haar, the mist off the North Sea, drifts inland, enfolding and darkening the tall stone houses, casting a dank gleam on the slate roofs; beads of moisture cling to your hair, and you ponder the phrase 'chilled to the bone'.

Or sky and sea merge and the tossing gulls are indistinguishable from the foam flinging up off the waves. Then the east wind comes whipping in sheer and sharp, freighted with the snows of Siberia. At night in bed you can't sleep for thinking of those lines from Wordsworth's 'The Idiot Boy':

His teeth, they chatter, chatter still,
Like a loose casement in the wind.

You will never be warm again. Conversely, if you decide you can bear it no longer, and go to the beguiling, decadent South (England), you will not need an overcoat for many years – not until that primal immunity has worn off. All this I know because I spent four years at boarding school in St. Andrews. Enough of that. There is a great deal more to St. Andrews than the plaint of a shivering schoolgirl.

Mary Queen of Scots came here, staying in a room which is part of my old school's library. As her ship neared the lowering, wind-beaten cliffs, according to William Shakespeare:

the rude sea grew civil at her song
And certain stars shot madly from their spheres
To hear the sea maid's music.

Some would have it that these lines refer to certain political displacements. I prefer the image as it is. What music? 'Plaisir d'Amour' would suit. The doomed queen planted a hawthorn tree in the grounds of the ancient university, the oldest in Britain after Oxford and Cambridge. The hawthorn lives on, couchant rather than rampant, lovingly supported. The university has brought forth many great scholars, not least of them Andrew Lang:

St. Andrews by the Northern Sea
A haunted town it is to me,

he wrote and he found Oxford something of a disappointment later. The students' scarlet gowns mingle and separate around the grey buildings in a poignant counterpoint. Youth and age, colour and its absence. My grandfather studied Divinity here, here my parents met when they were students. The scarlet gown hung on the back of our nursery door, but not one of us took it up.

St. Andrews is to me a city (and it is a cathedral city, not a town) plangent with regrets and sorrows. The past has seen terrible violence, murders, beheadings and burnings at the stake. You can still see the window in the ruins of the castle from which Cardinal Beaton, lolling on silken cushions, surveyed the Protestant martyrs as they turned to charred bones.

The emphasis on the silken cushions is peculiarly St. Andrean. Would the scene have been any less horrible if he had knelt on the cold stone window ledge? The presence of the church dominates St. Andrews, even in these secular days. Like Oxford, it is a city of tolling bells.

Its very bleakness is fraught with wild romance; it is the perfect setting for a tragic love affair, Héloise and Abelard or Tristan and Iseult. If you walk towards the city along the West Sands, you will see it in its most sorrowful beauty. This is one of the great views of the world. It is both a *memento mori* and a monument to endurance.

I suppose I must also mention that St. Andrews is the golfer's Mecca. And summer comes there, and the sun does shine.

But these are not my concerns. One of these days I hope to become a ghost. Then I will float above the shadowy seals and dancing waves of Elie, and I will drift with the haar about the towers of St. Andrews.

MOMENT OF TRUTH
Unedited interview with Colette Douglas-Home

All my life I loved poetry and longed to meet a poet. From the age of 12 on, I used to pray to the moon with tightly clasped hands and pray 'Bring me a poet.' I had read George Barker's poetry before I met him and had that marvellous kind of thunderclap feeling – that 'Wow . . . I love this!' – and the tingling spine. And then I did meet him.

I was about 21 I think. I was living in Scotland at the time and had come down to London to see an old friend, Donald, who was in fact living in Rome and had met George there. George was also in London visiting Elizabeth Smart and his children and old friends. So we met up.

Donald took me over to meet George at Elizabeth's flat. I had met Elizabeth already two or three times and got on very well with her. George was not living with her, but staying with her. She had a huge rambling flat in Paddington and there was always room for him. He was living with another lady in Rome. That relationship was breaking up but I knew nothing about that at that time. He lived in Rome full stop.

And so we met and got extremely drunk. I think both of us drank whisky at Elizabeth's flat and George and I got on very badly indeed. Yes, well I was rather straight laced. He showed me his book called *View From a Blind Eye* which is in some ways the one I like least of his books. He showed me some poems that were meant to be funny and I didn't think they were funny and was drunk enough to say so. That caused such explosions of wrath. Nobody had ever been so rude to me ever and I was still young enough and Scottish enough, and, you know, well brought up to expect one was polite to one's elders and one's elders were polite back. I just couldn't believe it.

So anyway there was this massive bloody great row and the only odd thing about it was that Donald who was with me got fed up with me and went off to Chelsea where we were staying, so there I was. George's son Sebastian said I could sleep on the floor of his bedroom, no strings attached or anything. So when, at last, clearing up the whisky glasses time came, I made my way up to Sebastian's bedroom and George uncharacteristically pursued me upstairs saying 'Where are you going?' I said Sebastian had said I could sleep on his floor and he said 'Oh no you don't.' So he woke his daughter Rose up and forced her to get out a camp bed and even made some motions of pretending to help her make it up. I was to sleep in Rose's room.

And you know retrospectively I realise this was the most uncharacteristic behaviour. I have never known George to do this. He never gave a damn where anyone slept. Well anyway we met in some pub a few evenings later and I expected him to apologise to me which he didn't do. So in fact I cravenly apologised to him. I did think he might then bring himself to apologise to me but he just said 'I forgive you my dear' and I thought 'You bastard'.

I wasn't attracted to him at this stage. I thought his poetry was fantastic but he had been so volcanic and horrific there was nothing but a kind of shock still in me.

But then we started drinking and then we started talking and then we started laughing and then I realised you know there was a completely different side to him. I went back to Scotland and he came to visit me. There was no romance whatsoever, just talking, and a good deal more drinking, scandalising my father.

Then I went to London to try to seek my fortune all over again and fell in with another friend of George who was planning to go out to Italy to visit him. He asked if I would like to come along and he wrote to George saying is it all right to bring Elspeth and George sent a telegram back saying 'Thank you for thinking of such a nice present.'

So this chap Tony and I went out to Italy and Tony warned me against George all the way. George by then had split up with his wife in Rome. I call all his ladies wives because I think they deserve status. There is no other way to describe a serious relationship producing children, lasting many years. To say 'that woman' or something is unfair, it's wrong and I dislike the word partner. I dislike it very much. Mistress is wrong too. It is too louche to describe a domestic situation so I think wife will do fine. It may be unemancipated but *tant pis*.

So George was living in a most lovely cottage out in the Alban Hills near Lake Nemi of the *Golden Bough*, if you know James Fraser's *Golden Bough*; a fantastic sort of haunted place where the priest king, the king that had to die used to pace those woods. There was a great deal of ritual connected to it, the worship of Diana and this high priest known as the priest king guarded the sacred grove until such time as somebody came to supplant him and he was murdered. He knew he had to die. It was a very strange haunted place; and guarding the golden bough with his sacred branch and a green volcanic lake where the Emperor Nero once kept his pleasure boat.

It was a most romantic place, wild chestnut woods, white violets and in the summer wild strawberries, very delicate . . . elegant. So anyway there we all were going for long walks (again I have retrospectively discovered this was completely out of character with George) and talking about Horace and love of poetry and oh it was just absolutely heavenly. Tony was still there and then George got fed up and kicked him out and asked me to stay on; the romance having burgeoned by then. Actually it was the night Kennedy died. You know that classic 'Where were you then?' Tony then came bursting in through the french windows into our bedroom shouting to me 'Get to your room'. It was so funny I just started laughing. George shouted at him 'Get out of my house. Get out. Get out.' Tony then dramatically went off with his easel and his paints and got the last tram into Rome; suddenly departed to a Greek island where he has remained ever since. There had been some rows before that. He had hoped to be a romantic partner. He tried to strangle me in fact in the sacred grove of

Nemi, but having been brought up in a boys' prep school I was able to deal with that.

So then we continued to live in this marvellous cottage. There was an ancient contessa who was our landlady who lived in a villa at the top of the gardens, the huge garden grounds with mimosa trees coming into bloom. The scent of mimosa is very evocative of that time. And so we took off from there.

I did have some wild and dreadful thoughts about 'Oh dear what will my parents say about all this?' I'd written some lies about acting as a personal assistant to this poet, well they had met George before, under rather drunken circumstances. Then we wanted to have a baby and that was duly accomplished.

Marriage didn't bother me. It was only when I thought of my parents' reaction I thought 'Maybe I should be married. They will not like this'. But it didn't bother me. I suppose I was on a headlong go-for-broke. I was aware of George's track record but I also had the ludicrous arrogance of youth, you know 'I can do it', and I also thought if I can't do it I shall destroy him in revenge for what he has done to other women. He didn't know that.

Fortunately the positive rather than the negative side developed so we eventually came back to England in time for the first baby to be born. Elizabeth would say he wasn't husband material and he wasn't really, but he was a fantastic father to all his children, adored all his children and they get on very well with each other.

He was not good husband material because he was a poet. Poetry mattered more to him than anything else in life except possibly his children; so one was always really playing second string to the muse. It could be very trying. I am a very undomestic person and, you know, trying to cope with things like builders and coal and lighting fires and keeping the car taxed. He didn't do much. He drove. I mean he drove with great verve about the place but you had to do a lot of kind of bullying to get things kept remotely legal. It's not that one cares particularly about being legal but it is a bloody nuisance being caught, no tax, no MOT etc, and bills have to be paid or the telephone is cut off.

Little things like that. and if somebody is scribbling away and the milkman is beating on the door and they won't hand over a cheque . . .

At that time I had no money whatsoever. I was interested in babies, I wasn't interested in having a job. It was very self-indulgent of me. George adored them once they arrived. He was dubious every time I got pregnant. We didn't have little chats about 'Let's have another baby'. I just got on with it.

I suppose that meeting George totally and utterly changed my life irrevocably. We were together almost 30 years until he died last October and it got better and better and better.

George, despite the age gap, was completely ageless. He was just George. You wouldn't have thought 'Oh he is 78' which he was when he died. You know he used to like to say broodily in his cups 'Man is a spirit' and he was a spirit and I trust is a spirit and I feel his presence around a lot, not in a kind of fanciful way, but an overseeing power.

I suppose at first I was still very overawed by George as a poet, as aside from being George, and gradually you become accustomed to that. But poetry was the mainspring of our lives together. He always got me to read anything that he was writing and talk about it and so on. When we get drunk we always read poetry to each other. Drink is another important feature of my life. Saturday nights were drinking time really. George was very disciplined about it. He could not work with a hangover because he always drank vast quantities and so he had to work during the week; but Saturday nights were massive drunken occasions. That was actually not too easy to handle when the children were small. We were trying to get them to go to bed and they would come down and there were always loads of people round and you were trying to cook them some filthy spaghetti or something. You can imagine. But of course the children get older and it all sorts out.

We couldn't get married before we did because George was married once when he was young. Initially when we came back to London after the first baby was born he did say 'Let's get married', but we couldn't trace his first wife. She was somewhere in America. We did go to a lawyer and so on but he was just very incompetent and then after a bit it really didn't bother me.

My parents, after a bit of initial reluctance and crossness, accepted my dubious status and then eventually we did find out where his wife was. She was living in Kentucky in a kind of home and she had Alzheimer's disease and there was no way you could . . . it would have been very distasteful really and George was a Catholic as well. But she did die in the year we got married and we decided it would be a nice thing to do. It would be a sacrament. So it was just a sort of confirmation and a consecration of our time together. I thought it might be very nice for the children. But it had never occurred to the children that we were not married so they were all very shocked. I think they thought it was quite funny.

In a way my upbringing all tended towards George. My parents had been so fond of poetry themselves and they had always encouraged us to learn by heart and so poetry was always threading a way into one's head anyway and so it was a right true end to it all even if it did break a few rules. For the future my writing and my children are the two things. I don't want to marry again. I have done that.

BY HEART
Elizabeth Smart: A Life
Rosemary Sullivan (1991)

'NATURE was kind that night in supplying a large round moon and warm breezes. The fair-haired Betty wore white organdie. It is generally known that she plays the piano beautifully and writes a little.' Thus the Ottawa Letter in a 1934 *Mayfair*, when Elizabeth Smart was 20 years old. A few months before, she had been presented to the Governor General amid a 'lovely bouquet of winsome girlhood'. She was blonde, rich, beautiful, surrounded by admirers; she had gratified her mother, a glittering hostess to many 'notables'. But she had gratified her for the last time, for beneath the white organdie beat a heart bursting with aspirations to heroic love and literature, in terror of talent wasted and time passing by.

Elizabeth's father, Russel Smart, had worked his way through university, studying both science and law. He became an attorney and then a patent lawyer, building up an international practice based in Ottawa. Louie, her mother, made their house a social hub and gave her daughters the feeling that 'one was the best there was'. She was witty and charming, but would explode into shocking rages and lie shrieking on the bathroom floor. She gave and withdrew love at will.

Elizabeth experienced this withdrawal for the first time when she was two and her sister Jane was born. She became fearful and solitary; she learned to be devious and to placate. Her mother's long, graceful neck mesmerised her; she had a recurrent dream of its growing so long that the head fell off: 'It was my fault. I could prevent it by loving her enough.' Jane tells a story of the furious Louie pushing seven year old Elizabeth into a cupboard. Elizabeth screamed and screamed. When the door was opened they found her fingers jammed in the hinge, maimed and bloody with two nails lost.

Such images underpin what was a conventional middle class upbringing, with governesses giving way to carefully chosen schools and a busy, talkative and intelligent family circle. There were frequent unsettling moves to larger houses, but Russel's unconditional love and generosity rebuilt some of the confidence eroded by Louie's moods.

Summers were spent by Lake Kingsmere in the Gatineau hills, and there Elizabeth discovered a mystical delight in landscape and plants. Six months in bed with the fashionable ailment of a leaking heart valve had fostered her pleasure in books; during this time, at the age of 11 she started to write stories. She also learned by heart the poems she loved.

At 18 she went to London, to study music, which she soon abandoned in favour of writing. This was the first of many trips across the Atlantic; by the time she was 24 she had crossed more than 20 times. Her yearning to become a serious writer struggled against the duty and fun of being a blonde. Louie warned her about Men's Desires and wrote of a mother's anguish.

Elizabeth ignored Louie's moans, enjoyed flirtations, but also sought out men to give her literary encouragement and criticism. Among these was J. M. Barrie, who like everyone else said 'Write'. He also said: 'A clever woman doesn't let you know.' She conceived the notion of a demon lover, who would awaken her spirit. And so she abandoned the white organdie and the seductions of luxury and sought true love and literary life in Europe.

Her story becomes increasingly spectacular, played out against stunning landscapes among remarkable people, not least the preposterous Mrs Alfred Watt, who took her on a work tour to promote the Associated Country-Women of the World (77 meetings in New Zealand alone). Unsurprisingly, this trip did not further her passionate quest and she began to hate Mrs Watt. 'So fragile was her creative ego, so strong the dichotomous pull between the social world and the world of the imagination, that to write would require a death,' remarks Rosemary Sullivan. (she often says things like that.)

However, Elizabeth escaped and found herself in a series of artistic households where the women, writers or painters, were Muses, slaves and concubines to the priapic and creative male. She became involved with Varda, 'the Greek collagist': 'He was a wild, manly gale. He smelt of brown earth and grass.' He also, according to Henry Miller, encouraged women to 'bound like an antelope or canter like a palomino'. He was known as Yanko to his friends and one can't but yearn to call him Wanko. However, Elizabeth was happy with him for a while, and continued to meet him on both sides of the Atlantic for some years; in 1940 she was living with him on the 700 foot cliffs of Big Sur, California, when she at last encountered her demon lover.

Her passionate love affair with George Barker, whose poetry she had loved for years with equal passion, needs no documentation from me, his widow. Its guilty, grim and glorious consequences, literary and physical, have become the stuff of legend. This was Elizabeth's choice, 'what my heart first waking whispered the world was', and despite lonely pregnancies, financial difficulties, solitude and exhaustion, she believed to the end that she had made the right choice. Her first obsessions remained constant. Tied to her parents by financial need, she never resolved her fear of her mother, her desperate yearning for her love. Her wonderful garden in Suffolk was the triumphant expression of early delights at Kingsmere. She wrote three books, including the celebrated *By Grand Central Station I Sat Down and Wept*, and was a dazzling journalist. But exhaustion, work, child rearing and confusion stifled her writing, and she was haunted by the sense of time passing. She would have been happy to see the current renewal of interest in her work. She had her great love affair and did not want another one. And she had her four children. In the end (she died in 1986) she believed that to have children was the most important thing of all.

Her story can be seen in many different ways – as the struggle of an unmarried mother in the 1940s and 1950s, the passionate survival of a free spirit, the triumph of the heart over reason, the difficulties of a woman trying to write. Rosemary Sullivan, in my view wrongly, chooses this last as her dominant theme.

Her deep and honourable regard for Elizabeth leads her to disparage anyone who seems to stand in her way or even disagree with her. This is particularly apparent in her comments on the men in Elizabeth's life. On George Barker, for example, Elizabeth felt 'there was no man as witty, as intelligent, as passionate'. 'And one might say as slippery,' adds Sullivan. No, one might not. There is far too much of 'one might say' in this book; there is also too much kindly explanation of incidents and quotations which already speak for themselves. Certain phrases lose all their strength through recurrence: 'the cruel sexual bargain', 'the extraordinary thing is. . .', and worst of all 'the womb's ethic'. She is also guilty of double standards, for while she criticises men or their ambiguous dealings with women, she condones this behaviour in Elizabeth. Barker finally left her because of her affair with a photographer, but when her children asked her why he was never there she would say 'Ask him', or 'George is so unjust. It's all lies.' No blame, as they say, but a biographer should be morally consistent.

I have the feeling that Sullivan has been obliged to finish her book more quickly than she might have wished. It covers 72 years and a myriad of characters, all carefully indexed and annotated, but there are still a great many inaccuracies, much turgid psychobabble – 'the introjection of the parental archetype', etc – and a conspicuous lack of humour. But it is informed with enthusiasm and tells its remarkable story vividly. Most importantly, from time to time one has a powerful sense of Elizabeth's presence.

Elizabeth's heart dictated her existence, made her choose perfection of the life rather than perfection of the work. She gave and did not count the cost, fought and did not heed the wounds. In the end, like very few, she could say with her heroine Dido, 'Pervixi'. It will all make a wonderful film.

THE CHAMELEON POET

The problem with being a literary widow is that, sooner or later, one inevitably gets stalked. This is the price of being married to a genius, which is how T. S. Eliot described George Barker, the man I later married. George was then a 24-year-old poet, and by the end of his life he had written more great poetry and fathered more children – 15 in all – than most writers. He travelled the world and drank in Soho with Francis Bacon and Dylan Thomas – who didn't in the Fifties? Elizabeth Smart, his lover and the mother of four of his children, was inspired by her great love for him to write *By Grand Central Station I Sat Down and Wept*. He is an immovable part of literary history.

I met George in the winter of 1963, at a gathering of Elizabeth's, where he stood leaning against the mantelpiece, snarling. In 1967 we moved to Norfolk, after Graham Greene had helped us secure a lease on a house George had found. We had 28 years together but, after he died – on the day the clocks went back in October 1991, having just asked me, 'Has anyone ever told you that you have the most remarkable eyes?' – I suffered for a while from a condition I now recognise as post-mortem dementia. Sometimes I uttered strange cries, alarming the dogs. I shook a lot, but it was winter, so I may just have been shivering in my windswept kitchen. I lost three stone, could not read or watch television and had great difficulty in writing, telephoning and general locomotion. Gin was my sustenance and I had no hangovers.

It was during this period of limbo that I became obsessed with finding a biographer for George, immediately, before everyone who had known him died, too. People did suggest waiting a while – years even – pointing out how unnecessary it was to have living witnesses, citing Victoria Glendinning's *Trollope* and Richard Ellman's *Wilde*. I paid no attention. My requirements, I believed, were modest. The biographer should be a poet, a Catholic, a friend, a man and, of course, a good writer. Everyone I approached was either already engaged on some magnum opus, seriously ill or not a biographer. Finally, I thought of Robert Fraser, who fitted into some, though not all, of my categories, but had edited George's monumental *Collected Poems*. He had written various critical and literary studies, none of which I had read. Faber inspected these and agreed to go forward. Fraser received a substantial advance and, in a surprisingly short time, a first draft came through my letterbox. I went through this text with gathering astonishment, then fury, and, as I read, I annotated. Annotation resolved rapidly into scribbles and expletives and crossings out. It was clear to me that Fraser had little understanding of the characters concerned. How could my husband's life story have been taken over in this way? It was boring, and from the foreground of every chapter loomed the figure of the author. I telephoned the editors at Faber to say a thing or two about Fraser.

They had not yet received the script and were bemused.

Fraser appeared at my house to discuss what he called 'any minor alterations'. As he had not even photocopied his script, he was obliged to study in detail my corrections and comments. He claimed not to have met the word 'naff' before; he left with a working knowledge of its application. My pig was screaming her head off because the vet was trying to cut her toenails. Fraser refused to fetch her anaesthetising bowl of mulled wine. I made sure he didn't have any, either. He tried to make me light the second bar of the Super Ser heater. Some hope. Rage kept me warm; he shivered in his grey pelt. I spoke of the charm of my glacial bathroom and the tablet of Wright's Coal Tar soap to no avail.

Another two or three drafts followed, still containing errors. For example, inspired by a photograph of myself and a friend gathering brushwood for a picnic fire while on holiday in France, Fraser stated that when we ran out of money on this jaunt, we 'helped local farmers with the harvest'. Two pregnant women and two often inebriated poets making hay? I think not. Or, of the evening George died: 'To comfort her, for she was very distressed, a friend brought her a copy of that day's *Sunday Times*.' Gosh, yes, that would have done the trick.

Eventually, and with my enthusiastic agreement, the whole project was abandoned. That was nearly three years ago. I was, and am, deeply ashamed of my folly, which cost the publishing house much time and money. And I am still baffled by the way a person whom George and I had known for years, and whom I had respected professionally, had portrayed my husband in such a way.

A few months ago, Cape informed me that it was about to publish yet another draft of this eternally recurring volume. I told them that this was lousy news. The new (unauthorised) version is improved and a great deal of work has gone into it, although it seems to me vulgar and dull. I hope that, in time, there will be another biography by another writer.

But vengefulness and anger are bad for the soul, and, at my age, I must look to mine. George loved Keat's phrase 'the chameleon poet' and would have been delighted to have it applied to himself. I've little doubt he would have been amused by my troubled relationship with the whole goddamned project.

MEMORIES OF GEORGE BARKER

Much of late has been written about George's wild, bad life style, in reviews of Robert Fraser's biography, *The Chameleon Poet* (2001). Since when was it the business of a reviewer to moralise? If they had persevered to the end of this very long book, they might have noticed that for the last twenty eight years of his life, George stayed in one place, with one family, a present and devoted father to our five children, who adored him then and now. It is not for me to criticise his earlier behaviour, nor will I deny that our time together was often turbulent. It was also vivid and passionate and treasured. To countervail that spiteful litany of blame, I offer a few glimpses of the George I knew.

Unsurprisingly, as the father of fifteen children, George loved babies; babies responded, eyes shining with delighted recognition and conspiratorial glee. Few men of his generation were happy, as he was, to push a pram, and entertain its occupant through the streets of London. 'Babies are cherubimos', he would say. 'They have wings.' Before I met George I had never liked them one bit; he made me see things differently. The early morning tea ceremonial began the day in Norfolk. Panels of river light and leaves flickered on the bedroom walls; the five infants rolled and bounced about us. In the brass knobs at the far end of the bed our reflections were strangely curved and elongated, like the Henry Moore king and queen who sit alone and brooding on a Scottish hillside. Or a Saturday night memory: George as usual behaving badly, drunk, dangerous and belligerent, but at last, to everyone's relief, gone off upstairs, and someone realising that she'd left her six-week-old baby wrapped in her shawl on the bed. There they both lay in deep sleep, George saintly as an effigy, the baby moth-like clasped on his chest.

Saturday nights did have their good moments, before the ravening ghouls he observed in Robert Colquhoun came to taunt him in his turn. He would alarm and entertain visitors by his singing habits. Leaning on the drinking room mantelpiece he would grasp a vase and intone plangent cowboy songs or Thomas Moore's lyrics. Sometimes he played an invisible violin. At dinner people scrambled to sit next to him, to be out of his missile firing line. But when he chose to read poetry aloud, seldom his own, often Hopkins or Yeats, or the anonymous 'Quia Amore Langueo', he held the room spellbound. Not everyone was a poetry lover, not everyone could cope with the badness and madness, but they would still turn up on Saturday nights.

During the week he didn't drink at all. His discipline was rigorous. Apart from hangover Sunday, he wrote every day, sequestered in his study. If he was going through a barren phase, he would still keep the pen moving, into prose or rude limericks about fellow poets. He kept his notebook with him at all times, and if it was full, would use the nearest book. Georgette Heyer was the only twentieth-century novelist he was prepared to read, and the house is scattered with curling paperbacks containing scatological overspills. The Muse came first among his women, and she was the only one to control him.

He had great enthusiasm for all forms of sport. Part of Saturday ritual involved the wrestling on television, Big Daddy and Giant Haystacks. The Grand National was for him the first day of spring, a joyous family sweepstake and an epic of courage and nobility. I thought, after he died, that if any occasion could bring him back, this one would. I held a solitary sweepstake, allocating horses and money, but it didn't work.

Cars were another obsession. He was a skilful but lawless driver; I would never go in the front with him, sitting instead behind, rigid with fear. Sometimes this made people take him for my handyman driver. In a few weeks he could reduce a perfectly viable car to wreckage, by inventive tinkering; baked bean cans, lawn mower plugs and chewing gum played their part. He had some unusual ideas about motoring. 'In fog always drive on the wrong side of the road.' 'Never change down at junctions.' 'Indicators are for women.' Driving, like drinking, was to him a non-domestic activity, ideally separate from the rest of life. Sometimes we had two cars, and I would creep along in the death-trap reserved for women and children, while he swept about the countryside in something flash. He hated to part with a wrecked car and often the garden became a scrapyard. Even now his 1960 Mercedes Benz continues its disintegration in an open-sided shed, conspicuous and immovable.

When someone has died, it is tempting to see their manifestation in another form, a hare, moth, the shape of a cloud. For George I fancy the white owl, who at dawn shrieks defiance from the ridge of the roof to a parliament of owls heading home from hunting. And each autumn, in the churchyard, a solitary specimen of the brazen mushroom *phallus impudicus* rears from his grave. That would amuse him.

THE LONGEST GOODBYE

It is a year now since my husband died. On the day he most hated, when the clocks turn back and our days pitch into cold and darkness. It seems like yesterday. Everything that has happened since is like an incident recorded in the chapter summary of an old history book, remote events impinging on someone else, seen through the wrong end of a telescope, the print almost too small to read.

My daughter and I sat in the registrar's office, eyeing a Thank You

For Not Smoking sign. The kindly lady behind the desk handed out Benson & Hedges. 'My boss said someone to do with a poet would be coming in,' she told us. 'He'll be sorry to miss you. We haven't had a poet before.' The window looked out on nothing but stormy sea and sky, both the colour of muddy milk. Beyond the horizon was more featureless horizon, mile upon mile of freezing wind and water stretching on until the Arctic circle. It was the right place to be that afternoon and I would have liked to have stayed there.

Moving about was peculiarly difficult; the days seemed endless. One step at a time, one hour at a time. None of us could eat; we drank a great deal and we had no hangovers. The evenings were almost bearable, when we sat round the fire and talked about George and laughed. Mornings were dreadful, each day renewing the knowledge of loss; but they also brought sheaves of letters, extraordinary and unexpectedly moving. To read anything longer than a letter was impossible; it was weeks before I managed to go through the obituaries, months before I was able to write. At first I shook a lot; I still do sometimes. I don't know why. It is not *timor mortis.* But I have been afraid of grief, afraid of drowning in it.

Even in those first numb days, there were moments of inadvertent mirth. There was the fund-raising letter from the Samaritans which arrived the day after George's death – 'Dear Mr Barker, Have you ever felt you couldn't last one more day?' – then the early-morning call from the undertakers, intercepted by our daughter Raffaella, as she spooned porridge into her baby. 'Sorry to disturb you, Mrs Raffy Elly. We just wanted to know if you'd like your Dad's grave dug extra deep? So your Mum can go in too.' Such moments smoothed a little time away.

Going back to work was weird and alien. I felt ill when I was away from home, except when exploring derelict mansions at sunset – a pastime provided by house-hunting relatives. The cold red sky, the rooks calling through ebbing light in unfamiliar terrain, the knowledge that another day was almost over were oddly cheering, a small respite.

I am aware that I am fortunate in being part of a large family but the state of grief is essentially solitary. Talking to friends who have been bereaved helps a little, but only a little. There are numerous well-intentioned books dealing with every aspect of loss. Jeanette Kupfermann writes movingly and courageously of her experience of widowhood in *When The Crying's Done* (Robson Books), but in the end it does remain her experience. Bel Mooney has brought out *Perspectives For Living* (John Murray), a collection of interviews with bereaved people; it makes for harrowing reading. While I can only admire the strength and goodness of the human spirit which illuminates its dark pages, I was left feeling horribly distressed and somewhat voyeuristic. A few common needs emerge: for ritual, for talk with others in similar circumstances, for physical warmth, for dreams of the deceased. Much more apparent is the unique nature of each person's grief. There is no assuaging, unless it be brought by time. This I have yet to see.

I find death absolutely unacceptable and I cannot come to terms with it. I can no more conceive of utter extinction, of never, than I can conceive of infinity. I cannot believe that all that passion, wit, eloquence and rage can be deleted by something so vulgar as the heart stopping. Where have they gone? As I see it, there are only two possibilities: that the spirit exists in some other plane of being, with no relation to our living selves, or that the spirit exists on some level that is still connected with us. Naturally I prefer the second idea. To say I believe it is too strong a statement; but I wish to live as though it were so. I am not a widow, I am George's wife. Why must our marriage be nullified by his death? Sons, daughters, aunts, friends all retain their relationship. I shall retain mine.

But *O the heavy loss now thou art gone.* When a lover, husband or wife dies, the survivor has also lost his or her own self, the self that was refracted and reflected by the other, and all their shared and private past. No dialogue, no jokes. And what of the dead person's belongings, objects that mattered to him, objects from his earlier past? It seems to me a denial of his existence to dispose of them or lock them away. I am not making a shrine of these things. I simply feel that they have rights. Possibly, of course, I am off my head.

Be that as it may, the living spirit pushes up through the stone carapace of grief like tendrils of convolvulus and one composes one's own small survival rituals in honour of the departed. Each to their own. Mostly I watch the dawn; I am waiting for a time when I feel that I can look forward to the day. For now, the past is what matters.

BROKEN HEARTED

This is a grey north country morning, still and soft, a harbinger of the changing season, heavy with melancholy. In the little wood doves begin to call, tentative then dazzling in urgency; other doves respond; they repeat the notes over and over until all the air is clamorous, sobbing and calling and crying.

Beyond the trees the steep harvest land sweeps to the sky in a perfect curve of tarnished gold. 'Don't do it, don't do it,' warn the doves, sharp with anguish; and the sorrowing choral resumes: 'I mourn for my love, I'll be chief mourner.'

In this quiet place one rainy afternoon 500 years ago, 13,000 men spent two-and-a-half hours hacking each other to death. This was the battle of Flodden; it destroyed the entire ruling class of Scotland and their king, gained nothing for either side and need not have taken place. But, like the first world war it left an aftermath of inconsolable grief, generations of widows and spinsters who remained bound to those men they had lost and not only could not, but would not, replace.

I remember them well from school days, those unmarried dedicated teachers and I remember, too, our hideous unkindness when we spoke of them, for we assumed that no one wanted to marry them and this appalling state of affairs was entirely their own fault. Consider that hand-knitted magenta jumper, that bristling mole, that steely glare. Consider instead the broken heart, and the silent gallantry of its bearer.

One of the characteristics of the broken heart is silence. No talk may cure it, no therapeutic chat. Hans Andersen's Little Mermaid was dumb throughout her suffering. Dido's wound of loss sat deep and silent in her heart; only when she transfixed herself with her false lover's sword and moved metaphor into reality did the heart cry out. Sorrow drains the world of its colour. Dido's last time of happiness, as she rode out to hunt with Aeneas, glows with sunshine and gold and purple. After that there is only monotone and darkness. Tennyson, in passionate grief for Arthur Hallam, abandons his customary richness of sound and image for a language that is bleak as pain:

> *He is not here. But far away*
> *The noise of life begins again*
> *And ghastly through the drizzling rain*
> *On the bald street breaks the blank day.*

The idea of the broken heart is not itself peculiar to a romantic tradition, although other cultures have placed the seat of the emotions elsewhere, in the head or even in the solar plexus. But one must be careful to distinguish stylised stylish suffering from the genuine article, for it is confusingly entwined with Pre-Raphaelite attitudinising, and with memory, distance and death.

Absinthe drinkers and wan lovers may be pale and wretched from obsession but not from irreparable internal invisible damage. Even now the state may be recognised; certainly in my childhood people still talked of dying of a broken heart, a condition both pitiful and virtuous; so in fairy stories and myths the victims of the broken heart may pass through tribulations to redemption, but not to reinstated happiness.

MOVING ON

Five years ago my husband died. I am still not used to his absence. I still can't accept the fact of death, the notion that one must come to terms with it. How? It is an outrage, a violation of all our day-to-day precepts. We live as though it were not so; then suddenly it happens and life is irredeemably altered. And one's head is screwed round to a different angle, a new way of looking.

I remember a hospital ward in Siena; an elderly man had just died, propped on his pillows. Across his chest his widow lay screaming: 'Where are you? Tell me where you are.' The other inmates went on eating their lunch and reading their newspapers and through the window the August sun poured down. Where are they indeed? And why, with all that time now available, should they not make a few brief appearances just now and then? Dreams aren't good enough.

I find that there are two kinds of dreams. In some, life with the dead is as it used to be, pre-mortem, vivid and turbulent and funny and real. One wakes then into the renewed and shocking gulf of bereavement and it will not be a good day. But are these visitations or are they simply delusive memories? I must cling to the fancy of a visitation, however painful it may be to waken. Then there are the other dreams; it has all been a terrible mistake. He didn't die at all but we went and buried him and now he isn't in a very good state but he is back or coming back and the house is full of people who will put him in a rage, and *what has happened to his car*? 'Considering you've been dead for five years you're looking really great,' I babble, untruthful and placatory. This is all anger and guilt and nightmare and I wake, appalled to find that I am relieved that he is dead after all. So what's all that about?

There are daytime confusions too. A huge beech tree stands in my garden. We buried my husband beneath an identical one up in the village churchyard, a beautiful situation, shaded in summer and nobly rampageous in the winter gales. Beside the grave there is a tiny mouse hole, and in the evening miner bees return from their labours and go processing in, two by two, underground. Their decorum is broken only by the occasional foray to sting my dogs. They ignore me. It is soothing to sit there on the bank and watch the bees and consider mortality and my own ultimate inhumation in this spot.

Down the hill, I can hear the voices of our grandchildren as they play in the stream. This year, in February, on a white morning still and cold as death, there came a crack of a rifle from the churchyard. The great tree had split from its roots and lay spread-eagled over the graves. Not a single stone was displaced; the branches encircled, caressed, bypassed every one of them. Beside the colossal trunk on my husband's grave, a glass of snowdrops remained upright and intact.

And within the trunk another swarm of bees was hibernating. Honeycomb dripped down its fatal hollow vault. People tried to save the bees but they died, of shock, of cold, who knows? But this summer, for the first time ever the beech tree in my garden has been loud, day in and day out, with a swarm of bees. Do the dead send coded messages or is one just a neurotic wreck?

Without that defining person in one's life, one is cast off balance, seeking a new identity. I certainly don't want to find myself, having spent half a century avoiding any such thing, but I need some point of fixity. That sense of being alone on a wide, wide sea is disquieting. It makes me dizzy. The evenings are very long. Sometimes it seems to me that there is no evidence now of those 30 years of shared past; they might have never been.

I heave out the photographs, I look at the photographs for a long time and I drink a lot. Once I read all of Shakespeare's sonnets to the photographs, once I and absence conducted a sweepstake on the Grand National together. I was obliged to take the winnings.

I am told we are expected to let go of the dead; what if the dead wouldn't want us to let go of them? Or do their wishes cease to matter, let alone one's own? Have they any idea of what we might be getting up to? I cannot yet believe that all that passion and wit and knowledge and rage can be obliterated by the failure of the beating heart. There are so many questions which seem unanswerable, set aside behind the spurious smokescreen called Coming To Terms With Death.

MOVING ON

The word widow derives from the Latin *viduus*, empty; the drained vessel, the barren gourd. Great. It is a peculiarly colourless word with few and depressing associations; widow spider, Widow Twankey, that weird-looking young woman in a sort of mantilla advertising an insurance company equally weirdly called Scottish Widows. Or the widow bird who sat mourning for her mate. While the married state is undoubtedly preferable, I find myself doomed to solitude, monogamous beyond the grave.

It pains me when people suggest that after five years one might be forming new relationships; it seems cruel and disloyal. At first I could not enjoy anything at all; I also felt that I had no right to enjoy anything. This at least has passed. But I am aware of an abiding loss which qualifies everything I do and at times is overwhelming.

Certain landscapes, scents and sounds, the lighting of the fire on a winter evening, a collection of boxes containing pen nibs and old clock parts and coins can all without warning reform and metamorphose into Hokusai's towering glassy wave, suspended over the simple concourse of survival, the great doom's image. How could a heart not be broken?

CHERUBIM

It certainly isn't worth it, the day term begins and life is supposedly reverting to drab and normal.

The dawn light yet again reveals great muffled shapes, wearing boots, on every sofa. It is worse in the kitchen where, the previous evening, I set the table with a keen eye to the assertion of Family Values (dinosaur mugs and blue stripy bowls) in the face of drunken revelry. Now there is a moraine of overflowing ashtrays, sodden cigarette packets, half empty beer cans, spilt wine. I hurtle about the sofas, screeching. Nothing happens. In one room I plug in the Hoover and leave it turned on and roaring at the sleepers; in another I send the remote control New York police car into action, siren wailing, horn blasting, lights flashing. There is a distant chatter of machine-gun fire. I fling open windows and hurl coats into the rainswept garden. I drop a few cats around. Silently the shapes rise, clear up the kitchen, retrieve their dripping coats from the puddles. The air is heavy with injured innocence, unspoken reproach.

I remember the hymn our headmistress thought appropriate for the first day of boarding school term: 'Can a mother's tender care/Cease towards the child she bear?/Yes! She may forgetful be . . .' Oh God, I think. Soon they'll all be back in London, and then I'll miss them. I didn't really have to chuck their coats out. Suddenly I am exhausted, my heart begins to thump and guilt comes seeping in. One of them gives me a cup of tea, complete with sugar and milk. My heart brims with gratitude. Oh, happy is the mother whose child, unbidden, gives her a cup of tea. Third son used to say that he would look after me when I was old and mouldy. I am no longer the murderous harpy of ten minutes past; I am old and mouldy. Does he notice? I am a mental and physical wreck and it is all their doing. 'They fuck you up, your mum and dad'. Philip Larkin had it the wrong way round. Mind you, I'm glad he wasn't one of my children.

So where have they gone, the cherubim, the magical babes, each of them once the world's most beautiful? Sometimes I dream of them and wake in tears of loss and bereavement. And other sunderings follow. The time when their friends become more important than their parents; teen time; leaving home time. My fourteen-year-old daughter ceased to kiss me goodnight because of her great hatred for me. I knew a lot about this hatred because I used to read it up in her diary. But one evening she had a school friend staying. This friend embraced me warmly at retiring time; whereupon the hissing viper of my bosom followed suit and bade me goodnight with a breathtaking show of filial devotion. That Judas kiss caused me acute pain for a long time.

Much later, during a friendlier period, she returned from a holiday in Spain. I was very excited; she had never been away for so long. As

I drove, fearfully and illegally, a great distance to collect her, I planned a happy mother and daughter evening, enhanced by a bottle of gin to indicate her new adult status. We'd been home for seven minutes when she was off with an unknown youth in a bright orange sports car. 'Thanks for fetching me, Mum. I'll be really late, so don't stay up.' I shared out the celebration meal between the cats and dogs. Then I drank the gin.

Boys torture their mothers in a different way. They do dangerous things and they often look very peculiar. One son decided his ears stuck out; he glued them to his head with Superglue. He combed the woods for small dead creatures and simmered them in a great cauldron on the Aga so that he might extract their bones to make necklaces in the manner of the Plains Red Indians. He also threaded bones into his hair. His brother, pogo dancing, split his skull on a nail protruding from the ceiling, and had to be rushed to hospital. He was dressed as an Egyptian mummy and the cere cloths and bandages were very serviceable in soaking up the blood. Another fell off a motorbike and smashed his leg. Another ate a bumper packet of firelighters. I have spent a great deal of time hanging about hospitals, waiting for them to be mended.

At night I still lie awake, inventing accidents more improbable even than the ones which have occurred, on the quaint principle that if I've thought of them they won't happen. You are never safe again after you've had a baby, terror and loss lurk around every corner. You are perpetually alert, straining after the ghostly voices of children long grown, an infant crying in the night.

I would like to be one of those wooden Russian dolls and have them all packed neatly back inside. I am a non-PC mother, with matriarchal tendencies. It seems absurd that one should go through the mighty travail of rearing children, only to wave them goodbye. 'You go your way/And I'll go my way'. I seem to recall that the next line is 'Nothing seems to matter any more'.

But they do matter, just as much as they did when they were little. And those babies, the cherubim, haven't really gone. Behind each adult child hovers a recession of all his or her earlier incarnations, like an inversion of the line of Banquo's unborn sons who appear at one of the cheerier moments in *Macbeth,* a jolly dinner party, I believe.

Contrary to ludicrous statistics, you don't need a lot of money to bring up children. You need persistence and guile, ruthlessness, resilience and imagination. You will learn to bow gracefully to the inevitable (most of the time anyway) and you will become impervious to public humiliation. You must be able to laugh. And above all you must be able to love. All this they teach you. All this you owe to them, and in the end they owe you nothing. They are a privilege beyond accounting. Recently one of my sons won a bottle of Armagnac in a fancy dress competition; he was disguised as his mother. A dubious enterprise, but he gave the Armagnac to me. Definitely worth it.

A HANDBOOK ON GOOD MANNERS FOR CHILDREN
Erasmus of Rotterdam
trs Eleanor Merchant

We live in an age of aspiration fraught with self-doubt. Help manuals proliferate, advice columns feature in every magazine, private schools flourish. From nine months children may spend all their waking time being educated or enhanced by classes, groups and clubs. They are pampered and protected beyond the imaginings of previous generations and mostly they seem pretty horrible. You wouldn't want to sit near them on the Tube. Or on the bus. Or at your dinner table. I suppose there are some nice ones, but they are a rarity, usually closely related to me. The actor Sanjeer Baskhar was asked in a recent interview to choose something extinct to be brought back to life. 'Good manners,' he said.

As we know, the child is father of the man, and in the past the homunculi were expected to have manners. In the 14th century William of Wykeham founded Winchester School with the thunderous motto Manners Makyth Man. 'In courtesy I'd have her chiefly learned' wrote Yeats for his newborn daughter. 'Hearts are not had as a gift, but hearts are earned.' Courtesy, the art of making other people feel comfortable, valued even, the art indeed of imagining what it is to be another person, is derided these days as a form of hypocrisy. *O tempora, O mores.* What's so awful about being wished a pleasant day?

Erasmus of Rotterdam (the unkind said Gouda), the great humanist scholar, brought out this little book on children's manners in 1530. It was an instant success and was translated from the original Latin into all the tongues of Europe; Erasmus had actually chosen to write in Latin to provide gentle instruction for his eleven-year-old pupil. His basic tenet is that good manners will spring from 'the ability to ignore the faults of others and avoid falling short yourself.' This is the first book in Western literature to focus entirely on a child's behaviour in society. Erasmus's ideal is the attainment of civilitas through familial devotion, a liberal education in the arts, an acceptance of the duties of life, and, most importantly, the practice and observation of good manners. He himself was born out of wedlock and grew up in various households and institutions. As an ordained priest, he did not marry or have children, but he adored family life, most especially enjoying it on lengthy visits to his beloved friend Thomas More who was deeply involved in the upbringing of his numerous children. The book is divided into seventeen sections, each dealing with one aspect of social or physical presentation – the Eyes, Posture, Table Manners, and so on. His voice is kind but authoritative: 'Puffing out the cheeks is a sign of disdain, whilst deflating them indicates despondency.' Really it is all very humane and sensible; do not indulge in hysterical mirth, do not stagger in the theatrical manner favoured by bishops and Swiss soldiers, be civil and cheerful at mealtimes, never mentioning the drunken behaviour of others, ignore obscenity, rise above shyness by associating with older people and play-acting. While some think that standing with one hand on one's groin is elegant and soldierly, Erasmus doesn't like it; but it's better than going around with both arms bent behind your back, which looks 'sluggish and thieving' (male royals NB). At all times strive to avoid a running nose and an imbecilic expression, *id in Socrate notu* – as may be observed in Socrates. No argument, but he offers a polite formula for contradiction: 'It was told to me very differently by . . . .' Only in Church is there a strict decorum, for Christ and his angels are all present; and those angels are always there, wherever you may go; behave accordingly. There is room for imaginative kindness: 'We should allow those who are less well off the comfort they take in their own modest pride.' I like that very much.

Erasmus's concerns are touching and unexceptionable; he is writing to a child but every point made applies equally to adults and is relevant enough today. 'Was it not ever thus?' demands the translator. Well, yes and no. That this book was produced at all is an indication of a leisure gap in turbulent times. His friend Thomas More was beheaded five years later. God, war, and the axe shadowed his life. Merchant's breezy, determinedly contemporary style promotes the notion that they were really just like us, those doubleted geezers back in the 16th. They weren't.

And millennial aspiration is entirely concerned with self-fulfilment expressed by the material. Erasmus's spiritual hope for 11-year-old Henry is simply that through these precepts he may influence 'the fellowship of all children' and be worthy to serve. Finally, although in his will Erasmus left 'a portion' for young women, in these pages females are to keep silent. As for dwellers in the countryside, they are too uncouth to mention. Would he could visit London today.

JEALOUSY

If the infant is primitive so is its earliest vice, jealousy – probably the most innate vice of all. First comes love, then jealousy, an unholy, uninvited symbiosis.

Once there was a great gaunt dog called Griselda, who lay, snarling softly, in an alcove beside the blacksmith's furnace. With clash and with clangour he shod Bonny and Beauty, colossal Clydesdales, and Griselda's yellow eyes narrowed and flickered in the spark light. One day she had a litter of squally pups. In the late afternoon, as darkness gathered and Mr Gould shook the sweat from his hair and damped down his fires, she ate them. You could see she did not want them.

I told my mother and she said, No, it was Mr Gould's fault, they should not have been near all that noise and disturbance. That was clearly rubbish. If it were true, why had my mother not eaten her babies? I wanted her to eat them. I stumped about shouting. She smacked me hard. 'Don't be ridiculous,' she said. 'What on earth's the matter with you? The trouble with you is that you have a nasty jealous nature.'

How very true. I longed to be called Griselda and it was with intense relish that I read the ballads of my native land. They have a swift way of dispensing with nuisance. 'The elder came and pushed her in./Sister o Sister, sink or swim' or the betrayed wife, Annie: 'Gin my sons were seven rats/Rinnin oer the castle wall/And I mysel' a great grey cat/I soon would worry them all.' My brother and I tried and failed to despatch one sister; for a while I considered losing others in the forest. It became obvious, not that it was wrong, but that there was no point. The world expanded and it contained greater attractions than self-laceration over siblings. Even so, the occasional frisson lingered. Contemplating a roast suckling pig in a wondrous shop in Soho, called I think King Bomba, I considered the possibility of my youngest sister served thus, with an apple in her mouth. I studied Euripides's *Medea* with an enthusiasm which contained nostalgia; how fine a dinner I might have offered to my parents. That would have shown them.

Jealousy, of course, should not be confused with envy. In the teen years one may yearn to have smooth blonde hair or (as in those ancient days) a dirndl skirt or divan beds with matching candlewick bedspreads, or a mother who wears white lipstick, but this is not the consumer, the passion, the 'green-eyed monster which doth mock the meat it feeds on'. The carrion beast slinks on scene again with boyfriends, husbands or whatever one calls them. Although I have been mainly fortunate in avoiding its attentions I have experienced them and have become again a murderess. I have stood at the top of a flight of stairs ready to drop a stone cross on an unsuspecting but guilty head; only the presence of a baby against my shoulder stopped me. The monster's only joys are violent and transitory; but its poison is all pervading and irreversible. It is no wonder that the jealous person's countenance is traditionally tinged with green. The only cure lies in oblivion.

Female jealousy is associated with witchery, bitchery, dementia and underhand behaviour. Its manifestations are often inventive – the abbreviation of a chap's Armani suit or other bits, the share-out of his wine cellar, the mutilation of his motor. I know a woman who has taught her much younger husband's beloved parrot to address him in her voice, uttering sweet blandishments, offering evening drinks. 'Just so he'll be sorry later, when he's with someone else.'

Men seem more straightforward. They just kill the woman. You are doubtless aware, but it is worth repeating, that marriage or similar makes a woman 70 per cent more likely to meet a violent end, at the hands of himself. The word zealous and the word jealous have the same ancient Greek origin signifying an eager rivalry, an uplifting admiration, a passion with nobility. Plato set it in opposition to envy or *phthonos*.

There is a handy old expression *oudeis phthonos*, or as some still say, no sweat (man). Othello, literature's great jealous man, is constantly described as noble, even when behaving in a manner that is frankly ludicrous. After endless bombast and drivel over the missing handkerchief, he goes storming off. Emilia says percipiently: 'Is not this man jealous?' Desdemona is stunned: 'I ne'er saw this before. Sure there's some wonder in this handkerchief.' The noble Moor then reappears: 'Handkerchief – O Devil!' (falls in a trance). Later of course he says 'Wash me in steep-down gulfs of liquid fire' and therefore can be forgiven anything. Nonetheless, that cry of Handkerchief seems to me to share a little place in the great scheme with Lady Bracknell's Handbag.

Personally, I eschew all that sort of thing these days and am more interested in trying to write a villanelle or discovering thirty useful things to do with radishes. The monster has shambled off over the hill, though sometimes I still see its shadow. Or not? Recently, I sat in a hospital bed, wearing a seductive hospital nightie, ashen-faced, hollow-eyed, drips and tubes tangled about me. Mad Bertha after 50 years in the grave. Someone I do not like remarked: 'You're looking 10 years younger.' 'How could she say that?' I screeched at my daughter, 'Don't worry, she's just jealous' said the beguiling nymph.

When I was little I associated jealousy with jellyfish. I often encountered these creatures while swimming in the far-from-unpolluted waters of the North Sea. I have no intention of ever again setting foot in that icy ocean; nor shall I be jealous. Jealousy, jellyfish, see if I care. Or as one might say, lemon jelly, kiss my belly.

MOVING ON

It was in the brilliant light of the Antipodes that I saw myself plain. And plain is the word; a number of others slither to mind; middle-aged is their sum total. There I was, strolling along, not exactly singing a song, but merry and bright. And there I was, reflected in that awful full-length mirror, a shambling, shapeless, she-bear, with tired eyes and a drooping mouth.

Hide, I thought, hide from the gaze of the world; and don't come out again until you're several inches thinner and 15 years younger. If you never try on new clothes, if you believe the camera always lies, if you shrink from long mirrors as a vampire recoils from the cross, you can pretend you're getting away with the flying years.

The soft focus of presbyopia helps as well. Presbyopia was the harbinger of this new era. At first, one has difficulty reading in bed. After months of holding the book further and further away, arms extended into the freezing penumbra of a bedroom without central heating, concessions must be made.

I have a friend who snipped the sleeves off old jerseys to make arm comforters, but he too, came to the day of reckoning, the day of the cheap, magnifying spectacles available from the choicest newsagents.

'Only for reading,' the new wearer proclaims. Soon they are also for chopping vegetables and then for eating anything that requires a delicate approach. Because I lose my spectacles every 35 minutes, I am obliged to wear them slung round my neck on a black string. They swing out and smash my grandchildren's tiny noses as I stoop to struggle with zips and shoelaces. And if I am too vain to wear them during dinner, I may be punished later by an eyeful of risotto, slyly captured on the lenses' pendant plateau.

Last summer I was in France with a friend who also required spectacles. Only for reading. Neither of us had yet evolved into string wearing. This meant we had to stop every 20 minutes for her, every 35 for me, to check we hadn't lost them. I was managing rather well, better, dare I say, than she, until I found myself, speechless and sightless, confronting a menu.

My son read it out to me in rural high school French, while my bespectacled friend mused in silence. I noticed she was wearing my specs. Mine. 'So sorry darling, they looked just like mine.' Anyone could see they didn't, if they could see at all. We found hers under a bar stool at the hotel.

Thus have I learnt that strings are good, vital even. They also stop you propping your specs on funny places, like your chin. And you can still see far away, into a great distance.

'We look before and after, and pine for what is not,' said Shelley. Satan, too, offers this vista of temptation to anyone in middle years, a little surprised to find themselves in Dante's dark wood or, as in my case, in the dazzling sea light of the Pacific. I speak as I find. To look before and after is a sort of tautology. Which is which? Are they the same? A completing circle bringing you back to square one? I will try to look backwards, maybe before.

Well, I certainly know that I wouldn't want to go through childhood again. The anxieties, the nightmares, the foreverness of school, the longing to be a grown up, for they were always so nice to each other. And then the big jumps, university, boyfriends, utter disillusionment. In darkness lost.

Then I had happier times, babies, five of them, spaced in a desired but unplanned manner over 10 years. Now I am privileged to have grandchildren and to repeat some of those entrancements. It seems so short a time ago that their mother played in the barn, swung off that tree branch, lovingly attended by an evil little swish-tailed Shetland just as they do now.

At other times I think that I have lived as long as anyone could. My infancy is so far away, across a wide pale strand and at the end of the shore is darkness, a cave, origin. 'Look homeward Angel now, and melt with Ruth'. But no malingering.

Ahead, the great doom's image lifts slowly over the horizon. Friends die, mortality moves into the immediate. I am shocked and astonished as never before by the great numbers of people in the world each, like oneself, leading their one and only precious life. I am aware, with a certain fatality, of the beats and the missed beats of my heart.

What the hell, Mehitabel? What of now? Now is as good and as ghastly as ever. I, who have skulked on the peripheries and used most tricks to get out of the serious business of living, am startled to find myself embarked on a strenuous new life with new sets of obligations. My children are grown up, and still my favourite people. They are also as alarming and nerve-racking as when they were small. My husband is dead. 'You're on your own now, baby,' he informed me more than once and gleefully from his hospital bed.

I miss the discipline they all imposed on my days and I find it hard to structure life around myself, despite the necessary impositions of work. This perhaps will come with practice. But from this new freedom I have learnt a great deal about what I do and don't need; I have also learnt to be careful about wishes, for they often come true.

And I realise now that this is a fine time. I don't care about being young or old or whatever. I am past the anxieties of earlier days, no longer concerned about image or identity or A-levels, no longer fearful of shop assistants or doctors' receptionists. I can admit without giving a damn, to being a slut, liking salad cream, holding certain politically incorrect views. I can still change and grow, mentally and physically.

At this interesting point in life, one may be whoever and whatever age one chooses. One may drink all night, smash bones in hunting accidents, travel the spinning globe. One may teach one's grandchildren rude rhymes and Greek myths. One may also move very slowly round the garden in a shapeless coat, planting drifts of narcissus bulbs for latter springs.

LITERARY LIVES

ALEXANDER THE GREAT
The Invisible Enemy
John Maxwell O'Brien (1992)

Alexander the Great was born to Philip II of Macedon and Olympias of Epirus in 356 BC. He died in Babylon aged 32. In life he deliberately created his own legend; after his death it multiplied tenfold. People have written about him for more than 2,000 years, some with unqualified admiration, some in hostility, most presenting a hotchpotch of gossip and fact. No complete contemporary account has survived. But beyond all the speculation and romanticising stand his extraordinary achievements as leader, liberator, conqueror and explorer.

At the age of 16, after years of tuition under Aristotle, Alexander began his military career. By the time of his father's assassination in 336, he was established as an outstanding warrior, a Homeric hero in the mould of Achilles. Despite family intrigues and quarrels and a proliferation of stepmothers, there was no serious questioning of his right to the succession, and the army immediately acclaimed him as king. At once, he began to implement Philip's cherished plan to invade Persia. Retracing the route that Xerxes had taken against Greece, he liberated the Greek cities of Asia, then moved south and west, occupying the Persian naval bases so that their fleet was rendered powerless. He took Phoenicia, Palestine and Egypt, then moved inland to Mesopotamia and the final confrontation with Darius III, who was routed at Gaugamela and murdered by his own men shortly afterwards.

At this point, Alexander's expedition had achieved its ostensible purpose. Persia was conquered and the kingship was his. However, he pressed on north and west, past the Caspian Sea, over Parthia to the Caucasus, then into Russian Turkestan on a campaign which lasted another three years. Finally he entered India, defeated Porus and took the Punjab. He had now been away from Macedonia for nine years and his armies had had enough. Reluctantly, he abandoned plans to push eastwards and made his way back to Persia across trackless desert, losing more men to sand and thirst than had ever perished in his battles. Disaffection and mutiny ensued. None the less, in his last weeks in Babylon he was planning new exploits – an invasion of Arabia, to link Egypt with India. His death is thought to have been caused by an acute fever, possibly malaria, aggravated by alcohol.

Professor O'Brien's minutely researched book takes Alexander's relationship with alcohol, both in its material form and in the numinous aspect of the god Dionysus, as its central theme. The Macedonians were celebrated drinkers, viewed by Athenians as barbarian boar hunters; 'moderation in all things' was not their credo. Philip himself was known as *Philopotes*, drink-lover, and Olympias was involved in Dionysiac rites. Symposia, lengthy and competitive drinking parties, were an accepted part of drinking life, celebrating with equal vigour weddings, funerals, victories and relief from the tedium and stress of long campaigns. Alexander's greatest friend, Hephaestion, died after ingesting a half gallon of chilled wine for breakfast, and 35 men died during a drinking contest to commemorate the self immolation of the ascetic philosopher Celanus.

As a young man, Alexander criticised his father's excessive habits, but as he grew older he followed suit. This does not seem abnormal. O'Brien would have Dionysus overshadowing Alexander's life, but in fact Alexander, who was exceptionally zealous in sacrificing to the gods, seems seldom to have bothered with him. He razed Thebes, the city of Cadmus, Dionysus's grandfather, to the ground, and did feel later that this was a sacrilegious act, but he encouraged an actor who should have been leading Dionysian festivals in Athens to abscond from his sacred duties and come out to perform for him in Asia. He also ignored Dionysus's special day of worship on several occasions. It is possible, of course, that he feared the wrath of an affronted god, but it is more likely that his increased drinking was encouraged by a combination of heredity, social expectation, exhaustion and anxiety.

Alexander won great victories but also committed horrible and impious crimes, and many of these took place before 330, when O'Brien believes alcohol began to destroy his psyche. He had dragged an enemy general behind his chariot, he had burned down the great palace at Persepolis and slaughtered the people of Tyre. He had displayed what O'Brien quaintly calls 'creative religiosity', by manipulating the calendar so that he might fight in the forbidden month. As a very young man he had pulled the Pythian oracle priestess off her sacred stool. Yet at the same time, both before and after 330, he was deeply attentive to the needs of his men, sharing every danger with them personally, organising their medical aid, looking after their families. He was able to perform astounding feats of strategy, as in the taking of the 7,000ft Rock of Aornus or his confrontation with Porus and his elephants. He was able to summon up rhetoric which moved an army in mutiny to tears, and to weep himself at the mangled body of the dying Darius and the fate of the mutilated Greeks he met in the desert. The chivalric honour he paid to worthy foes remained constant, as did his courtesy to women.

None of this suggests a brain ravaged by alcohol. His troops were weary of endless campaigning, nine years of bitter cold alternating with desert conditions or the Indian monsoon and plagues of snakes. They loathed his policy of orientalisation, involving ritual abasement to a Macedonian king dressed in Persian robes and a conical hat worn at a sharp angle. There had been attempts, or rumoured attempts, on his life; it is not surprising that he should become suspicious and quick-tempered, or that he should deal ruthlessly with dissidents. As O'Brien says in his preface, one can only guess at the truth of his nature, and it is questionable to suggest that it was perverted by drink rather than by the natural outcome of circumstance and years.

Although one must respect Professor O'Brien's scholarship, this is an uneven and unsatisfying book. The first part, dealing with Alexander's boyhood, is full of conjecture, and there are some cringe-making twinkly remarks: 'It was no small task to be great, when measured against Philip of Macedon'; or, concerning a mythic brawl involving Zeus, Pericles and Apollo: 'Members of this family insisted on having things their own way and Alexander, who thought of himself as a direct descendant, was no exception'. At this point, the book reads like a *Boy's Own* story. However, the remaining two thirds, covering the campaign, murders and demise in Babylon, are lucid and compelling. Two jarring notes persist. One is O'Brien's constant desire to mingle the mythic and the factual, with gods smiling to themselves as Alexander commits some headstrong impiety. The second, which is profoundly irritating, is his arbitrary rearrangement of lines from the *Iliad* and *Bacchae* so that they read like lisped messages for those of small concentration span:

Winning for myself
great glory
and
for
my
father.

In the end, the lines which best explain Alexander's driven and exacting life and early death are not the irreverent ones prompted by the early pages of this book:

Do you remember an inn
    Alexander,
do you remember an inn?

but those assigned to Cleopatra, in origin also Macedonian:

Bring me my robes, put on my
    crown.
I have immortal longings in me.

TENNYSON
Peter Levi (1993)

Tennyson hated biographers, journalists and tourists. 'He would have wished,' said his friend Benjamin Jowett, 'that, like Shakespeare, his life might be unknown to posterity.'

However, people wrote about him constantly, providing a running commentary on his jokes, his smoking habits, his taste in food, as well as his marvellous poems. So there have been many biographies, beginning with his son Hallam's memoir in 1897, four years after the poet's death. Peter Levi, Tennyson's latest biographer, delayed writing his book until the 1990 publication of the final volume of Tennyson's letters, and he acknowledges his special debt to Christopher Rick's edition of the poems.

Tennyson was born at Somersby Rectory in Lincolnshire in 1809, the third of 12 children. His father was a bitter and reluctant parson, pushed into the church by his own father and eventually destroyed in a welter of alcohol and violence. Tennyson's mother loved animals; she travelled about the Lincolnshire lanes in a wheeled chair drawn by a Newfoundland dog; her children trooped around her, declaiming her own compositions as they went, or listening to her read from James Thompson and Mrs Hemans. They all wrote poetry – Alfred, Charles and Fred with distinction. By the age of 11, Alfred had filled a notebook with Latin elegiacs; when he was 18, he and his older brothers brought out a book of poems.

This degree of literary precocity was not unusual at that time, but the family themselves, as Levi admits, 'were extremely odd'. Their cook put it more strongly: 'If you raked out Hell with a small toothcomb, you we'ant find their likes.' A profound melancholy intermittently afflicted all of them, driving Edward to madness and permanent asylum at the age of 18, Septimus to serious depression, Charles to laudanum, and Arthur to drink. Yet they remained a strong family, and there are many glimpses of happy times; playing with Alfred's monkey; dancing through summer dusk to the music of Emily's harp; and tramping about the Lincolnshire landscape which always haunted Alfred, even though the family left the rectory at Somersby when he was in his late twenties.

At Cambridge, he made a wide circle of friends and won a poetry medal. Following the publication of *Poems, Chiefly Lyrical*, his reputation as a great poet began. His father died; he left Cambridge and brought out *Poems*, which was less well received. Then his dearest friend, Arthur Hallam, died, plunging him into agonised grief. He began work on *In Memoriam*, his masterpiece, revising and rearranging and adding to it for almost 20 years. At the same time, he was writing *Ulysses, Morte D'Arthur* and other important poems. But he published nothing for 10 years. He was also now estranged from Lincolnshire. Though he wrote prolifically, his spirits remained low. By 1841, he was smoking his shag tobacco for 12 hours a day, using the edges of his manuscript as spills, and drinking two bottles of port each evening.

Despite his elation at the great success, in 1842, of *New and Revised Poems*, his melancholy did not leave him. It was aggravated by financial anxieties. Aubrey de Vere observed that Tennyson 'will not be right until he has someone to love him exclusively'. This was not to happen until 1850, when his long-postponed wedding to Emily Selbrook finally took place. 'The peace of God came into my life before the altar,' he said. In the same year, *In Memoriam* was published, and Tennyson was made Laureate. It was at a time when he had declared that he might have the greatest mastery of the language of any poet since Shakespeare, but he had nothing more to say.

Through 40 years of great domestic happiness, he continued to revise and improve earlier poems and did produce astonishing new work, notably *Maud*, whose sales enabled him to buy Farringford on the Isle of Wight. It is extraordinary to consider the enthusiasm of

Victorian England for verse: even *Enoch Arden* sold 17,000 copies on its first day of publication. Tennyson enjoyed his Laureateship, but was obliged to write many dull poems on public affairs. *Idylls of the King*, once hugely popular, now seems a pre-Raphaelite embarrassment. 'Superlative lollipops,' said Carlyle; 'a huge botch,' says Levi. Yet his best was as good as ever. No one has surpassed him as a poet of landscape or of grief; only Milton can rival the music of his language.

Peter Levi's enthusiasm informs and illuminates on every page. I particularly enjoyed his discussion of *In Memoriam* and *Maud*, and of Tennyson's inspired alterations, often consisting of one or two words only: the revision of 'the sweet narcissus' to 'the shining daffodil'; or 'after many a summer dies the swan', previously 'the rose'. The book is a triumph of condensing, for everything about Tennyson was huge – his family, his range of friends, his work, his intellectual curiosity, even his voice. The deep affection which infuses Levi's clear, genial, and witty prose cannot but involve the reader. I have never before finished reading a biography with such a sense of loss and grief:

Ah Christ, that it were possible
For one short hour to see
The souls we loved, that they might tell us
What and where they be.

WRITING DANGEROUSLY
Mary McCarthy and Her World
Carol Brightman (1993)

In her story 'C'est le Premier Pas qui Coûte', Mary McCarthy describes her fictional self as 'one of those cowards who are afraid not to be brave'. But it is that fearful knowledge of necessity which creates bravery, and her courage, as much as her intelligence, formed and sustained her remarkable life.

Five idyllic years of infancy in Seattle ended abruptly with the deaths of both parents in the 'flu epidemic of 1917. Mary and her three small brothers were fostered by grim and cruel relatives in Minneapolis, fed on pigs' feet and chicken necks, beaten regularly with hairbrushes or razor strops. Mary won an essay prize at school and received a special thrashing to prevent conceit. On Saturdays she was given electric shock treatment, apparently as some form of bereavement therapy. The local Catholic church and school provided her only aesthetic pleasures.

At the age of 11 she was retrieved to Seattle by her prosperous Protestant grandparents, but her brothers were left in boarding school. Surrounded now by warmth, opulence and affection, she began to resent her grandparents' over-protective regime. At school she demanded attention and achieved notoriety by losing her faith and acquiring lovers twice her age. At the same time she loved the idea of justice and order (as personified by her grandfather) and, oddly, Julius Caesar. Vassar, 'a Forest of Arden and Fifth Avenue department store combined', fed her intellectual ambitions and her passion for literature.

Socially, however, she felt uneasy, and she made few friends. 'We were afraid of her brains,' said a classmate. Many another would say this in times to come. Vacations were a torment, for Seattle was too far and she could not be seen lingering, an unwanted wallflower, in college. Mercifully she received invitations. 'I am a person who has a special feeling about holidays,' she declared endearingly. It is not often that she is endearing; the pride which insisted that she appear invulnerable also renders her rebarbative.

Immediately after Vassar she married Harold Johnsrud, an actor, and embarked on the Bohemian life she craved, playing Sancho Panza to his Don Quixote. They had no money but they did have parties. She began to write book reviews and meet left-wing radical writers. The intellectual status of American Communism attracted her but she disliked its canting proclamations. The parties went on and she joined protest marches in evening dress.

At the age of 25, when her marriage had collapsed and she was living a life of amazing promiscuity in New York, she met Edmund Wilson, 'the era's Boswell and Johnson', through the *Partisan Review*. She passed out during their first dinner together. A few months later they were married. Seven turbulent years ensued; Wilson claimed that McCarthy was subject to fits of insanity and aggression; she accused him of drunken violence. None the less, bullied or encouraged by him, she now wrote the stories in *The Company She Keeps*, which established her as a writer.

She married twice more after leaving Wilson, had innumerable lovers, and continued to write fiction, book reviews, theatre reviews, and two books on Renaissance Art. She lived variously in New York, Paris, Warsaw and Italy; she sent back roving reports from Vietnam and enraged her compatriots by stating that: 'It is manifestly untrue that all men are created equal...The inalienable rights to life, liberty and the pursuit of happiness appear, in practice, to have become the inalienable right to a bath tub, a flush toilet, and a can of Spam.' Of Simone de Beauvoir she famously remarked: 'She's not utterly stupid.' Satre declined to meet her. William Carlos Williams said that her fiction was written mainly 'for those it attacks'. Koestler said that she had a 'wholly destructive critical mind'. Her McCarthy relations saw her writing as 'a scream of persecution for profit', underpinned, they implied, by the Jewish streak inherited from her maternal grandmother. And in October 1979 she crossed that narrow line between courage and folly and accused Lillian Hellman on the Dick Cavett Show of dishonesty: 'Every word she writes is a lie, including *and* and *the*.' The colossal row and interminable lawsuit which followed probably contributed to the wasting illnesses which killed McCarthy 10 years later.

This book is meticulously researched and contains a biographical glossary, notes, notes on notes and a vast index replete with lively sub-headings: 'Edmund Wilson, drinking habits of, sexual appetites of. . .etc.' There are 714 pages, about 300 too many for the average reader's appetite. Much of the detail will be of interest only to students of American intellectual life during and after the Second World War. There are occasional inaccuracies: Caroline Blackwood is described as 'a former lady-in-waiting to Princess Margaret' – 'It's defamatory to us both,' Lady Caroline declares. The writing is clear and unfussy, blessedly clear of pyschobabble, and most of the central characters are vividly conjured, though it is hard to see Edmund Wilson as the squalid, lying, priapic pig who heaves and grunts through these pages. Her obvious affection for McCarthy does not blind Brightman to the chilling selfishness, sexual rapacity, lack of compassion and snobbery, but the courage and intellect shine through, and while *The Group* does not withstand re-reading, *Memoirs of a Catholic Girlhood* and the stories remain true works of art. McCarthy's radiant smile remains too, beaming from pages of photographs: the smile of one who must be seen to be having a very good time, and the smile on the face of the tiger.

OTHER PEOPLE
Diaries 1963-66
Frances Partridge (1993)

Frances Partridge is Bloomsbury's oldest survivor, but this, the fourth published volume of her diaries, does not belong to the perennial Bloomsbury retrospective. It deals with the period in the sixties which followed the sudden death of her son Burgo, less than three years after the death of her husband, and it is first and foremost a testament of courage and tenacity, charting her progress from the numbing black ice-water of grief to a point where she has re-created a way of living, a new look at the world through a different lantern slide.

All grief is intensely personal, but anyone who has suffered bereavement will recognise certain of its torments here – the fear of drowning in the isolated self, the sense of irrelevance to others and the lack of 'the warmth of being loved and having someone with whom I can laugh and who is interested in anything at all that I've done or thought, and vice-versa'. But here the pain is tempered for the reader by Frances Partridge's utter refusal to indulge in self-pity, her acerbic sense of humour and her generosity to friends, family and humanity. This is no blueprint for survival, but it is a vivid account of one person's way of coping.

She is surrounded by friends who variously offer or demand support, and as time goes by her involvement in their concerns increases. It is clear that she is much loved, and deservedly so. Her kind, calm intelligence, open mind and unprissy adherence to standards all offered a refuge from the turbulence and sheer silliness of Sixties London life. Julia Strachey, Raymond Mortimer, the Cecils, Janetta Jackson, David Garnett, babies, lunatics, labradors crowd about her. And she works, almost unceasingly, through weekends and Christmases wherever she may be, translating and annotating, eager as soon as she has finished one thing to start on something new.

She travels a great deal too, amazingly even forcing herself to Italy with Raymond Mortimer a couple of weeks after her son's death. As time goes by, her descriptions of these trips become increasingly sharp and fresh, especially illuminated by her delight in colour. There are compelling and unexpected details in her accounts. She finds the painted walls of country villages near Bantry in Ireland reminiscent of buildings in Leningrad. She notices that certain awful truths about the natures of friends are brought out by travel; she loves them nonetheless. She sleeps uncomplainingly under a coverlet cobbled together from her host's underpants, she admires the improvement in Gerald Brenan's domestic arrangements ('there is only one cat and the house smells less than it did'), she learns Turkish, learns Russian, exults in the top floor of the Post Office Tower, adores Herodotus.

People move in and out of the same clear focus. Diana Cooper's startling fixed blue gaze during a railway journey (she is asleep but has had so many face lifts that she cannot close her eyes); C P Snow, snowman-like dissolving in the golden rays of a bottle of whisky; Iris

Murdoch seen as Joan of Arc. Conversation – 'when two people together weave a cat's cradle of ideas' – remains the greatest pleasure of all.

Although Frances Partridge provides notes on some of the foremost dramatis personae, there is often an element of frustration: there are so many people here with so many children and ex-husbands and boyfriends, and you can't always work out who belongs to whom. A Bloomsbury family tree would have been useful and interesting, for there has been much intermarriage between its descendants. But these are mere quibbles. This a moving and affectionate book whose conclusion is that time does not heal the knowledge of loss but does alter it.

GAVIN MAXWELL: *A Life*
Douglas Botting (1993)

Gavin Maxwell was three months old when his father was killed in the First World War. 'I kept Gavin very much as the child of my anguish,' declared his mother. Melancholy pervaded his life, disappointment ended all his endeavours, but his wild, perverse spirit sustained him, driving him headlong into adventures of increasing eccentricity. One of his final projects was to set up a breeding colony of Eider ducks on a Hebridean island furnished with children's windmills, tinkling bells, flag bunting and little tents of pine branches.

Birds were his first love. His early childhood was spent on the moors of his family estate in Galloway, collecting and studying all manner of flora and fauna. By the time he was sent to boarding school he had met only ten children, including his three siblings, and he found his new life intolerable. 'You must try to be like other people,' they told him. His education fizzled out when he became seriously ill at the age of 16;

from then on he was plagued by ill-health. This prevented him serving overseas in the war; stationed in the Highlands, he became an instructor in the SOE and attracted the notice of the medical officer as a 'creative psychopath'. He enraged his superiors by asking for compassionate leave when his pet flamingos flew out to sea, but he also made a number of close and lasting friends.

After the war he set up a shark-fishing business based on the island of Soay, attracted by adventure rather than commerce: 'We sailed into a dream sea in the dark and the eerie phosphorescence, towed by the wounded shark far below.' Eventually his impracticality and total lack of business sense obliged him to sell up and seek some new way of earning money. In turn he became a portrait painter, a poet, a racing driver at Silverstone and an explorer. His poems were printed in the *New Statesman* and in 1952 his first prose book, *Harpoon at a Venture*, established him at once as a brilliant descriptive writer and a cult figure, to some the White Knight, to others Captain Ahab, forever in pursuit of the elusive indefinable.

This myth had some truth, but there were other sides to Maxwell, most of them conflicting. His publishers found him the most tiresome author they had ever dealt with; he was constantly demanding royalties and advances which would be swallowed immediately by his latest series of debts. At the same time he claimed that money was of no real importance to him. He could be wildly generous and absurdly mean. He was reclusive by nature but he found solitude unbearable. He persuaded Wilfred Thesiger to take him on an exploration of the marshlands of Iraq; here he found himself extraordinarily, mystically happy in a desolation of water and sky which seemed to him to exist outside time and space. Thesiger's view of his companion was more prosaic: 'Dead baggage,' he commented. And when Maxwell's baby otter, the first of many, died, the extravagance of his grief seemed merely lunatic to Thesiger: 'He should be locked up.'

But now began the lifelong thraldom to otters. Accompanied by a second marsh otter, Maxwell returned to Britain and moved into the house in the Western Highlands which he called Camusfeàrna, the centre of his dream kingdom by the sea. Although he still travelled, notably to Sicily and Morocco in search of material for further books, the demands of otters gradually dominated his life. He was no zoologist: his attitude to his animals was entirely anthropomorphic. The otters had their bedrooms, their personal assistants, their crates of eels dispatched from London.

The struggle to support them and Maxwell's series of huge and powerful cars forced him into continuous writing, a task he found loathsome. All his books were rapturously received by the critics, but until he wrote *A Ring of Bright Water* he earned little money from them. This book made him rich, albeit temporarily, but it also destroyed the private world he had constructed with such labour; it brought literally hundreds of visitors to Camusfeàrna and immersed Maxwell in a ceaseless whirl of interviews, lectures and lurid publicity. Disasters, previously regular, now occurred constantly and with accumulating seriousness, until the final night when the entire house burnt down. Two years later Maxwell was dead from cancer. His ashes were buried in the rubble of Camusfeàrna.

Douglas Botting tells his story vividly, with a few lapses into journalese. He is himself an explorer and writer who shares many of Maxwell's interests, particularly his intense love for northern landscapes. Maxwell emerges as a fascinating, difficult and complex man who wrought his own doom and involved many others in it, testing the loyalty of his friends to the limit of endurance. They are the quiet heroes of this book, which reads more like a novel than a biography, scattered as it is with poltergeists, ghouls and a sorceress in the unexpected form of Katherine Raine. Maxwell's life itself is so extraordinary that these presences seem perfectly appropriate – and there are heavenly photographs of otters.

IN EXTREMIS
The Life of Laura Riding
Deborah Baker (1993)

Laura Riding possessed a large patchwork rug. Made of 'the finest silk and velvet rags that I could command from others', its squares had been worked, to her order, by 20 Cumberland ladies. The rug supplied her with a revealing image of her place in the world: 'And so each who made a square was my subject. And so I became Queen.' Power-crazed and despotic, Laura rampaged through the first half of her life in a self-promotional binge of destruction, portentously described as 'the search for truth'. What truth? What did she mean? Why was she so monstrous? What led to her mythic identity as Robert Graves's muse, his three-faced goddess? Her biographer, in time-honoured mode, trundles into her childhood for an answer.

Laura, not actually Riding but Reichenthal, was born in 1901 to impoverished parents, German-Jewish immigrants who settled in Brooklyn. Her early days sound depressing, but not dreadful. She had an adoring older half-sister who married a publisher and fostered her literary interests. She had a younger brother who aroused the not unusual reactions of rage and jealousy. Her father was involved in socialism, had a lively mind and encouraged reading. Her mother was plaintive, ill and odd: 'She wore a stocking round her eyes whenever possible; at home a white stocking; abroad a black stocking; and occasionally . . . a grey sock of my father's, fastened at the back of her head with a safety pin.'

Laura married Lou Gottschalk, a lecturer at Cornell, when she was 19; she dropped out of college, only returning to alarm her contemporaries with hints about sex and douches. She was writing obsessively; in 1924 she won the Nashville Poetry Prize and began to meet other poets. She left her husband and went to live in Greenwich Village; pursuing an illusory affair with Allen Tate and seeing her work published in magazines. Robert Graves wrote from England: he admired her poems and invited her to accompany him and his family to Egypt, where he was to lecture. Graves appears to have expected a literary secretary; Laura anticipated rather more. Tate had wearied of her. 'The maddest woman I have ever met,' he called her.

Laura returned triumphantly from Egypt; she had become Graves's confessor and advisor. Now she lived in a *ménage à trois* with Robert and his wife Nancy in London. She took an Irish lover; one fine morning he rejected her. She ran downstairs, picked up a bottle of disinfectant, returned to her fourth floor room and drank it in front of Robert, Nancy and the Irishman. No one stopped her. She then leapt out of the window. This, amazingly, resulted only in broken bones, but it brought an end to Graves's marriage. He left his wife and four children and on the proceeds of *Goodbye To All That* went off with Laura to live in Deya on Majorca. There Laura dressed in extravagant gypsy clothes, and flaunted a shawl embroidered with a 'representation of her damson-coloured surgical scar'.

For ten years she and Graves wrote and lived together, attracting numbers of fellow writers and painters to join them on lengthy visits. Laura had her kingdom; from its security she continued to issue hostile blasts of didactic theory to the English literary scene. With Graves she had already brought out *A Survey of Modernist Poetry* in which she dismissed Pound, Wallace Stevens and Eliot; this is her only influential piece of work. Now she reiterated her windy notions of restructuring experience, purifying language, ridding it of 'stale, historical and mythic associations', but the verses she wrote were opaque, clumsy and repetitive, rendered almost incomprehensible by inverted syntax and an entirely personal use of words. As Virginia Woolf said, she was 'a damned bad poet'.

In Deya she developed her female-centred aesthetic theories. She stopped sleeping with Graves: 'I think that bodies have had their day.' Visiting couples were obliged to leave their bedroom doors ajar. She encouraged a young woman to spend a few nights with Robert, but when the girl became pregnant Laura insisted on an abortion, witnessed it, and then banished her. Despite her claims that women were fundamental and men secondary, she required the adulation of men and was hostile to women. She bullied and alienated innumerable friends; they saw her treat Graves 'like a dog'. She stopped writing poetry and embarked on sickeningly coy fairy stories with characters called Mr Thinking-Hard and Mr Thank-You-Very-Much. She planned a new moral order, a world reorganised on matriarchal lines, her First Protocol. And all this time Graves continued to support and idealise her.

With the Spanish Civil War, fascism reached Deya and they were obliged to leave. Laura's *Collected Poems* were published in America and reviewed enthusiastically by the critic Schuyler Jackson. In England, for years now, her work had been published only as a sop to Graves, whose *I Claudius* was enjoying world success. She felt an outsider in London, no longer a queen (but a 'Queen-bore' according to Geoffrey Grigson), and persuaded Graves to accompany her to America. There they met up with Jackson, his wife and family. Laura focused her basilisk eye, Jackson's wife was driven crazy, he abandoned his four children, they ran off together and married. Graves returned to England and, ultimately, to Deya. For the remaining 50 years of her life Laura lived in Florida, working on her husband's citrus farm and restyling her past to suit herself.

This goes a little way to excuse the confused and two-dimensional effect of this biography. Deborah Baker makes it clear that she had no help from her subject and wrote the book against her wishes. Riding was notoriously hostile to interviewers and she and Graves issued many mutually contradictory statements. The book focuses on their 14 years together, and this is entirely legitimate. But one derives no real sense of either as a human being. Laura is all persona; Graves is potentially far more interesting, but he remains a vague, background figure.

It is hard to read 400 pages about a woman so intrinsically unpleasant. The author's attempts to exalt her poetry and, somewhat in desperation, to present her wit, fall flat. Many of Baker's sentences are scarcely literate: 'Too much pain . . . than was practical', 'endearing' when she means 'enduring', death's 'veraciousness'. Clichés abound, complex paragraphs begin with serial unrelated subordinate clauses;

chapters plunge forward in time and then move smartly into reverse, making you feel you've travelled a long way for nothing. Really you can't wait for it all to be over.

Was there any point in starting? I think not. There is a story to be told, but it belongs to Graves. This is a bad book about a very bad woman.

PATRICK HAMILTON: *A Life*
Sean French (1993)

The novel *Hangover Square* is one of the great books (and has one of the great titles) of this century, most apposite to the dog-end of our festive season. Have you ever tried to give up smoking and drinking in one fell swoop? Here is a canny wee ruse (though not for mixed company). Drown the last third of a cigarette in an inch or two of whisky; retire to bed with this elixir adjacent to your pillow, balanced perhaps on top of your Good News Bible. Retain relative positions for as long as possible. An equally effective and infinitely pleasanter solution, if I dare use that word, is to read the novels of Patrick Hamilton, recently re-issued by Penguin, Cardinal and the Hogarth Press, presumably in the hope of a revival of interest in his work, consequent on the publication of two biographies in the last two years, Nigel Jones's *Through a Glass Darkly* (1991) and now Sean French's *Life*.

It is not often that one meets anyone who has read Hamilton's books, although it is moderately well known that he Died of Drink. His life offers the vicarious appeal of self-destruction in our time of self-regard, as prevalent in the caring Nineties as in the uncaring Eighties, and with Eighties vulgarity the word 'failure' is applied to him, prefaced perhaps by a caring 'tragic'. This view of Hamilton was originally fostered by his brother Bruce's memoir *The Light Went Out*; one of the virtues of Sean French's biography is that he exposes that book for the rubbish it is.

Hamilton was born in 1904, the third child of middle-aged parents, both of whom wrote. He did not enjoy his childhood, although in later life he said that it was as pleasant as could be expected. Indifferent nursemaids and a father rendered inscrutably sinister by drink brought about a sense of instability and anxiety, the beginnings of the 'malady of our doubt' which shadowed all his life.

To look at the photograph of the adult Hamilton on the book jacket is at once to recall Housman's 'I a stranger and afraid / In a world I never made'. Tentative, diffident, almost disengaged, he seems poised for flight. But the family, father excluded, remained remarkably close, 'united', said Bruce, 'in love and understanding', and even the father's monstrosities eventually became merely comic, significant to his sons only for the dread possibility that they might one day resemble him.

All three children were devoted to their mother. Patrick liked to address her in the extravagant language of the novels she wrote – 'my exquisite', 'my angel' – signing himself 'your infatuated Patrick'. When, old and ill, she chose to commit suicide, her children were her passive accomplices. Odds and ends of jobs and studies succeeded school, which Hamilton managed to leave at the early age of 15. He wanted at first to become a poet. But, after working in the theatre and touring the provinces with his actress sister, he focused instead on the novel, where he was able to use the dramatic techniques he had absorbed.

He had no romantic illusions about writing, describing it as 'hard labour in solitary – something to which even illness is preferable'. The most fascinating parts of this book contain Hamilton's thoughts on his trade and how to conduct it. He believed that it required utter dedication, 'a life-of-labour-from-day-to-day-gospel . . . expecting nothing from life, but using oneself unremittingly and fighting with endless courage a winning or losing battle.' In the matter of discipline he distinguished between mild self-control and 'something partially fanatical', backed by his faculty for 'stored observation', which enabled him to transform his glum choice of subject matter – run-down boarding houses, squalid pubs, the unrelenting extinction of hope – into masterpieces of atmosphere and detail.

Sean French quotes from *The Plains of Cement*, where a man searching for his card has 'bent his head down, not unlike a parrot diving into its feathers, to rummage more deeply', and from *Hangover Square* he cites the evil and mindless Netta, described as 'something seen floating in a tank, brooding, self-absorbed, frigid, moving solemnly towards its object or veering sideways without fully conscious motivation'. Netta was the sort of cheap manipulator Hamilton detested, and he domiciled her by the crossroads in Earl's Court where he had been hit by a car, a hideous accident which ripped off his nose and left him mended but maimed mentally as much as physically.

His relations with women were uneasy. He drifted back and forth between two dutiful and devoted wives, but his mother and his sister were his enduring loves – they both provided a safe haven from the sado-masochism which he saw in all other adult relationships. He did not drink when he was writing, and he evolved a number of strategies to outwit the demon. Gathering depression at last overwhelmed him; the deaths of family and friends, the demands of the Inland Revenue and the hostile reception for *Mr Stimpson and Mr Gorse*, which is now seen as one of his finest books, brought him to a state of suicidal apathy. After ECT treatment he felt better but wrote no more. He continued to drink, funded as always by the great success of his earlier work, especially his plays. His liver failed and he died, cheerful in a negative, numb sort of way, at the age of 58.

Sean French's rather colourless biography relies on lengthy quotations from Hamilton's letters and work, and these, far more than the text, give one a real sense of the man. He turned an odd but unremarkable life into remarkable literature, and he maintained his own rigorous standards. He won his battle. He was a writer who drank, not a drunk who wrote.

ROALD DAHL
Jeremy Treglown (1995)

Towards the end of his life, Roald Dahl claimed that if he walked in to any house in the world where there were children, he would be greeted with excitement and delight. Throughout his 74 years he made numerous bids for glory, none entirely without substance, but often exaggerated to the point of fantasy. Here, however, he spoke with more truth than usual; it may well be that the subject of this new biography by Jeremy Treglown is better known than any other English-language author of the second half of this century.

Generations of children have grown up with Dahl's books and have been able to enjoy reading them to their own children. These books have been translated into innumerable languages, filmed and televised. Their saturnine author enjoyed replying in rhyme to school-children's fan letters: 'Oh wondrous children miles away / Your letters brightened up my day'. A supportive teacher might be disconcerted to find herself hailed as 'lovely, gorgeous Sheila'. Benevolent, quirkily paternal, the 'Sparky' father he ordained as an ideal, Dahl made himself mythic, fantastic as Mr Fox, subversive champion of the lonely misfit. The malign fantasy which informs his writing permeated his life, a life which in return flung up a series of allegorical challenges. Milton's 'two-handed engine at the door' smote him not once but over and over. His head was bloody, but unbowed. Some people, he wrote, 'have an indomitable spirit and nothing . . . will cause them to give up'.

Dahl was born in Cardiff in 1917, to prosperous Norwegian parents. His father, a shipping broker, had settled in Wales some years earlier, with his wife and two small children. Suddenly widowed, he remarried. Sofie, his new bride, cheerfully took on the existing family and soon had four infants of her own. Roald, her only son, was the third baby, the special one, later nicknamed the Apple. When he was three, his eldest sister died of appendicitis. Two months later his father died. That autumn another daughter was born. Sofie, devoted and matriarchal, brought up her children, did what she believed best. In the summers they went to Norway to her family. There her father, a naturalist, fostered Roald's interest in birds and insects. Aunts and cousins told stories of trolls, witches and haunted forests, and Treglown informs us that they 'ate fresh fish and burnt toffee'. This sounds so odd that for a moment one sees the whole family as trolls, as Maurice Sendak creatures.

At school at Repton Dahl was good at games but otherwise undistinguished. Those few of his contemporaries who remember him remark only on his unkind humour and competitive spirit. His finest achievement, it seems, was the invention of a sadistic mousetrap which plunged its victims into a bowl of water; its slogan 'Catch as Cats Can't' rings true to Dahl. He was bullied and he bullied in return, more verbally than physically. At home he was surrounded by adoring womenfolk.

The outbreak of war found him working for Shell in Tanganyika. He enjoyed the opportunities for local exploration and the colonial comforts, but he was often bored; the excitement of joining the RAF and learning to fly over the Kenyan highlands remained with him all his life, providing images both magical and nightmarish for his writing. Flying an unfamiliar plane over unfamiliar territory to join his squadron in Egypt, he crash-landed in the desert and spent seven months in hospital recovering from serious injuries whose aftermath never left him. He later converted the acute pain and frustration of this episode into fictive heroic exploits. He declined convalescent leave in Britain and fought with gallantry in the hopeless air defences over Athens and then the Peloponnese. Five weeks later he was sent home, suffering blackouts and excruciating headaches which ended his active service. He had, however, become a war hero.

In due course he joined the British Embassy in Washington as assistant air attaché, liaising in what now seems a strangely casual manner with British Intelligence. But here, unlike at Repton, Dahl was valued for his wit, his service record (factual and otherwise), his looks and charm. Washington was wildly social, rich women swarmed about him and he discovered that he could dominate a room full of people with his fantastic stories. C. S. Forester asked him for RAF anecdotes to be used as propaganda, received the romanticised account of Dahl's plane crash, and sent it to the *Saturday Evening Post*, where it appeared in 1942 as *Shot Down Over Libya: An RAF Pilot's Factual Account* and marked the inception of Dahl's unintentional career as a writer.

His stories began to appear regularly in magazines and Disney attempted to make a film of his *Gremlins*. Although this project collapsed, the malevolent elves were perpetuated in a Disney book published in a fair storm of argument over their provenance. Despite the fact that gremlin stories were rife in the Air Force, and several other books about them had appeared, Dahl was happy to take credit for their invention. Isaiah Berlin took a sardonic view of this: 'He initiated gremlins, that is to say they were already there, in the air force, but he put them on the map. He was extremely conceited, saw himself as a creative artist of the highest order, and therefore entitled to respect and special treatment.' Half a century later, Dahl's exasperated publishers could have made the same comment.

Back with his mother in Buckinghamshire, he found post-war Britain flat and depressing. He was trying to make a living by writing, but he was outside the literary scene and there he remained. He was often in pain from his accident, racked with anxieties and doubts over his own writing abilities. He managed to sell a few stories to the BBC, and to American magazines, which paid him astonishing sums. His Washington friend and patron, the newspaper magnate Charles March, involved him in various philanthropic trusts, administering funds to poor families in the East End. Dahl performed his duties with zeal but was unable to resist mocking both benefactors and recipients whenever an easy target presented. He also collected furniture, paintings and china for Marsh to ship back to the States. Eventually, in 1951, he followed him there.

In New York he plunged back into an intensified version of the social life he had enjoyed in Washington, drinking and boasting, gossip and malice, manipulation and name-dropping, reflected in his stories with a satirical edge which he did not bring to his own behaviour. Through his friend Lillian Hellman he met Patricia Neal, young, beautiful and already famous as an actress. Despite the misgivings of certain friends, they married in 1953. Dashiell Hammett remarked that 'the ring isn't bad-looking, and I told her I was glad she was getting that out of it because she didn't look as if she was getting much else'. Neal and Dahl moved into a house in Buckinghamshire (paid for by Neal and her mother-in-law) but continued to spend much of the year in the States. Knopf now brought out Dahl's flying stories, *Someone Like You*, to wild success. Dahl was in his element, claiming that he was a literary Picasso breaking away from Corot and Monet. In England the book was received coolly. Critics noted its cruelty.

Seven busy years succeeded. Neal's acting career continued to bloom; Dahl's writing was erratically received, until in 1960 he had a new triumph with *Kiss Kiss*. But it was in this year that the first series of personal catastrophes occurred. Baby Theo, aged four months, was struck by a cab as his nanny pushed his pram across a New York street. His skull was smashed and he was not expected to live. Ultimately and incredibly he did recover, after years of desperate illness and suffering. It is clear that it was Dahl's resource, energy and refusal to lose hope which finally saved him. Working with his son's consultant and a friend who was an aircraft designer, Dahl pioneered the Wade-Dahl-Till Valve, which has since been used to treat thousands of children with brain injuries. But before these terrible anxieties had subsided, Olivia, their eldest daughter, died of measles. She was seven, as Dahl's dead sister had been. Gradually Neal was able to return to acting; as a writer Dahl was utterly disabled by his grief. And two years later, shortly after receiving her Oscar for *Hud*, Patricia Neal suffered three violent strokes, which left her insensible and crippled.

Again Dahl refused to accept the grim prognosis. He set about bringing her back into the world with an astonishing determination, which often shocked onlookers by its brutality and ruthlessness. Nonetheless, it worked. Eventually she was to return to acting and to a full and normal life. Eventually their marriage collapsed under so long a strain.

Dahl not only re-created his wife. He ran his household, adored his children, planned the garden, wrote screenplays (unsuccessfully) and continued to produce stories. At last even in England his books were selling well, and he had a substantial income from translations, TV adaptations and the eager US market. But his health was poor and he was constantly exhausted. In 1983 he married Felicity Crosland and enjoyed seven years of renewed happiness, contentiousness and productivity before his death from Leukaemia in 1990.

Dahl's profound attachment to his family is the one consistency in a life of veering contradictions. Patricia Neal remarked cynically that he had 'an enormous appreciation for anything he generated'. In his life and in his work there is an undoubted element of misogyny, but it is balanced and outweighed by his sympathy with children. He enjoyed striking attitudes, provocative whenever possible. He badly damaged his reputation by an ugly anti-Semitic book review written in the Eighties. There was a certain truth in his self-mythologising; he was in many ways a hero who performed astonishing feats. He was also cruel and irascible, attention-seeking and selfish.

Jeremy Treglown treats his complex subject with admirable objectivity, shading at times into coldness. In outlining Dahl's life and character he is economical, lucid and convincing. This is not an authorised biography, and there are certain blank areas. We are given only a most superficial impression of Patricia Neal, and little feeling of the warmth which existed between Dahl and his children. His daughter, Ophelia, is the designated biographer and she will perhaps redress the balance here.

Treglown dwells at unnecessary length on sales figures and publishing politics, and some of his accounts of editor's minute revisions of Dahl's manuscripts will be of interest only to specialists. Treglown's tone is dry and unemotional, almost to a fault. He is at his best when discussing the stories and their relationship to Dahl's own life, at his worst when describing a schoolboyish incident at the Washington embassy in a style of breathtaking vulgarity.

As a final quibble, I disliked his habit of referring to Dahl from the age of 60 as an *old* man. There is just a whisper of the unjustifiably patronising here. But overall this is an honourable intellectual account of an extraordinary man, a fitting complement to any more emotional and subjective treatment to come.

ROBERT LOUIS STEVENSON
Frank McLynn (1994)

It is Edinburgh, 1853. Wrapped in blankets, safe in the arms of his nursemaid, the infant R.L.S. stares from his window into the winter darkness; the street lamps glow and he can see gas burning behind other windows, where other small, fevered children wait interminably for morning. When he was not kept awake by illness, Louis' nights were fragmented and fearful with nightmares. At the nursery fireside his devoted nurse told him tales of body snatchers, ghouls, ghosts and the vengeful god of Calvinism. These were supplemented by his father's bedtime stories and his dreams, tangled in monsters and Jacobite conspiracies, hooded horsemen, infinite tenement staircases. The romance of the past, the terror of the supernatural, the unrelenting anger of God provided an imaginative reality as solid as the cool Hanoverian terraces of the New Town, as menacing as the swooping wynds, dark archways and seething slums of the Old.

Besides these, the awful weather and the marvellous landscape, (Stevenson said that the climate made the Scot metaphysical) the Calvinist ethos of sobriety and the Celtic tendency to intoxication, the yearning for order, the desire for a world free from duty which ineluctably goes rolling into chaos, all conspire to wreck the Scottish psyche. So it was in Stevenson's day and so it is now. He found the sound of Edinburgh's Sabbath bells one of the world's most dismal uproars, and by the age of twenty two had fallen out seriously with his parents over what he saw as 'the disloyalty to Christian love' of Presbyterianism. He did little work at Edinburgh University, but read and wrote for his own pleasure. He avoided most lectures on the grounds that the act of concentration might bring on brain fever. His father overlooked this as he assumed that Louis would be following him into the family tradition of lighthouse engineering. Their relations grew worse as Louis began to publish reviews in Leslie Stephens' *Cornhill* magazine and wandered off to France, spending time with painters amd loose women in Grez and Barbizon. He returned to Edinburgh and actually qualified as an advocate in 1875; however his legal career earned him only four guineas in his whole life. Money 'i.e. happiness' was to remain a desperate desideratum and a humiliating tie with his parents. But meanwhile in Paris he had met and fallen in love with Fanny Osbourne, a married woman ten years older than himself.

Fanny had left her faithless husband Sam in California and with her two children was staying in the Anglo-American colony of painters at Grez. She was dark haired and olive skinned, a heavy smoker and a gun toting sharp shooter. She had artistic pretensions but little talent. At first she was more attracted to Louis' beloved cousin Bob, who was himself more attracted to her daughter Belle. She clearly did have feelings for Louis, but was equally drawn to him by the prospect of his father's money. She returned to California to try to arrange a divorce from Sam, while Louis set forth on the walking tour in the Cevennes which became *Travels with a Donkey*. The donkey reminded him distressingly of his absent love, and when the book came out it was much criticised for its sexual overtones. At last, after a year spent in America with and without Fanny, she obtained her divorce and in 1880 they were married. His parents were desperate that he should come home and offered him £250 a year. His health had deteriorated under the stresses of his new life and he had experienced his first haemorrhage, but he was reconciled with his father. Years of travelling about Europe in search of the ideal climate for his chest problems ensued. Fanny also became ill, usually in places where R.L.S. felt better. Despite gathering anxieties, he wrote constantly, short stories including the marvellous *Thrawn Janet*, and then *Treasure Island*, which was his first public success. *Black Arrow* and *Prince Otto* followed. His parents bought them a house in Bournemouth and this was the improbable venue for the writing of Jekyll and Hyde; he achieved the first draft in three days while ill in bed. At last, with the death of his father, he had some financial security and he set forth with Fanny, her son Lloyd and his mother for America and ultimately for the Pacific islands. In Samoa he found a climate which suited him; they built an extravagant house and made a garden and a farm. For a while Louis was wildly happy. 'There is nothing so interesting as weeding'.

They played cricket with unripe oranges, gave extravagant parties for native chiefs and visiting warships, and ran an extended household containing nineteen island servants headed by the pleasingly named Henry Simile. For Stevenson this life had elements of the chieftan/clan relation of his chivalric fantasy and the island people appealed to his Jacobite sentiment. But he was increasingly aware of his isolation from his literary friends, and he began to miss Scotland, 'that indescribable bite of the whole thing at a man's heart which is – or rather lies at the bottom of – a story'. On December 3rd 1894 he suddenly collapsed and died two hours later from a brain haemorrhage. Such are the bare facts.

Frank McLynn tells the story vividly with a well judged accumulation of detail and just enough repetition to be reassuring. He is particularly good at creating a sense of place, often using Stevenson's own words, and he introduces his characters objectively, allowing most space to those whom R.L.S. loved most, his father, his cousin Bob, Colvin and Henley. The glaring and undermining exception to this is his treatment of Fanny and her children, who can do nothing right. Fanny may have been a flawed and difficult woman, but it is inconceivable that Louis would have tolerated and indeed loved her all those years if she had been the monster depicted here. The most damning thing Stevenson has to say of her is, 'I am what she has made me, the embers of the once gay R.L.S.', and this was in the midst of his row with Henley and during a period of deep depression, a condition which recurred throughout his life and alternated with euphoric serenity. To say that the Osbournes unscrupulously abused Stevenson's generosity is to ignore his own pride and family feeling and to insult his intelligence and resolution. Stevenson's luminous personality invests the whole book; his wit, his charm and his astonishing courage dazzle. McLynn discusses his work to moderate effect, most interestingly when he traces the influence of Melville and most boringly when he becomes psycho-analytical. Stevenson knew himself and was his own modest assessor.

Three of his remarks contain much of his essence: 'Man is not truly one but truly two.' 'What genius I had was for work', and 'I ought to have been able to build lighthouses and write.'

HENRIETTA
Henrietta Moraes (1994)

Henrietta Moraes is a survivor. 'I never gave in' is the refrain of her book. It charts the passage of a remarkable and tempestuous life from baffled, loveless infancy in the 30s to painful self knowledge in the 90s. Her early years, spent with an increasingly violent grandmother and an indifferent mother, forged a spirit well versed in human mutability and incapable of compromise. At the age of 3 she became a boarder at convent school, bathing in a white cotton tent to save the Holy Mother's blushes, and force fed on scraps of congealed fat. The next school was even more punitive. 'The flames were reflected on the grimy white walls and it seemed all leaping shadows and dark piles of coal and this great old boiler and gigantic nun towering above, spitting and belching.'

A happier interlude in a big country house and a jolly girls' public school led to London, secretarial college and escape to Soho, jazz clubs, the Gargoyle and serious all day drinking. 'I didn't know how people behaved' she remarks 'so I just did as I wished, probably the best thing to do anyway'. The demon angel Alcohol took her under his wing. Her drinking companions became life long friends, difficult and dazzling, violent, vituperative, witty and mutually forgiving. Lucien Freud, John Deakin, the Bernard brothers, David Archer, Francis Bacon, John Minton, Francis Wyndham – their names are legion and luminous. She married, divorced, remarried, had two babies, had typhoid, divorced again, took on an assortment of shortlived jobs and lived in the riverside house which Minton left her after his suicide, a house haunted by the spirits of imported slaves, manacled to the dripping walls 200 years before. A third marriage, to the poet Dom Moraes, disintegrated. The death of her beloved Irish housekeeper and mentor precipitated a dark night of the soul. The swinging sixties brought her amphetamine psychosis, methedrine, an addiction to cat burgling and a spell in Holloway. She lost her house; her children lived with friends. Here for the first time a twinge of self criticism appears: 'I know now that my children suffered a lot and if I could change anything in my life it would be this'. But for then it was a headlong embrace of hippiedom, into the Afghan robes and godhead via LSD. At Brian Jones' memorial concert Henrietta and her friends scattered hundreds of tiny silver packets into the crowd. 'Acid, acid, acid' we called, like Christina Rossetti's goblins. Like so many other goblins they went back to nature, trundling haphazardly round South West England in a gypsy caravan drawn by stout skewbald Rizla, nicking purple hearts, amiably colliding with cars and occasionally burning themselves down. This bit of the book is pretty annoying.

The demon angel, banished in favour of drugs, now reappears: 'I had moved into the Newcastle Brown stage of my life'.

There are druggy, drinky adventures on the Welsh borders, in Sri Lanka and in Ireland. The Irish period lasts 5 years but ends again in tragedy, with death, banshees and broken bones. Back in London Henrietta finds a room and a gardening job, a joyous renaissance, only to learn that she has cirrhosis of the liver. The closing pages which describe the harrowing complexities and eventual serenity of a sober life are extraordinarily moving. This reads as a memoir rather than an autobiography. The voice is conversational and rambling, sometimes repetitive. The characterisation is thin, with a couple of exceptions. With such a density of material the book could be twice as long. None the less it is compelling and vivid, not so much an account of the spirit of its times as of Henrietta Moraes's own spirit. She speaks as she finds, and is as uncritical of others as of herself. There is no self pity and not a mean word here, only a poignant freshness and affection, affection which is clearly returned in equal measure by her huge assortment of friends who have helped out endlessly with houses, jobs and companionship at no small cost to themselves. In an odd paragraph she claims to have a literary rather than a visual imagination. I venture to disagree. The book will make a brilliant film. It is crammed with images, bright and disparate as a lovingly disorganised photograph album, a brave attempt to set some order upon chaos.

Pity about the title.

EVELYN WAUGH
A Biography
Selina Hastings (1994)

'Furniture is so useful,' observed Evelyn Waugh's mother Kate. 'He would have been happier designing furniture'. It is startling to discover that even after the beginnings of his literary career, with his biography of Rossetti completed and *Decline and Fall* under way, Waugh still believed that his real future lay in cabinet-making. His fascination with elegant craftsmanship began in infancy with his mother's sewing box, its minute compartments and accessories, and continued all his life, becoming a metaphor for his other preoccupations, writing and Catholicism.

Evelyn was born in Hampstead in 1903, the second son of Arthur and Kate Waugh. Arthur worked in publishing, loved literature, amateur theatricals and cricket. He was the author of several books, including a life of Tennyson and a series of bicycling poems. Kate was a devoted wife, mother and homemaker, reacting against her disorderly upbringing. They were mild, kindly people, and Selina Hastings' account of their marriage, with its innocent pleasures and modest aspirations, is infinitely touching. Evelyn, as an adult, saw them as shamefully Pooterish; he despised his father's literary achievements and resented his preference for his older brother Alec. Alec, meanwhile, noted Evelyn's resemblance to Lupin Pooter and was entertained.

After a happy childhood spent racketing around Hampstead Heath, Evelyn endured the rigours of public school at Lancing. Here he was unpopular, arrogant, sharp-tongued and devoid of team-spirit. Although he was writing prolifically by the time he was 16, his greater interests were in calligraphy and book binding. Lifelong misanthropy had set in: 'the increased insight into people's characters led, I found, mainly to increased dislike'.

A history scholarship to Oxford began three years of resolute idleness in that 'deregulated nursery', where he formed intense and lasting friendships with other newly liberated drinkers, including Frank Pakenham, Harold Acton, John Betjeman, Anthony Powell and Hugh Lygon, whose family was the source of the Marchmains in *Brideshead*, written 20 years later. Through these friends he became familiar with the great country houses of old Catholic families, which offered him an ideal of aesthetic and spiritual continuity, a domestic counterpart to the church.

Waugh left Oxford with many debts and a third. A wretched period of teaching was made tolerable by drinking bouts in London and

Oxford, and concluded abruptly by a commission to write a biography of Rossetti and a vague job on the *Express*. With the acceptance of *Decline and Fall*, he abandoned thoughts of cabinet-making for writing and after a long engagement married She-Evelyn, flirtatious, lively, reader of 'Prousty-wousty' and owner of a handbag which was shaped like a Pekinese and known as Androcles. In Islington they played house; a friend likened them to a pair of squirrels with their 'round eyes and reddish nutkin colouring'. Both had married to escape from their families and to set some order on their lives. He-Evelyn spent periods of solitude writing in country hotels; She-Evelyn, lonely and depressed, returned to flirtation and parties. Inevitably, the marriage collapsed. Horribly shocked to find himself divorced, Waugh embarked on several years of travels of increasing improbability and pointlessness, funded by various newspapers and publishers.

Vile Bodies had been well received but his travel pieces were not successful; as Selina Hastings observes, Conrad's dictum that the writer should study human nature in unfamiliar surroundings to avoid superficiality simply didn't work for Waugh. He wrote best about the world he knew best. But in such a time of emotional chaos, despair and accidie he found that the Catholic church offered an 'unarguable historical truth', with discipline and order leading to salvation through a series of dove-tailing doctrines; the priest was the craftsman. He was admitted to the church on 'firm intellectual conviction'.

At last, after the protracted annulment of his marriage, he was able to marry Laura Herbert and achieve a stable loving home life in the country. Almost immediately war was declared and his life was again fragmented. He knew active service once only, in Crete, and was disgusted by what he saw as the cowardice of the British Army. Due to his unbridled obnoxiousness he was never given responsibility. Indeed, it was suggested that he would be shot, and not by the enemy, if he attempted any form of leadership. Although he was able to write for long periods through the war and spent a surprising amount of time with Laura and friends, he came out of the army in deep depression into an England which had changed forever. For 20 more years he wrote and drank and tortured himself and others, none the less sustaining his old friendships and tolerating rather than enjoying family life with six children and the silent Laura, who had become obsessed with her herd of cows. He died on Easter Sunday 1966, after Mass, at home, and in unusually good spirits. His family said that he wanted to die. He had said 'I believe that man is by nature an exile and will never be self-sufficient or complete on this earth.'

Selina Hastings has written a remarkable biography, uncensorious but never indulgent. Her style is supremely elegant and her eye for detail brings dazzle and wit to every page. She is admirably unintrusive to the narrative, allowing incidents and individuals to speak for themselves; in the 600-odd pages she steps forward twice only, once to be a little sharp on Diana Cooper, 'voracious for admiration, indifferent to sexual love', and once, when a friend remarks àpropos of Laura that 'wives must have *some* life of their own', she comments 'there was never to be much chance of that'. Indeed it would have been interesting to learn how Laura endured or enjoyed those long lonely years and so many pregnancies engendered but often unwanted by Evelyn, who saw children as 'defective adults' of inferior worth to his library: 'A child is easily replaced, while a book destroyed is utterly lost.'

Discussion of the books is brief and to the point, linking Waugh's life and associates to his fiction. She is sympathetic and lucid on his very personal version of Catholicism and its particular role in *Brideshead* and the *Sword of Honour* trilogy. She is also wildly funny on the bizarre language of *Helena*, notably when the Emperor Constantine mentions his formal green wig: 'just a little thing I popped on this morning. I have quite a collection. You must ask to see them. Some of them are very pretty.'

This is a monumental book, leisured but never monotonous. She says in her foreword that she aims to give an impression of what it was like to know Evelyn Waugh, even what it was like to be Evelyn Waugh, and certainly one has by the end of the book a most powerful sense of someone who has just gone: not merely the lasting image that Waugh offers of himself – 'I just saw myself in a mirror . . . like a red lacquer Chinese dragon, and saw how I shall look when I die' – but a complex striving and solitary soul. Could he have been happier as a furniture maker? Never.

CHRISTINA ROSSETTI
A Literary Biography
Jan Marsh (1994)

In the bleak mid winter, 100 years ago, Christina Rossetti died. She was 64 years old; to the end she had prayed, believing that in heaven there was an afterlife for the deserving, but that she had 'A Father in Heaven not incapable of slaying forever'. On that cold dawn, four days after Christmas, she died in great distress and pain, but also in silence true to her precept, 'no moaning will I make.' She died as she had lived, stoic, for more than half a century. She had achieved high recognition for her writing and expressed herself finally satisfied. But no one now, she said, could be 'Mother, Sister, dear friend to me'. As snow had fallen, snow on snow, so loss upon loss had assailed her. It is fitting that 'In the Bleak Midwinter' should be by far her best-known work – so well known, indeed, that few recognise its author. It is always there at Christmas. She had a modest wish to be remembered at her death, 'And then remembered or forgotten it will be well with me', she added with urgent and characteristic self-effacement. Her passing, like much of her work, seems sad, unresolved and cold.

In the beginning, things had been otherwise. In 1830 Christina was born into a warm Italian family, fourth and youngest child of Frances and Gabriel Rossetti. Her maternal grandfather, Gaetano Polidori, had settled in England and married an English girl. Frances's brother John Polidori was Byron's eccentric friend and physician, author of *The*

Vampyre. Gabriel Rossetti was a political exile from Naples. Academic, poet and patriot, he was a charismatic focus for London's Italian community. The four children were brought up in a loving, lively and talkative open household. From infancy they were bilingual. They played word-games, went to the opera, read, acted, painted and wrote. Christina was acknowledged as the poet of the family. They were precocious, bright and adored, all their lives remaining an exceptionally close family.

But when Christina was 13 her father became ill, and he was obliged to give up his post as Professor of Italian at King's College. Frances took over the family finances, working as a governess; sister Maria did likewise, and the boys, Gabriel and William, continued with their education while Christina stayed at home looking after an increasingly wretched and resentful invalid. For Christina the spectacle of her father's slow erosion by illness was catastrophic. She herself became acutely ill and changed from a vivacious, boisterous and demonstrative child to a melancholy, withdrawn and untrusting young woman, haunted by nightmares and afflicted by self-loathing. Spiritually she and her sister came under the influence of Pusey and Dodsworth at their local church by Regent's Park. While Maria developed a radiant faith and many years later became a nun in Pusey's Anglican Sisterhood, Christina's self-doubt and scruples multiplied under fears of the Second Coming, the Day of Judgement and the flames of Hell. Even Maria suffered from an anxiety that the General Resurrection might take place when she was among the mummies in the Egyptian room at the British Museum.

On a more cheerful note, grandpa Polidori printed and circulated among friends and family a limited edition of 42 of Christina's verses. The enthusiastic reception of this first collection confirmed her literary aspirations; the following year she sent two poems to *The Athenaeum*, which published them when she was still only 17. Her brothers were also writing poetry, and Gabriel printed Christina's work in the Pre-Raphaelite Brotherhood's short-lived magazine *Germ*.

Christina maintained an affectionate but distanced relation with the PRB, detached by social convention from its wild extravagances, but a willing sitter and amused onlooker. Over the years she had three muted romantic understandings with friends and colleagues of her brothers; none of these came to anything, and they left her stricken and wretched. The first and most wounding was her engagement to James Collinson, who rejected her for the Catholic Church. The image of the yearning, agonised heart recurs throughout her poetry: 'I turn my face in silence to the wall/My heart is breaking for a little love.'

Love, locked out, displaced, an unwanted gift returned to its donor, was to be Christina's lot. She had a wide circle of friends, but her closest relationships were with her immediate family, and especially her mother, whom she outlived by only eight years. Hope deferred and redemption through suffering had become guiding principles. Her contemporary Dora Greenwell paints a chilling picture of the unmarried woman 'fading into neutral tint' and 'taking up less and less room in the world, and seeming to apologise to it for even the little space she occupies'. Humility and modesty were the part of women, to serve mankind in Christ's image and to perpetuate the uncritical ideal of maternal love. When Christina's first book, *Goblin Market and Other Poems*, was published in 1862, the *London Review* praised it especially for having 'none of the violation of reserve' which it claimed spoiled the work of George Eliot, Charlotte Brontë and others. Although her book received excellent reviews, its initial publication owed much to the persistence of her brother Gabriel, as did most of her subsequent printed work. Christina had a strong sense of her literary destiny, but was unwilling to further it by argument or what she saw as self-promotion. While she was well aware of society's double standards for men and women, she declined to support the movement for women's rights, citing Christian authority on male and female roles. She actually wrote a poem which began 'Woman was made for man's delight'. Her social conscience drove her to assist in a Home for Fallen Women, but she avoided all other forms of charitable work, preferring to campaign against vivisection.

As her literary career developed, her personal sorrows multiplied. The cruel early death of so many of her family and friends and her own recurring illnesses deepened her faith but rendered her 'inflexibly puritan': many people found her reserve intolerable and she had increasing difficulty with friendships. In middle age she assumed the self-protective mantle of an old woman; from this security she permitted herself the odd self-mocking remark 'A fat poetess is incongruous, especially when seated by the grave of buried hope', or 'I wrote such melancholy things when I was young that I am obliged to be unusually cheerful, not to say robust, in my old age.'

If only more of her irony permeated this biography. One longs to feel passionately for Christina, but it is impossible. She remains remote, exasperatingly nebulous or painfully censorious, standing back, skirts furled, lips curled and nostrils flared in anticipatory scorn. Only the hooded, dolorous eyes speak of her inner desolation. But too long a suffering makes a stone of this reader's heart. I had a guilty desire to be off having fun with Gabriel in his Chelsea house where he kept wild women and Swinburne and a Brahmin bull and wombats. Why couldn't Christina have had a wombat? She loved them ('When wombats do inspire, I strike my disused lyre') and often visited them at the zoo, taking 'A goodly bag of eatable'. Surely there was something furry or frivolous in her life? How did she pass all those long gloomy days? This book gives a sense of her as a writer, as a Christian, but not as a human being.

Jan Marsh indulges in a fair amount of speculation: 'doubtless', 'one imagines', 'perhaps', occur too frequently, and there is some gruesome writing. Concerning Gabriel, 'The appearance of *Verses* alerted him to the fact that his kid sister was growing up with a distinct gift.' Concerning James Collinson, 'He gave his heart to Christ rather than Christina.' I found Marsh's comments on some of the poems informative, but more often they are tiresome and tendentious or over-explanatory. Some, no doubt, will be enthralled by the pages which deal with Marsh's proposal that Christina was sexually abused by her father. Here is a scrap of evidence: 'The figure of a crocodile who sheds tears to allure his victim, is an apt image for a sexually abusive father.' Oh? Cape's publicity sheet makes much of this, and of

Christina's work for Fallen Women, in a pathetic attempt to lure the prurient. This is an act of gross dishonour to a most fastidious and private woman.

I'm not convinced by Marsh's attempt to present Christina Rossetti as a great poet. Far better to turn to the excellent Everyman *Poems and Prose*, where one may make one's own judgement on a selection from the work. There is a concise introduction giving all the facts and omitting the nonsense and tedium, with a helpful chronology. Meanwhile the National Portrait Gallery is celebrating (as they quaintly put it) the centenary of her death with a rich exhibition of portraits, photographs and manuscripts. Here you may see and wonder at the difference between Gabriel's ecstatic maidens and his sister's excruciated soul.

FISHER'S FACE
Jan Morris (1995)

For nearly half a century Jan Morris has been haunted by the face of a man whom she never met, a man who died six years before she was born. She keeps his enlarged photograph pinned, mysteriously, on the inside of her wardrobe door. Perhaps as Fisher swings slowly out to meet her in the morning she ponders the possibility that here is her spiritual reflection, or again her complement; a doctor once told Fisher that he should have been born twins. The young James Morris wanted to be Fisher: 'That's the man for me,' he said when first he saw Fisher's photograph; he began to collect a great volume of material which swelled alarmingly over the years. Now the older Jan Morris has settled for an affair in the afterlife and written a self-styled *jeu d'amour* and caprice, an extravagant conception of breathless adulation, gossip, games and war.

Much has already been written about Fisher's life and this book makes no claim to be a biography. It outlines his career but focuses powerfully on the complex personality behind the strangely contemporary face. Jack Fisher was born in Ceylon in 1842; aged six he was sent to relatives in England and did not see his family again for 25 years. After prep school he joined the navy as a cadet sponsored by Nelson's last surviving captain and by Nelson's niece. His first ship was Victory, he had just read Southey's *Life of Nelson* and at the age of 13 he began a life dominated by Nelson's heroic image. The navy was to be his 'intellectual obsession and emotional passion'.

As an Admiral he commanded the British Fleet in the Atlantic and then the Mediterranean, eventually he became First Sea Lord. He served all over the world during the period of the Navy's transition from sail to steam, and he was an enthusiastic technologist, an inventor, designer and constant advocate of progress. The paramount importance of the Navy was his credo: 'No soldier of ours can go anywhere unless a sailor carries him.' He had a keen sense of social justice and he reformed conditions and career prospects for the ratings. He saw the potential of the submarine when colleagues would not take it seriously: 'Underhand, unfair and damned un-English'. He launched the first turbine-driven warship; the Grand Fleet he had armoured forced the surrender of the German Fleet in the Great War.

He knew everyone from Bismarck to Garibaldi to the Tsarina. He yearned for his own Trafalgar but saw little active service, for these were the long years of the Pax Britannica in which his Navy kept the peace, maintaining Britain's imperial sway over a quarter of the world. The Navy also often interfered in matters which were not its concern. 'Tell these ugly bastards that I am not going to tolerate any more of their bestial habits,' boomed one commander, poking his nose uninvited into a tribal dispute in rural Turkey. Morris paints a richly beguiling picture of the Victorian Navy, its profound inner security, its glorious assumptions, its extravagant social life and its traditionally eccentric leaders.

Fisher was adored by his men; most of his colleagues adored him too, forming a devoted and protective circle known as the Fishpond.

Women, says Morris, would want him as a lover; and men would simply want to be him. He was generous, witty, enormously charming and quite unpredictable. Besides the Navy his grand passions were the Bible (Old Testament) and dancing. He used to take two midshipmen with him to balls so that when he had danced the ladies off their feet he might still have partners. He was wildly demonstrative to men and women, an unashamed self-publicist, and a crafty flatterer of journalists: 'The most masterly thing you ever penned. It was BOVRIL!!!'

Inevitably he acquired enemies, notably the wondrous Lord Charles Beresford who had a hunting scene tattooed on his backside, and a wife whom he called 'My little painted frigate'; this lady is said to have worn false eyebrows. Such details make this book a constant delight. Morris wanders about Fisher's life, dwelling now on his taste in clothes, now his religious impulse, now his political intrigues, conjuring up a series of *tableaux vivants*. 'Fisher is still alive for me,' she declares. 'I shall go wherever he goes, as infatuates do.'

Although Morris hankers after that affair in the great hereafter, her persona strikes me as Fairy Godmother rather than lover. The voice is indulgent, effusive, only occasionally sardonic. Exclamation marks abound, but for once they seem appropriate. It is all such fun, a terrific thrill to be shared with everyone.

Now and then she really overdoes it. There is a completely deranged vision of Fisher, back from the grave, flirting with Mamie Eisenhower and stealing red roses from her bouquet. And Fisher's Garboesque retreat from the final debacle of his life as a statesman is just too much: 'His face a mask of bitter hauteur at the window of his sleeper, our Jacky steamed away into his closing chapters.' Yet even these hyperbolic frissons are somehow enjoyable; and if in the end the hint of coincidences and double identities and fusions of past and present remain a tantalising blur, one still feels oddly privileged to have looked at Fisher's face through Morris's eyes and shared with her his 'genius for delight'.

ANGUS WILSON
Margaret Drabble (1995)

Angus Wilson died four years ago after a long illness. During his lifetime and after his death his reputation as one of this century's greatest novelists has stood firm among those who knew his work. To others, over the last 15 years, his name has become increasingly unfamiliar and his books, until their recent re-publication, were hard to find. Indeed many people today confuse him with A. N. Wilson. Ironically part of the reason A. N. Wilson uses his initials was that it was thought at the start of his writing career he might be confused with the more eminent Angus. Margaret Drabble's bright and loving biography should go far to create a new readership for novels whose power and wit are timeless, and whose recurring themes of wanton cruelty, complacency, 'willed ignorance' and self-deception are all too relevant.

Wilson's life was the mainspring of his writing, and his childhood its acknowledged primary source. He was born in 1913, the youngest of six sons; his next brother was 13 years older and his parents already middle-aged. His father came from an impoverished line of Scottish landowners. Willie Johnstone-Wilson was a gambler, a flirt and a man about town who never worked and lived in constant debt. The family moved regularly, between the south coast and Kensington, renting a house or reduced to taking rooms in boarding houses. Angus was a 'child among adults, an eavesdropper', later a spy and go-between. Charades, theatricals and family legends fed his imagination; two years in Natal, visiting his mother's family, left him with a lifelong yearning for sun, colour, exotic flora and fauna.

His brothers left home as soon as they could. When Angus was 15 his mother died and he became his ageing father's keeper through schooldays at Westminster, through his three years at Oxford, and on into his working life at the British Museum. This burden of premature responsibility increased his sense of being old while young and at the same time held him in a timewarp, a fledgling who might not fly.

Like many other precocious and sensitive misfits he survived at school and university by playing the freakish jester, the storyteller. Although he made lasting friendships he was often mocked as 'an amusing but hardly human pet'. Freed at last by his father's death in 1938 he began to enjoy an eccentric and brilliant social life and a series of homosexual affairs, overshadowed and qualified by the looming horror of war. After the bombing of the British Museum he was sent to Bletchley Park where he worked on deciphering Italian naval codes. Here he was tense, rebellious and desolate. An analyst suggested he try writing as therapy; finding that he could only produce 'pastiche Dickens' he gave up almost immediately.

At the end of the war he returned to country lodgings, travelling in to London to work at the museum; still disturbed and unhappy, he found himself loathing pubs and clubs, blackmailed by pick-ups and involved in a turbulent triangular love affair. Then, at a loose end one Sunday afternoon, he was bullied by an elderly village neighbour to jot down some thoughts on village life: 'I just wrote a story.' He continued to write stories, overwhelmed by a sense of 'miraculous delivery'. Cecil Connolly printed two in *Horizon* and in 1949 Secker and Warburg brought out a collection, *The Wrong Set*. This was rapturously received and Angus became an instant celebrity, fêted and praised, the focus of attention both socially and at work. There, as deputy superintendent of the British Museum reading room, he was a fine sight on his dais: 'a colourful bird, in a vast circular cage, bowtied, blue-rinsed, chattering loudly . . . .'

Colleagues and readers provided endless material for his stories, as did friends, family, the now tolerable past, and the changing orders of post-war society. He had also now begun his enduring relationship with Tony Garrett. More stories, *Such Darling Dodos*, were published, and then a book on Zola. He was in constant demand for talks, reviews, sustaining a full-time job and writing his first novel *Hemlock and After*, ostensibly a tale of village life. Wilson loathed the limited nature of the English provincial novel and the complacency it engendered in its reader. Here he wrote of the narrowness and hypocrisy of rural life. 'I'm getting to know all your little movements dear,' a neighbour once told him.

He also wrote of homosexuality and bisexuality, of accepted social limits and their transgression. This brave, funny and controversial book brought him more serious attention and a reputation as an 'investigative social analyst'. In 1955 he left the museum and went to live with Tony in a remote Suffolk cottage. Now he lived entirely by his writing, while Tony worked as a probation officer. His life assumed a pattern which was to continue until his final illness. His year would be spent in a punishing series of lecture tours abroad and at home, reviewing, writing the next novel, suffering from desperate anxieties now about writing, now about money; at the cottage with Tony he gardened, entertained streams of visitors, and subsided into brief and random periods of unbroken privacy.

As a public figure he was involved in campaigns for homosexual law reform, for public lending rights, for funding for authors; he worked tirelessly for the Pen Club, the Arts Council, the National Book League. He taught at the brand new University of East Anglia where he became professor, he was awarded the CBE, he travelled literally all over the world. And he was unfailingly sustained by Tony Garrett. In his later years he became profoundly depressed by the philistinism of Thatcher's Britain, by the cult of violence promoted by television, by a vision of 'Benthamite, high-producing, technological workday people who after work simply watch and eat and never come alive.' He began to feel he had lost touch with his times. The greater his success, the more painful his work became: 'so much is expected of one all the time.' Bad reviews terribly distressed him. He felt 'over-worked, horribly poor, depressed and frightened by the future'. Nonetheless, driven by financial necessity, he vowed even in old age and illness 'I'll go on writing until

I fall.' As much as anything, this book gives a chilling account of the hazards of a writer's life.

Despite homosexual law reforms and a new tolerance, prejudice was still rampant. At a university in the States he was greeted by a huge sign, intended to read 'Welcome Angus Wilson' which had curiously lost its g. When he was knighted in 1980, the *Daily Express* celebrated 'our latest nancy knight'. Tony had lost his job and thus his independence, due to malicious gossip years before. He and Angus had shown great courage in declaring themselves and continuing to live in the homophobic countryside.

Margaret Drabble's own eye for detail is a constant delight. She shares her subject's dry wit and his passionate anger at the small and dangerous meannesses of the human soul. Her writing is uneven, with occasional lapses into journalese: 'They taped a long interview with a grey-suited, velvet-tied Angus while they munched chocolate biscuits and sipped tea by a smoking log fire.' But the main fault in this fascinating book is that same love of detail, which leads Drabble to interminable lists of names and irrelevant information: 'Serikawa records that the salmon was boiled, but Tony says it was poached.'

However, she is able to convey a character of great complexity, a life triumphant and tragic, as paradoxical as any in his books, with such warmth and utter credibility that one shares her affection for him. Concerning biography, Wilson had said that 'in the last analysis the human personality is not open to invasion'. Allowing for this decent reticence I like to dwell at last on the image of Angus and Tony 'pottering around the countryside with the Pevsner in the glove compartment', for a little while oblivious to Angus's 'high distant overtone of perpetual woe'.

PAUL GAUGUIN
A Complete Biography
David Sweetman (1995)

'Everyone knows something about Gauguin,' remarked Robert Hughes famously. Everyone likes to have an opinion about Gauguin, too, usually hostile. Grounds for hostility vary; that he was a stockbroker and middle class as well, that he abused women in art and in life, that he threw everything up and went to live in a dream island and got away with it (apart from dying in agony from syphilis), that he was a foul-tempered monster whose unkindness led to Van Gogh's self-mutilation and madness. David Sweetman's long biography strives, as one would expect, to disengage man from myth and it is to some extent successful; certainly he has researched minutely and travelled far.

Paul Gauguin was born in Paris in 1848; his father, Clovis, was a radical journalist, his mother, Aline, the half Spanish daughter of Flora Tristan, a celebrated early feminist. A great uncle was Viceroy of Peru; a more distant ancestor was Alexander Borgia. It was on a visit to the wealthy Peruvian relatives that Paul's mother 'was appalled to see Clovis keel forward dead from a heart attack'. At this moment, the family were sitting in a whale-boat off the coast of Patagonia.

They spent the next seven years in Lima, and Sweetman emphasises the role of the pre-Colombian ceramics which Paul saw there in his later choice of imagery – notably the recurring presentation of a 'shrouded skeletal figure similar to the mummies hunched in the foetal position, wrapped doll-like in cloths'.

Back in France he attended boarding school, where he was unruly and unpopular; he then joined the Merchant Navy. His mother remarked that he should 'get on with his career since he has made himself so unpopular with all my friends that he will one day find himself alone.' Later his guardian helped him to find a job as a sort of accountant in the Bourse, he married a cigar-smoking Dane called Mette, and in his spare time he began to paint in oils, exhibiting with the Impressionists.

When he decided to give up his job to paint full time, he plunged himself and his growing family into financial disaster. He abandoned them in Copenhagen and returned to France, painting in Brittany and in Paris and taking odd jobs. The resourceful Mette ultimately raised all five of their children by her own efforts in Denmark and Gauguin gradually left his place in their lives, although he continued to write to them for many years. A doomed attempt to wring money out of the Panama Canal venture took him to Martinique, where he spent six months painting exotic landscapes and women. Ill health brought him back to France where he met Van Gogh; that winter he joined him in Arles, and Van Gogh's tragic fate ensued. In 1891 Gauguin sailed for Tahiti, on 'official business'; he passed the rest of his life in Tahiti and in the Marquesas Islands, apart from a couple of years in Paris and Brittany again, spent painting and exhibiting. In 1903 he died of syphilis.

Such are the bare facts of Gauguin's life, and Sweetman elaborates them with a wealth of detail, description and anecdote, meanwhile providing a clear account of artistic movements from Barbizon through Impressionism, pointillism and synthetism into symbolism. He is lucid and painstaking in tracing Gauguin's many sources and influences, ranging from Kate Greenaway to Maori Gods. He exonerates Gauguin from most of the charges laid against him, and while he is non-committal over the Van Gogh episode, he describes it, and the weeks preceding Gauguin's death likewise, with delicacy and dignity.

Yet despite its glorious locations this is an oddly colourless book. Paradoxically, Sweetman doesn't seem to care much for Gauguin; yet he doesn't dislike him either. As a result one has very little sense of Gauguin's personality; he is choleric, sometimes aloof, sometimes gregarious, tactless, dedicated to his work; this is not enough. Other people take their identity only from their names and swarm through their busy lives as indistinguishable ciphers. There is a great deal of boring information about the French economic situation, or minor political movements in Spain, France and South America, and there is far too much speculation: 'what it must have seemed like then. . . one can only imagine.' Worse, the authorial voice is omnipresent and omniscient. 'What no one ever explained to them. . .' or 'he does not seem to have realised. . .' and, my favourite, 'this wild Bohemian was bound to bring trouble'. If only they'd had Sweetman there, how much better they would have managed. The patronising tone extends even to the 'now risible frock and pantaloon beachwear of the period' or Gauguin and Mette working at Peruvian embroidery: 'the thought. . . does raise a smile.'

Matronly pieties are scattered about judiciously, presumably to suggest that Sweetman, unlike Gauguin, is sympathetic to a woman's woes. This fails to convince, for the book is a testament to the prurience and salaciousness of its author and not its subject. From its earliest pages there are references to 'pert buttocks' and 'our own prime observation of her nudity' in a discussion of *The Spirit of the Dead Keeping Watch* – a grave and beautiful painting which Sweetman is anxious to establish as a work of pornography. His excitement mounts over a study of Gauguin's daughter: 'Aline was now four years old and in the painting her night shirt has rucked up to just below her buttocks . . . What on earth did Mette make of it, this image of her child. . .' This is grotesque enough, but there is worse to come. In Paris, when Gauguin meets a flirtatious 13 year old: 'the temptation must have been exquisite – the pubescent Judith, at the same magical age of 13 as Aline had been when he had last seen her'. I considered counting the number of times Sweetman uses the words 'bare breasts' and 'bare breasted'; 'naked girl' is another of his favourite phrases. I suppose it does provide a contrast to 'our old friend Pukaki, the monumental Tiki last seen in the Auckland Museum'.

Sweetman has a talent for describing the paintings, but these necessary sections of his book are largely flawed by his lascivious vision. It is impossible to take his interpretations seriously; it is impossible to honour someone who so dishonours his own subject matter.

LETTERS OF JOHN BETJEMAN
Volume II, 1951-84
ed. Candida Lycett-Green (1995)

John Betjeman occupies a unique position in the British psyche, a comforting dreamland of fire-lit nurseries, teddies and tea, suburban gardens, country stations, seaside holidays and golf. He presented himself as the common man of middle England, middle-aged, middle class, yet not so much *vox populi* as *vox humana*. Philip Larkin praised him for restoring 'direct intelligible communication to poetry'. Through the many films he made for television Betjeman reached the hearts and minds of millions more who might never read a poem but who felt that they knew him and shared in his delights. His modest aim was to make people use their eyes, show them 'things which are beautiful so that they will very soon realise what is ugly'. To Mary Wilson he confided 'your tastes are like mine in the Arts – and I think, though few will admit it, like most people's'. 'You understand things like Croydon as no one else would,' wrote his secretary. Through his enthusiasms he conferred a special validity upon decent, unambitious provincial lives. 'Eastbourne forever' he wrote to Cyril Connolly.

This second volume of letters selected by Betjeman's daughter completes the impressionistic biography and portrait which she proposed in the first; again it is richly supplemented by her own connecting passages of narrative. The period spans his vast success and fame as a poet, with his 1958 *Collected Poems* selling a thousand copies a day – 'what ho! I never remember such a dance since we published Byron's *Childe Harold* in 1812,' exulted his publisher Jock Murray – and includes his involvement in countless committees, writing columns and reviews, making films, lecturing at home and abroad and, most years, producing a new book of poems or prose.

But in 1972, when he became Poet Laureate, he was already suffering from Parkinson's disease. He struggled against depression and a melancholy which he believed had entered his life in childhood with the *Tales* of Hans Andersen. Despite his efforts, during the sixties much of the London he had loved was destroyed; Euston Arch and the Coal Exchange were gone; reluctantly he saw Liverpool now as England's architectural capital. His wife, the astonishing Penelope Chetwode, was increasingly away abroad, riding across India and researching her own books; their son and daughter were grown and the family home in Wantage had been sold. A cold wind blew through the tamarisks. He wrote to Penelope of death and of road drills; she wrote back describing buffalo racing. 'She likes me, but I am not essential to her,' he concluded. Elizabeth Cavendish, his 'other wife', provided the loving domestic life he missed so much. Candida Lycett-Green's treatment of her father's relationships with these two remarkable women is a model of clear-eyed affection and good sense. They complemented each other; 'as his daughter I found the situation completely without conflict.'

Betjeman received hundreds of letters each week and he answered them all, writing a minimum of 30 a day. He corresponds here with children, priests and fellow writers, with bureaucrats and most movingly with his family and legions of friends. Some of these letters are repetitive in content, pleas for the preservation of buildings, branchlines, churchyards, but they give a glimpse of the time and effort Betjeman expended. Most striking is his generosity to others, his unfailing encouragement and his personal modesty. Constantly he plays down the value of his own writing; Ardizzone's illustrations for his *Ring of Bells* 'are the verse; they are better than the verse'. It is clear that this is no false modesty.

He needed to write as he needed to pray, but he wrote very slowly, re-wrote and re-wrote, reading aloud as he went, crafting his poems with an urgent meticulousness which belies their apparent simplicity. Like many writers he had a deep sense of fraudulence and a fear that one day he would be caught out; he took to heart adverse criticism and was unconvinced by praise. 'Reviews don't count. Publishers' travellers are the only people who really sell a book.' And beyond self-doubt lay a greater dread: 'Never a day goes by without my thinking of my death and the lonely journey into eternity – will it be a journey or will it be blank nothingness?' In the last ten years of his life, as so many friends died, his letters affirm a belief in the afterlife, yet this was not a comfort which he could always offer to himself. Faith seems intermittent rather than constant. But it is good to read that after a nightmare once he awoke into knowledge of the love of God 'like a warm bath'.

Nonetheless, the prevailing mood of these letters is not one of gloom. Despite inner misgivings, failing health and financial worries, Betjeman radiates warmth, love and merriment. He writes a ballad to Deborah Devonshire that begins 'O Come wi' me tae Scratchwood'. 'For some reason (unknown to me) I reminded him of the service station just north of London called Scratchwood,' the Duchess confesses. There are also riveting references to his wife: 'Penelope is off her head and very active. There is a new kind of golf ball called Spalding Top Flight and the ones with black dots look exactly like her.' A lady in a sports shop remembers Betjeman declining to buy this brand, explaining that the resemblance would make them unusable.

Candida Lycett-Green matches her father in wit and generosity of spirit. Her descriptions of family life and of his final illness are intensely moving. These two volumes of letters are a brave and mighty labour of love; they have nothing to do with criticism and everything to do with true filial piety. Betjeman's image beams out from the photographs and his unanswered question lingers: 'What are we all here for if not for laughter and to see each other again?'

THE YEATS SISTERS
Joan Hardwick (1996)

Susan and Elizabeth Yeats, always known as Lily and Lolly, were born in 1866 and 1868. The forgotten sisters of the famous Jack and the very famous William, they formed the nucleus of an extraordinary family whose warring members strove for space and distance, but never disentangled themselves from their primal web of love, anxiety, exasperation and loathing.

Their mother, Susan Pollexfen, was raised in bourgeois comfort but found all hopes of material security blighted in marriage to John Butler Yeats, who abandoned his legal career and became a painter, moving his family back and forth between Ireland and England, uncertainty and poverty. Susan suffered three strokes and died in her fifties. She spent her last years silent and immobile in an upstairs room, her eyes, one blue, one brown, fixed unblinking on the sky.

Unlike their brothers, Lily and Lolly had little education and as they grew up, confined to the house by their mother's illness and domestic exigency, their pleasure in meeting visiting writers and painters was sadly qualified by a sense of intellectual inadequacy. When they met Maud Gonne, she totally ignored them, concentrating on the men. 'I could not see her well as her face was turned from me,' observed Lily; Lolly remarked on Gonne's slippers, worn with the insouciance of a woman who would not be setting foot on muddy pavements. In London Lily at last found work with their neighbour William Morris, embroidering and transferring designs to fabric; Lolly meanwhile combined household responsibilities with a Froebel training course. William took a dim view of his sisters' attempts to broaden their lives: 'They came out with no repose, no peacefulness, and their minds no longer quiet gardens full of secluded paths and umbrage-circled nooks.'

Lily's health was poor, and Lolly suffered acute exhaustion and anxiety as she combined household duties with teaching and writing a series of manuals on watercolour techniques. Yet the affection and the success of her pupils gave her a satisfaction which she could not find at home, where her tenseness, volubility and impatience irritated her family to distraction.

Their small earnings, supplemented by the occasional contribution from William and Jack, who had now moved out, kept the household going and supported their brilliant, extravagant and feckless father. As William and Jack became increasingly well-known, John too achieved success, exhibiting in Dublin and undertaking commissions which, however, he often abandoned. In London the girls wistfully revelled in news of these triumphs. But 1902 saw them all back in Ireland, with Lily and Lolly at last wholeheartedly involved in a venture which would stretch their energies, talents and imaginations for the rest of their working lives. With Evelyn Gleeson they set up an all-women embroidery workshop and printing press, committed to producing beautiful and functional objects made from Irish materials; they employed only Irishwomen. Lolly looked after the press whose first volume was William's *In The Seven Woods.* Lily was commissioned to embroider banners for the new cathedral outside Dublin. Jack designed for them and William recommended books for printing. This ambitious project became celebrated on both sides of the Atlantic and James Joyce referred to it (albeit left-handedly) in his round-up of notable events for Bloomsday: '5 lines of text and 10 pages of notes about the folk and fishgods of Dundrum. Printed by the weird sisters in the year of the big wind.' Success brought travel, professional respect and hordes of visitors, but financial problems persisted, and Lolly, working fanatically, became obsessed by the fear of losing her mind. A remarkable number of Pollexfen relatives had been put away in asylums.

The Dun Emer workshops, later known as Cuala Industries, were the sisters' proud creation and it is sad that today they are mentioned only occasionally in specialist catalogues. For almost 40 years they kept going, through feuds and squabbles with family and backers, through the Troubles, through the war. For Lolly they were perhaps more satisfying than for Lily, who yearned for a family of her own. Both sisters had hoped to marry, and found spinsterhood a sad and disregarded state, but it would be foolish and presumptuous to see their lives as impoverished. They had many friends, their days were crammed with incident; they saw their work valued and their family remained close. In old age Lily developed an intense hostility to Lolly, but after her death in 1940 she wrote a loving memoir. They were buried together in Dundrum.

Joan Hardwick writes with fairness and lucidity. I especially enjoyed her descriptions of Sligo and Rosses, the many family houses and the gallery of powerful relatives, as well as Synge, Pound, Lady Gregory, Parnell, O'Casey, Morris, Chesterton. What a novel could be written, what speculation might there be on the shaping powers of character and circumstance. Hardwick rightly turns her back on these temptations. She has produced a rarity, a biography of admirable understatement.

R D LAING
A Divided Self
John Clay (1996)

Ronald Laing was born in Glasgow in 1927 to a grim Calvinist couple, who curiously named him after the debonair film actor Ronald Colman. This tiny shard of frivolity glitters out of a glum moraine of childhood repression, unkindness and incomprehension, presented here with a degree of irritating psychological comment. The infant Laing was pre-natally doomed: jammed in the birth canal, he was assigned to a future of asthma, drink, drugs and uneasy relationships. According to his biographer, a Jungian analyst, he would also live his parents' unlived lives. He suffered from an overwhelming need for recognition because his father did not announce his birth for several days. And so on.

All the same, the facts are desolate. His mother burned his toy horse because he loved it so much. In a jealous rage, his father destroyed his new red dressing gown. He was not allowed to play with other children after school; they glimpsed him at the upstairs window, sitting beside his mother, staring out. Conversational limits were sharply defined: 'Ronald, we never talk about that sort of thing.' He developed eczema, and took refuge in music and reading. He went on to study medicine at Glasgow University, where he found himself increasingly troubled by unanswerable questions, 'the puzzle of human misery and the cruelty of the world.' He was profoundly moved by Antonin Artaud's attack on psychiatric practice. Artaud, himself a former mental patient, had said: 'a lunatic is also a man society does not wish to listen to, and whom it is determined to prevent from uttering unbearable truths.' Working in psychiatric hospitals, Laing found that he was able to align himself with the psychotic mind, enter its loneliness and share its experience. Experiments with LSD convinced him that here was a mirror of the schizophrenic experience, that 'special strategy for unliveable situations.'

John Clay gives a horrifying account of psychiatric medicine in the Fifties. There were no units for young people, patients led marginalised lives and their words were ignored. Lobotomy, leucotomy, insulin-induced coma and ECT were standard treatments.

For Laing, madness was endemic: 'Let no one suppose that this madness exists only somewhere in the night or day sky where our birds of death hover in the stratosphere. It exists in the interstices of our most intimate and personal moments.' Taking Heidegger's 'The dreadful has already happened', he questioned the nature and very existence of schizophrenia, most poignantly rendered in its literal translation, 'a broken heart'. Through regression he brought his patients into confrontation with the past, and set mental illness firmly in the context of the family.

The paperback edition of his book *The Divided Self* brought him enormous fame in the mid-Sixties. He became a guru whose ideas were uncannily in harmony with the spirit of the times. He made television programmes, joined sit-ins, published papers, wrote further successful books, travelled, lectured on Tantric sex and cavorted with

Timothy Leary, who was impressed: 'My eyes were riveted to his eyes. I was gone. Spun out of the kitchen in Millbrook. Spun out of time. Stoned high in a Sufi ballet. We were two organisms from different planets – communicating. I was an Eskimo on an ice floe.' 'My dad and his friends are potty,' said Leary's son. Another transatlantic wise man met up with Laing in London; after an LSD session they called on Laing's long-suffering and enraged wife and their five children. 'Coming as we did from such a delicate, silent space, it was an intense and somewhat trying visit.'

In 1965 he set up the Philadelphia Association, dedicated to relieving mental illness and researching its causes and treatment. He opened Kingsley Hall, a retreat where disturbed patients might take part in therapeutic experiments, or simply exist. Kingsley Hall was and is the subject of controversy. Undoubtedly it did good to many; others suffered. To some it was 'the Havana of the schizophrenia revolution', and to some it offered dangerous freedoms without responsibility. In 1970 it closed, but the Philadelphia Association went on to run eight more safe houses in north London.

It seems to me, as an amateur, lay person or what you will, that Laing's decline into dippiness runs parallel to his ascending fame and fortune in the late Sixties, an overdosing on *Zeitgeist* perhaps. His vision of the family as the centre of psychic violence led him to statements like: 'The initial act of brutality against the average child is the mother's first kiss.' He became obsessed with the business of birth, or rather rebirth, an elaborate ceremony involving rebirthing bags, helpfully made from gnu skins by his friend Francis Huxley. 'I am a better mother than your mother', was the dubious subtext.

Through the Seventies and Eighties, his life became increasingly turbulent. He continued to lecture at home and abroad, to enormous audiences, but he was losing his knack of supernatural sympathy: at times he misjudged their mood, or was too drunk to communicate. In London, 'for spiritual reasons' he hurled a bottle through the window of the Bhagwan Shree Rajneesh Centre. In Iona Abbey he informed his audience that: 'Calvinism has done more damage to Scottish society than drugs ever did. You can't even have a good fuck without feeling guilty about it.' Right words, wrong place. The depression which had overshadowed his life, that 'typical Scottish Calvinist involutional melancholic type of religious, nihilistic rumination' now overwhelmed him. He alienated friends and colleagues, resigned from the Philadelphia Association and was struck off the medical register. But during the last couple of years of his life he gave up drink, appeared to be revising some of his more extreme views, and planned a full-scale summary of his work. In 1989 he died of a heart attack.

This seems rather a strange time to publish a biography of Laing. The moral and intellectual climate of the Sixties has undergone severe and hostile scrutiny; its legacy of damaged children and a wrecked educational system cannot be denied. Laing's apparent glorification of schizophrenia, his advocacy of psychotropic drugs and community care are repugnant in the wake of recent violent crimes. It is a measure of the strength of John Clay's book that the reader's sympathies are utterly engaged. Apart from the uncomfortable beginning, this is a highly readable, sparse and dignified portrait of an extraordinary man. Whether or not his contributions to psychiatry prove of lasting importance, his very being is the stuff of legend. Avatar of the Sixties, melancholy psychopomp leading lost souls only to a greater darkness, humanitarian and innovator, archetypal Scotsman – Laing may be seen from many angles, but he undoubtedly has his place in the strange firmament of twentieth-century icons.

SELECTED LETTERS OF EDITH SITWELL
ed. Richard Green (1997)

At the age of 16 Edith Sitwell was sent out to pawn her mother's false teeth; the money went on whisky. 'Mind you,' she wrote many years later, 'I couldn't sympathise more with the owner of the teeth as regards that. The life would have driven anyone to it.'

Their terrible childhood bound Edith and her brothers, Osbert and Sacheverell, in lifelong devotion and mutual support. As the unwanted only girl, and the eldest, Edith suffered most of all. She said that her nervous system was ruined by the time she was ten, and in late middle age she wrote: 'The trail of what they have done is still all over everything.' Osbert spoke for all three when he observed to Edith, 'Our work is the true answer to such conduct.' Embattled, eloquent and often preposterous, the Sitwells took up their position *contra mundum*.

This handsome volume charts Edith's flight to London and her own flat, her developing literary success and her friendships and feuds over 60 years. It does not make a significant contribution to the study of women's writing, but it does provide insight, surprising and moving, into a difficult, cantankerous woman who possessed also courage, wit and a great generosity of spirit. Mostly, she claimed, her life was absolute hell. Ill health, money troubles ('I am in the soup as usual'), a pervading fear that her parents might somehow recapture her ('Do not let the Gingers know I am here...') compounded the brooding bleakness of her days.

Work, friendships and time spent with her brothers intermittently banished her natural melancholia. Her loyalty to her siblings led her to bizarre extravagances. Sacheverell was a genius 'on the same scale as Milton'. Osbert's failure to get into parliament was due solely to the crass philistinism of the 'worm-faced' British public. Critics are dismissed with withering contempt, and astonishing energy is expended on the strategies of war. Her lifelong feud with Geoffrey Grigson ('our Griglet') escalated into full-scale hostilities with, among others, Edward Marsh, Roy Fuller, Julian Symons, J. R. Ackerley, everyone at the *Listener*, the *Spectator*, the *Observer*... she claimed that Kathleen Raine had stolen her own imagery for her 'lady-maid's poetry'; she planned to spread a rumour that Enid Blyton was a *nom de plume* of D. H. Lawrence.

But her friendships were of equal importance. Her tastes in literature were, as she said, 'catholic' and she encouraged, supported and defended new writers; there are many unsolicited letters here of spontaneous warmth, expressing her immediate delight in work by Kingsley Amis, Denton Welch, Dylan Thomas, Allen Ginsberg, L. P. Hartley. On other friends she lavished affection and practical assistance. She nursed Helen Rootham, her former governess and companion, through ten years of terminal cancer, and she provided for Helen's sister all her life. When Dorothy Wellesley had been too drunk to appear on stage before the Queen at a poetry reading organised by the Sitwells, it was Edith who 'could not bear to think of her waking up in the night and realising that something dreadful had happened'. She wrote her a long letter of extreme kindness and delicacy: 'You had been (and still are) very ill with neuritis ... My dear, people do sometimes feel they can't go through a performance.'

Snobbery she used as a weapon against her foes, abandoning it entirely for anyone she liked. Her other weapon was her wit, and the most enjoyable letters here fizz with her peculiar brand of laconic acid. 'He showed me a sonnet the other day which began thus: "Fatigue sits in your breast like a spring hare/ Gnawing at the gross red cabbage of your heart".' There are dire glimpses of Edith's daily life: 'Captain J kept on picking ticks off his retriever's coat at meal times and throwing them under the dining table, wrapped up in pieces of fur to keep them warm, with the result that I imagine my feet are being bitten the whole time.' 'I want a message of hope for my dewlaps,' she announced to an apprehensive herbalist. Aspirant poets sometimes suffered too: 'Dear Mr Faber has sent me his own poems and I have written praising their integrity. That is my stock phrase now, and I think you might also find it useful. It saves a lot of trouble, and Integrity is a retriever-like, faithful quality that I find very trying. However nobody knows that.' Unhappily, her sense of humour did not extend to her own public persona. She, and to a lesser extent her brothers, did attract a vast deal of opprobrium, and were satirised in novels and plays by Wyndham Lewis, Noel Coward, Peter Ustinov, D. H. Lawrence *et al.* When a naughty man used a drawing of her for the cover of a volume titled *The Brighter Side of Birth Control*, Edith reacted just as he might have hoped: 'I have never heard of such a gross and filthy insult being offered to any decent woman. And the fact that I am a distinguished artist only makes it worse . . .'

She viewed her artistry with profound solemnity. Her poetry she saw as 'traditional, descended from Spenser, Milton, Marvell and Dryden . . . It is descended too from Baudelaire.'

This may be startling news for those who have tussled with her *Collected Poems* and perhaps turned to the introduction for assistance. Here she is, expounding on technique: 'These "a" (or "ai") sounds are echoed, farther on more insistently and with a deeper emphasis, by . . . "In the/ Corn, towers strain. Feathered tall as a crane,/ And whistling down the feathered rain, old Noah goes again" – where these assonances, while they are slightly counterpointed, are yet nearly as important as the ground rhythm given by "corn" and "tall".' But then for Edith 'everything is permissible as long as one succeeds in getting the effect one is out for.' Comparatively few of these letters deal with her literary theory, and just as well.

This is a long book, and some of its material is uninteresting and repetitive. A substantial body of letters could not be included, being subject to an embargo; these include Edith's correspondence with Graham Greene and with the Russian painter Pavel Tchelichew. The footnotes are set in maddening obscurity at the far end of the book and they are not always helpful. Identifications err on the side of economy and incidents are left unexplained. Most importantly, there is no biographical sketch.

None the less, the volume provides a welcome supplement to Victoria Glendinning's 1981 study, *Edith Sitwell: A Unicorn Among Lions*. Here we have the glimmerings of the soul behind Cecil Beaton's disconcerting portraits of the lady: gallant, malign, absurd and splendid. In 1954 she became a Dame. She wrote to L. P. Hartley: 'It will amuse you to know that as I advanced towards the Queen to get my decorations, the band played "Annie, Get Your Gun".'

SKATING TO ANTARCTICA
Jenny Diski (1997)

The heart of an iceberg is deepest blue, at its most intense at sea level 'where the ice is oldest and so compacted that all the air has been forced out'. This strange and brilliant book recounts Jenny Diski's journey to Antarctica last year, intercut with another journey into her own heart and soul, an examination of her childhood and her relations with her parents, a father who died in April 1966, a mother who two days later ran screaming out of her daughter's life for ever.

Just as Diski's visit to the bottom of the monstrous world is not a pilgrimage, rather 'a hopeful voyage in to whiteness', so she embarks on her inner journey without illusions. She does not seek solace or even an understanding of the forces which wrecked her parents' marriage and instilled in her a longing for oblivion so intense that she overdosed on her mother's Nembutal and now perpetuates her urge for 'whiteout' in her bedroom, in her flat, in her sudden compulsion to reach Antarctica.

Her satisfaction in the end is to find that her recollection is truthful, that her mother, mad and sad rather than bad, was the impossible creature whom she herself had of necessity excluded from her life well before her father's death, and thereafter tried to forget. She might be alive, she might be dead. Diski did not want to know. She felt neither anger nor affection. But even before she voyaged to Antarctica, her own 18-year-old daughter was discovering the bare facts of her grandmother's latter years; with reluctance Diski found herself looking in to the past, questioning elderly ladies who had once been neighbours, revisiting the block of flats where she spent 11 years of childhood; so she shored herself up against the outcome, probing the nature of memory.

Once there had been a small loved child called Jennifer. Her mother took her skating every day: 'You could skate before you could walk.' She was to be a star and her mother would share her glory. Both parents were children of Jewish immigrants; their daughter was to have the best clothes, the best education; she would achieve. By the time Jennifer was four the money had gone and the quarrelling had begun. Here is an extraordinary portrait of a solitary child determined to survive; 'portrait' is the necessary word for Diski tells us 'Any event occurring to Jennifer always includes Jennifer in the frame. The image is not from her eyes . . . but seen from the outside, from some eyes beyond the frame.'

Jennifer sits on her father's knee: 'What the hell I was doing there (if that actual moment ever existed and is not just a representation of a general memory), standing at one side, at a little distance from the armchair the two of them are sitting in, no more substantial than a pair of observing and possibly ironic eyes, I cannot say. Jennifer was frightened of ghosts. Perhaps she had every right to be.'

At weekends Jennifer and her father wandered blissfully round London, going to museums and cinemas and Chinese restaurants. At home her mother waited, angry and excluded. Later weekends were spent visiting her in a mental hospital, re-creating that early merriment on their long walks through the suburbs by knocking on doors so that Jennifer could 'use the bathroom. It became a game, a kind of roulette . . . Those brief visits belonged to the realm of our earlier museum wanderings; the house and people, the exhibits; our meeting people and seeing how they lived, like the stories my father used to make up about the things in glass cases. They were adventures in to unknown worlds, people whose houses, whose lives, looked to me so solid and stable.'

Until her books were taken by the bailiffs Jennifer read, played with other children in the block and ranged in total freedom about her domain, the limitless corridors, stairs, fire-escapes and surrounding pavements of Paramount Court. 'Even now I can't imagine any suburban or country childhood that would have provided me with so much.'

But within the flat, listening to nocturnal warfare, she repeated her prayers for peace a hundred times over, a hundred times tracing a star of David on her chest. She became nervous, elusive and wary of what each parent called the Truth. Her mother was hostile and critical, her father erratic; when she was 11 he left for good. Eviction followed, then years of constant moving, expulsion from school, passing back and forth between parents. Nembutal and mental hospitals. The mother of a school friend offered her a home, her father died and her mother disappeared. No one tried to find her.

There is not an ounce of self-pity in Diski's bleak account, and little warmth either. Images of ice recur, ice that is slippery, treacherous, cracking; a skating rink which promises infinity but brings the skater round and round in ever-repeating circles. In Antarctica Diski finds a Utopia, a no-place of floating Halcyon icebergs, constantly changing, melting, reforming; yet a place which 'would also remain essentially the same, its elements merely rejigged . . . Nothing there stays the same but nothing changes.'

Such paradoxes abound in a book of dazzling variety, which weaves disquisitions on indolence, truth, inconsistency, ambiguousness, the elephant seal, Shackleton, boredom, and over and again memory, into a sparse narrative, caustic observation and vivid description of the natural world. While Diski's writing is laconic, her images are haunting; her honesty transcends pain. The same honesty turns her away from the dream landscape of the ice world to a practical, perfect place, her cabin on the ship. Here there are white walls and white sheets. Here she may watch the snow falling silently from a heavy sky on to the sea.

THE NINE LIVES OF NAOMI MITCHISON
Jenni Calder (1997)

'Service and love above all Other Thinge' wrote the great 15th-century Scots poet William Dunbar. 'Adventure to the Adventurous' proclaimed a jug or mug (described as each in a book peppered with misprints) which Naomi Mitchison acquired in childhood. These three strands entwine to form the substance of her remarkable life.

Naomi Haldane was born in 1897 to an upper-class Scottish family of landowners, scholars, statesmen and writers. Her parents lived in Oxford, where her father was a fellow of New College, but holidays were spent on the family estates in Perthshire and Lothian, in a peculiarly Scottish ambience of romantic freedom and Presbyterian restriction, hill wandering and Sabbath ritual. Naomi and cousins were imbued with an ideal of service to the community and responsibility to the less fortunate.

She learnt to read at the age of three, attended the Dragon School (for boys), kept mice and observed her father's laboratory experiments. She became aware that while her mother expected her to be resourceful, independent and intellectually enquiring, she was growing up into a world which cared little for such qualities in women; her brother Jack went on to Eton, to university, and the 'common male destiny of achievement' while she and three other girls sat in the schoolroom sharing a governess. But she discovered adventurous literature by browsing in Blackwell's bookshop; she ran a guinea-pig stud and, in the spirit of scientific enquiry, performed post mortems and dissections. She took the stud with her to London when she worked as a VAD at St Thomas' Hospital in the war.

Her biographer is uneasy about this, suggesting that Naomi may have been 'unhealthily close' to her guinea pigs. 'Unhealthily close' is the sort of tedious phrase which creeps pointlessly into certain biographies; here we have also 'intellectually-prestigious' (dig that crazy hyphen) and, of course, 'burgeoning sexuality'. How close dare one get to a guinea pig?

Within the family circle Naomi knew a degree of social freedom, the house was full of her brother's friends, among them Aldous Huxley, whom the 16-year-old Naomi tried unsuccessfully to persuade to become her lover, doubtless again in the spirit of scientific enquiry. In 1916, aged 18, she married another staunch friend, Dick Mitchison, admitting later that she would have agreed to marry anyone in uniform. Nonetheless this union proved lasting and loving, while doubly unorthodox in that it swiftly, by mutual agreement, became an open marriage and yet survived, producing seven children.

From early childhood Naomi had kept journals; now she began to write fiction, transferring issues of her own life to a classical or legendary setting. Her early books deal with women's suppression or marginalisation, and the violently contrasting world of male bonding, comradeship and glory. She was an instant literary success and went on to publish eight books in six years, despite the demands of a huge household in Hammersmith comprising children, friends, animals and a substantial domestic staff whose presence was a mild embarrassment for an employer of radical political views. Naomi had an exceptional ability to write in unfavourable surroundings – the baking rocks of Africa, a rainswept fishing boat, a crowded drawing room and, most wondrously, while pushing a pram.

She joined the Labour Party and crusaded for women's rights, birth control, freedom in marriage and a social revolution whose ideal would be comradeship, both intellectual and physical, a loving and ceremonious communality, as expressed in the early Christian ritual meal known as *Agape*. She campaigned for a new work structure where jobs would be fitted to women and not women to jobs. On a trip to Russia, she saw Stalin as a sort of *Boy's Own* hero; her impulsive enthusiasms now make for poignant reading. Of communism she writes: 'through this system of belief, death and hardship lose their terrors, there is no such thing as boredom or individual fear, general love is made possible and happiness such as is very rare in other countries becomes a matter of course . . .'

Many of her friends echoed her views, for others she was too extreme. At this point her own comrades included E. M. Forster, the Huxleys, W. H. Auden, Krishna Menon, Indira Nehru, J. D. Bernal and Gerald Heard. In the States she took up the cause of Alabama sharecroppers, in Vienna she championed the politically oppressed. In the late Thirties, her writing began to meet with a cooler reception and her manifesto *The Moral Base of Politics* was virtually ignored. Exasperated by what she saw as an apathetic or anti-feminist literary establishment, Naomi withdrew to the Mitchisons' recently acquired house in Argyll, where she still lives. There she practised enlightened socialism, working the land, stooking corn and driving tractors, and started a local branch of the Labour party, suspecting the while that people were only joining because she and Dick were the lairds in the Big House.

During and after the war she was deeply involved in local politics, both on Argyll County Council and on the Highlands & Islands Advisory Panel. She worked tirelessly for economic regeneration, repopulation, transport and education in rural areas, and later for nuclear disarmament. Not all her causes prospered; an attempt to rally people into gathering sphagnum moss for bandages was notably unsuccessful, and she was often disheartened by Celtic inertia and the Highland characteristic of enthusiastically welcoming a project while inwardly determining to have nothing to do with it.

Yet perhaps at Carradale Naomi came closest to achieving her community, with family, politicians, fishermen, refugees, foresters, friends and lovers all assembling to bask in her 'passionate tenderness'. A splendid entry in her diary one Christmas reads: 'I wonder if I am normal for my age, or over-polygamous. Difficult to get data. I don't believe in promiscuity through the year: one hasn't time and it takes the mind off the things that matter, one's job and one's duty to one's neighbours. But at the life-giving seasons?'

After the war Dick became Labour MP for Kettering and Naomi flung herself into campaigning for him with habitual energy, fervour and recklessness, tempered by a degree of irony. In the Sixties she became obsessed with Africa, especially Botswana. In tribalism she saw again a realisation of her communal ideal. For the next 30 years she visited her adopted country annually; she set up libraries and community centres, she gave talks on educational methods and birth control; she initiated dam-building. Her efforts to stir women out of submission did not catch on; she came to realise that they had their own ways of coping. As in Scotland, she came upon apathy and inconsistency. She wanted to read Shakespeare aloud to her adored chieftain while he wanted to get drunk in the liquor store. She became a proscribed immigrant in Rhodesia and South Africa, a notorious 'career boat-rocker' 'anti-establishment gadfly'. But in Botswana she was given the status and title of Mother of the Chieftain. 'I have learnt to slip into an African skin,' she said. 'I cling like an old lizard to the rocks of Mochudi.'

And all this time she continued to write plays, stories, poems, articles and reviews: she has published more than 80 books. Her last two novels came out when she was 93. In her late eighties she went on lecture tours in the States and Canada. Life upon life indeed.

Her story is extraordinary and deserves to be celebrated, not least because beyond all her adventures and battles and achievements she has remained, as her husband said, 'true and brave and infinitely kind'. But this biography is sadly sparse, colourless and cautious. It is not often that one wishes a biography to be twice as long, but one does here. There is no sense of place, very little characterisation. Indeed, at times it is just plain boring, which, given the material, is outrageous. Such life as there is rushes sudden and vivid from Naomi's own words. Only in the last chapter, when Calder allows herself to speak personally, does she give any indication that she is capable of the rich, luminous treatment her subject deserves. If she won't do it, someone else must.

FANNY BURNEY
Claire Harman (2000)

Fanny Burney was born in King's Lynn, Norfolk, in 1752. She died in London in 1840. During her adventurous 88 years she met a prodigious number of writers, actors, musicians, philosophers, painters, almost every contemporary luminary, including Dr Johnson, Mrs Thrale, David Garrick, Sheridan, Chateaubriand, Talleyrand, King George III, Horace Walpole, Joshua Reynolds, Sarah Siddons. And she documented all this in her diaries, which span more than 70 years and have been in print since their first edition in 1842. She wrote four novels, inspiring Virginia Woolf to credit her as 'the mother of English fiction'. She wrote nine plays, one of which (*A Busy Day*) is currently on at the Lyric Theatre, starring Stephanie Beacham, who describes it as 'a really rich, rollicking Regency romp, and about as politically correct as Ali G'. In old age she brought out *Memoirs of Dr Burney*, a 'version' of her father's life which contains her own autobiography, using, reinventing, omitting material from her diaries in the interests of controlling information about her family and creating a pleasing self-portrait for posterity. Fanny herself and her (authorised) descendants also cut out, pasted over and inked through many pages of the diaries. With modern technology, however, much of the material may become accessible. Claire Harman mentions the Burney Project at McGill University, which has been working on this 'for some 30 years and is not yet within sight of an end'. Meanwhile, we are privileged to have this new and meticulous account of an extraordinary life, a life more than usually shaped by unwilled, external events which engulfed but could not extinguish a stoic character, a 'feeling heart' and an observant, sardonic eye.

Fanny was the third of the six surviving children of Esther and Charles Burney. Both parents were committed autodidacts, spending fireside evenings on a self-imposed reading programme, which included poetry, scientific tracts and Diderot's *Encyclopédie*. Charles Burney was a hugely gifted musician who became famous for his *General History of*

Music. The family moved to London when Fanny was nine, and through his talent and his amiable gifts as an 'arch networker', he rapidly achieved a web of acquaintances and friends including Smollett, Garrick, Christopher Smart and Dr Johnson. He met and admired Handel, on one occasion mildly reprimanding the choleric great man, who responded: 'I pec your barton – I am a very odd tog.' At home he was surrounded by adoring daughters, whose lifelong aim was to please him. His sons would go their separate ways, adventurous and eccentric, one to join the Navy, one to become a scholar, another to found a school for orphans in India.

Fanny did not read until she was nine and was known to her siblings as 'the little dunce'. But in a household thronged with bohemian visitors who talked, played music, recited and read aloud, she developed a gift for mimicry and a remarkable verbal memory. She learnt quantities of Shakespeare and Pope by overhearing her sisters' private lessons and, with the others, went regularly to the theatre. However, in a family which was conspicuously articulate, musical and witty she remained withdrawn, observing; her new title, from the age of 11, was 'the Old Lady'. Harman quotes a poignant story from the *Memoirs*. A wigmaker's family lived next door, in Soho. The children, playing together, found a cupboard of lawyers' wigs and ran shrieking about the garden in these 'dignified ornaments of the head' until one fell off into a tub of water and 'lost all its gorgon buckle'. The wigmaker was beside himself with fury; whereupon 10-year-old Fanny advanced, grave and composed. 'The wig is wet to be sure; and the wig was a good wig. But it's of no use to speak of it any more; because what's done cannot be undone.' 'The wig is wet' became a Burney phrase to describe the irredeemable. This alleged incident took place in 1762, the year of Esther's death. Perhaps from loneliness while her sisters spent time at school in France, perhaps from a need to create a less painful world, Fanny now began to write. Then and later, writing was for her an intensely private activity. In 1768 she burnt her juvenilia and began to keep her diary.

Ten years later, *Evelina* was published and was wildly successful. The talk of society, it was compared favourably to Fanny's idol

Richardson. Fanny's desire for anonymity led her into many bizarre situations and excruciating embarrassment. When she at last revealed herself, she found that her reticence was widely misinterpreted 'If you will be an Author and a Wit, you must take the consequence,' warned Mrs Thrale.

The consequences of celebrity were not all predictable. Sheridan encouraged her to write plays, a medium valued well above the novel in the 18th century. In fact only one of Fanny's plays was staged, years later, and despite a gallant performance from Mrs Siddons, it was a critical disaster. 'The Audience were quite angelic and only laughed where it was *impossible* to avoid it.' Under further literary pressure, she brought out *Cecilia* and was invited to become Second Keeper of the Robes at court after the Queen gave *Cecilia* to her daughters to read. Although Fanny's duties were minimal, she was obliged to be in constant attendance on the Queen and had no time for writing, no time even for going out. 'I am *married*,' she wrote to her sister Susan. Lassitude became her way of life. 'I only do nothing; that's all.' Harman brightens this sad episode with a brilliantly comic story involving one of Charles Burney's books, *The Present State of Music in Germany*. Queen Charlotte demanded a copy and Fanny received the book with 'the sensitive passages about German lack of genius marked in pencil, so she could avoid them when reading aloud.' Unhappily the Queen borrowed the book for the Princess Royal, 'who thought the marked sections indicated Fanny's favourite passages.' However, Fanny's terror over this incident – 'It's all over with us forever' – proved unnecessary, because it soon became clear that none of the Royal family had bothered to read a word of the book. In counterpoint, there is a most tragic description of Fanny meeting the poor mad King in the gardens at Kew on a cold February morning. 'He spread out his arms to embrace her (she imagined she was about to be attacked) and kissed her cheek, a most extraordinary gesture. The doctors "simply smiled and looked pleased", and the King entered into a rambling conversation with Fanny, during which he sang bits of Handel in a croaking voice and became tearful – "I have lived so long out of the world, I know nothing!" he said.'

Through the summer Fanny attended a Royal progress round the West Country. At Weymouth they bathed from machines, oblivious to the fall of the Bastille and imprisonment of Louis XVI. On their return to London, Fanny resigned from Court. In 1793, after the execution of the French King, Madame de Staël joined the wave of émigrés seeking refuge in England, and with Talleyrand and others set up home near Fanny's married sister Susan. Here Fanny met her future husband, Alexandre d'Arblay; they were married that summer and embarked on a rural idyll, growing cabbages with success (nothing else, however). The following year their son, known variously as the Bookham Brattikin or the Idol of the World, was born. Fanny's novel *Camilla* came out to indifferent reviews. Among the subscribers was the 20-year-old Jane Austen.

In 1802 the d'Arblays moved to France, intending to spend a year there while Alexandre's passport was sorted out. However, in 1803 Bonaparte declared war on England and for the next nine years they were trapped in France, deprived of news, of letters. In 1811, Fanny underwent a mastectomy, which she described in horrifying detail. Here Harman, who at times turns a caustic eye on her subject, comments: 'The value of Fanny's narrative as a rare patient's eye view of radical surgery has been acknowledged by medical practitioners and historians of medicine, but its greatest value is as a testimony to the inviolability of the ego.'

Returning at last to Britain, Fanny and her son travelled on an American ship. Unknown to them and unknown to the crew, the United States had declared war on Britain, so that the boat was seized by the British and impounded. It was at dinner that night that she saw 'a plate decorated with a likeness of Lord Nelson's head and the word "Trafalgar" written underneath and had to ask her hosts what "Trafalgar" meant'.

In 1814 her new novel *The Wanderer* came out, disappointing her readers and critics, both in content and in style, being a socio-political treatise devoid of satire and couched in ponderous language. 'Instead of the wind blowing through the trees, zephyrs agitate the verdant foliage of venerable branches,' comments Harman.

With her son Alex now established at Cambridge, Fanny joined her husband in France, once again at a moment of high drama: Napoleon's escape from Elba. She fled from Paris disguised as a friend's maid, ran into Chateaubriand while trying to post a letter, reached Brussels and was trapped there on the eve of Waterloo. After a series of calamitous adventures, she and d'Arblay returned to London, ill and exhausted, in the autumn of 1815. After his death three years later, she began to work on her journals for posterity; editing her father's memoirs and destroying many family papers. Her strange and unsatisfactory son died in 1837, never having fufilled his early intellectual promise, and her publication of the *Memoirs of Dr Burney* was received with scorn. 'An awful book,' says Harman; interfering, full of self importance and false humility.

Almost blind, but still talkative and still making new friends, including Sir Walter Scott and George Crabbe, she died in January 1840.

Much has been written about this 'strangely creative autobiographer', but Harman's account is full of special delights. She excels in the vivid presentation of scenes, the selection of detail. Fanny's devoted relations with her sisters are evoked with great delicacy, and Harman points out gently but firmly that we live in a time where we find it difficult to appreciate and easy to misinterpret such depth of feeling. The physical background of long, wasting and unexplained illnesses, ceaseless childbearing, desolating infant mortality and mortal fevers bears its proper weight.

The otherness of the 18th century is conveyed without over emphasis, lit by small details: the lack of privacy; the slowness of news to travel; the prominence of gambling. James Burney, Fanny's brother, led an equally extraordinary life, witnessing Captain Cook's death and dismemberment in Hawaii and yet bringing a Hawaiian dress back as a present to his sister – a dress which Mrs Thrale then had copied for herself. The difficulties a biographer must experience when dealing with such a manipulator of truth as Fanny Burney are scrupulously examined here: 'What's done cannot be undone,' said the child, but the adult novelist's subversion '*What if* it can?' persists without creating inconsistency.

Three powerful images, all purposely supplied by Fanny, linger: the child in the garden with the wet wig; the famous moment when Fanny, hearing of Johnson's approval of *Evelina*, dances with joy round a mulberry tree; and herself as an old lady marooned on a pinnacle of rock surrounded by a raging sea, accompanied by her dog whom she had hoisted up with her umbrella handle. No one has questioned the wig episode, but the mulberry tree did not exist, and rescuers removed Fanny from a stretch of shore where she was in no danger. Does this matter? To the biographer perhaps, but not to the reader. There's truth and truth, painstakingly dissected in this marvellous and beautifully written book.

MY FATHER'S PLACES
Aeronwy Thomas (2009)

Aeronwy Thomas was born in 1943 in London. Her father Dylan was off in the pub and did not meet her for several days. Her older brother Llewelyn was living elsewhere, with their mother Caitlin's family in the New Forest. This memoir focuses on the three to four years spent continuously in the Boat House in Laugharne, a great stretch of time for a child. She was six when they moved there; she was ten, in her first term at boarding school, when her father died in horrible and unresolved confusion in New York. Towards the end of this book Aeronwy says 'writing about my father's death was cathartic, though all my activity on his behalf, during most of my life, has been a form of reconciliation to his death.' The Laugharne years are the most vividly recollected time she spent with both her parents. Brother Llewelyn, older by three years, remains a shadowy, menacing figure on his occasional visits from boarding school. He chucked her doll's house over the cliff, making her consider how a person might go over. Baby Colm, born that first summer in Laugharne, was a cherub child whom Aeronwy adored, reluctantly. At his and her christening she took him from his pram and hid him among the gravestones. 'Mother was sure she had brought him.' Life goes on, he was found, they were both baptised.

This memoir is mostly about Caitlin, rampageous, unpredictable and violent, then suddenly 'a golden sun beaming'. She wore fabulous clothes, cartwheeled, danced on the table, drank, and swam in the nude with Aeron, who wore voluminous navy knickers. She cooked great stews of the perpetual sort for Dylan's solitary consumption. He did not eat with his family except on Christmas Day. Dolly from the village, who underpinned everything, provided the children with egg and chips and apple pies. Caitlin's stews bring about the only harsh remark in this affectionate history of parental neglect and oblivion. Dylan's chief patron, Margaret Taylor (wife of AJP), always neatly suited in coffee and cream, also made stews, 'green cat stews' coloured by cat pee, according to Caitlin. Aeron won't have this. 'Mother's, though more ordinarily brown, had bone marrow fat floating on the surface. She had no right to criticize anyone else's stew.'

We have no critical rights either. But here are some facts. These children were left alone every night of their lives. Aeron as a baby was left alone beneath the falling bombs of London. Her mother told her that if she had stayed in she would have lost Dylan. In Laugharne, Caitlin would beat her with a hairbrush so violently that she fled to friends or to her grandmother's bed, where she drew sheep and slept, in gorgeously described comfort and safety. Otherwise life offered its usual hazards, the unwanted attentions of certain visitors, the village deviant, precipitous bicycling, near death by drowning, crossing the road or the casually mentioned 'shooting incident at Majoda' when her infant form was stuffed up the chimney to escape the bullets. But

Aeron's greatest need was for her father's attention. She crashed her bike outside his shed, she screamed, she laughed, she showed him her special drowned sheep with its cathedral ribs, 'the lost sheep of my Bible stories that wasn't found'. He hated sunlight and noisy children in equal measure. Always, he disappeared into his shed. Once in the garden he looked at her blankly saying '"What are you doing?" as if I'd appeared out of the ground like a radish.' She made herself invisible, a listener and observer.

At one o'clock each day she would go to the pub to retrieve Dylan from his morning's drinking. From two till seven he was locked, usually by Caitlin, in his shed. Aeron would lurk outside. If she heard his voice it meant he was writing, for he pronounced every syllable out loud. If there was silence, he would be reading his green Penguins. Once a week 'steamy and wet as an African warthog', when Caitlin had rubbed his hair dry from his bath and cut his nails, Dylan read to her, *Grimm's Fairy Tales* or *Wind in the Willows*, or Enid Blyton. Yes! The Secret of Spiggy Holes! Just for a little of course, then off to the pub.

While much of the writing here is uneven, there are some sublime passages, a very Welsh tea party and a most haunting aftermath to Christmas Day. Just before the parents leave for their drinking spree, the child goes outside. 'The tide was creeping through the square hole in the garden wall and I rushed out onto the verandah to look down on the waters half filling the garden. Putting the tin whistle trumpet to my lips I gave a Christmas Greeting. A thin moon cast its pale beams on the estuary. As the tide came in, water rapidly cast its circle ever wider. The light from the sky painted silvery grey patches, which eddied towards our wall, entering the harbour like a determined but not unwelcome guest. Our lights and the moon made the rapidly filling pool of our back garden strange and eerie but not frightening at all.' This ghostly little figure provides the book's most arresting image.

'I decided that I belonged to all worlds' Aeron thought. She was nine years old then.

JANE'S FAME
How Jane Austen Conquered the World
Claire Harman (2009)

'She doesn't go to the see-and-be-seen parties. She's reticent with the press. There are nasty rumours that she engaged in an incestuous relationship with her sister, for God's sake. And frankly, she could use a makeover. But in this year alone, four of her novels have been adapted for the big and small screens. And with numerous World Wide Web sites devoted to her glory, she even holds her own with internet pinup Brad Pitt. Not bad for a British broad who's been dead for 178 years.' Thus *Entertainment Weekly* in 1995, already sounding oddly dated, unlike its subject, who has become a global industry, commercial, cinematic, literary, academic.

In this extraordinary book, crammed with scholarship and glittering with trivia, Claire Harman provides a valiantly detached account of every conceivable perception of Jane Austen through her short life and the near 200 years since her death in 1817. The Memoir produced by her nephew in 1870 prompted a great surge of interest which has swollen ever since and most vigorously since the films of the 1990s, but, ironically, it was also responsible for the generally received impression that Jane led a life of gentle sequestration, nervously concealing her writing, quite without ambition, happily engaged in domesticity and child play. 'Her performances with cup and ball were marvellous,' he tells us. She was excellent too at Spillikins. Her sweetness, wholesomeness and gentility were of course reflected in her writing. Another kinsman, Lord Brabourne, brought out in 1884 an edition of such of her surviving letters which was at variance with this notion. Jane's voice, here, is often cross, materialistic and nasty. Commenting on an acquaintance's stillborn child, she suggests the mother must have taken a look at the father. No one wanted to see the writer like this; the letters were set aside.

Harman, nonetheless, does show that from childhood Jane was spirited, competitive and proud of her writing, which she circulated happily around her wide circle of friends and family, many of whom wrote themselves. Her eldest brother was a poet and while at Oxford produced a literary magazine. Skits, burlesques, lampoons and amateur theatricals provided endless fun and Jane painstakingly collected her early writings into little books, her Volumes; Harman's quotations are enticing: 'A lovely young Woman lying apparently in great pain beneath a Citron tree was an object too interesting not to attract their notice.' She was working on full-length novels by her late teens, rewriting and reshaping in bursts of energy over long periods. An acquaintance then remembered her as very pretty, a husband-hunting butterfly; another saw her as a silent observer, still as a poker by the fire; later, as her fame grew, albeit locally, she became 'a poker of whom everyone is afraid.' Her books were anonymous, as was customary for women writers, but on receiving the joyful news of high praise in high society she determined to reveal herself with *Mansfield Park*: 'I shall rather try to make all the Money than all the Mystery I can of it. People shall pay for this knowledge.' But when she died the gravestone her family erected made no mention of her writing, her papers were dispersed, and despite sporadic interest over the decades, it seemed that a line had been drawn under her very existence, until that Memoir was prompted by some sense of rivalry with the Brontës' great celebrity and a growing annoyance at drifts of speculative gossip.

And so her fame spread, with new editions, illustrations even, and gathering critical acclaim, first notably from Sir Walter Scott who identified her as the creator of an entirely new way of writing, naturalistic and concentrated, unlike the traditional literature of drama and sensation to which he himself subscribed, 'the Big bow-wow strain' as he adorably put it. Scott and Macaulay were perhaps the first of many fervent male admirers (apart from Jane's beloved father) who have included Tennyson, Wilde, Fenimore Cooper (who wrote his first novel, *Precaution*, in the manner of *Persuasion*), Coleridge, G.H. Lewes, Bulwer-Lytton, even Robert Southey, who had been so rude to Charlotte Brontë: 'Literature cannot be the business of a woman's life, and it ought not to be.' (Austen turned down an offer of marriage for literature.) Disraeli read *Pride and Prejudice* seventeen times.

Mark Twain however expended much energy on her vilification. She was 'entirely impossible', worse than Poe, and should not have been allowed a natural death. He would like 'to dig her up and hit her over the skull with her own shinbone.'

The book offers so many delights. Byron's wife-to-be, Annabella Milbanke, adored *Pride and Prejudice* and is the first recorded admirer of Darcy. What a quirk of fate it was that later brought her detested sister-in-law, the scandalous, incestuous, Augusta Leigh to assist her in the birth of her first child, clasping a copy of *Emma*. Kipling was most poignantly moved to write *The Janeites*, his first fiction ten years after his son's death in battle at Loos. There is a marvellous illustration of the cover of *Storyteller Magazine* proclaiming this event and showing a soldier on a battlefield reading Austen. Her books were at the top of the Fever Chart devised for reading in military hospitals. As Harman says, 'It is odd to think of how many damaged and dying men in field hospitals and convalescent homes might have swum in and out of consciousness to the sound or the memory of Divine Jane's words.'

This is a fantastic compendium of absolutely everything relating to Austen, the tone calm and impartial despite severe provocation. It is another irony that in this most visual of times so many people's enthusiasm for her writing is actually an enthusiasm for the images of screen and artefact. A couple of years ago, the director of the Austen Festival in Bath sent, under a pseudonym and the title *First Impressions*, the opening chapters of *Pride and Prejudice* 'with proper nouns slightly adjusted' to eighteen British publishers, all of whom rejected them. Only one recognised the hoax.

But beyond all the hullabaloo, the need and yearning for Jane persists, perhaps because she is both most constant and most elusive. A lock of her hair in the Jane Austen House Museum, despite the interventions of Elida and Unilever, gives up no inkling of its original colour. As for her likeness, there is the 'horrid sketch' by her sister Cassandra and just one other verifiable image, which most wonderfully shows her 'in a pelisse and bonnet, out of doors on a summer day, with her back to the viewer.'

A JURY OF HER PEERS
American Women Writers from Anne Bradstreet to Annie Proux
Elaine Showalter (2009)

American women have been authors for more than three hundred and fifty years. Elaine Showalter's *A Jury of Her Peers* is quite astonishingly the first comprehensive history of these writers. Showalter is a literary critic celebrated on both sides of the Atlantic for her scholarship, wit and ability to convey complex arguments in simple and lucid prose. This prodigious undertaking reflects these qualities and moreover is written with a great generosity of spirit which leaves the reader inspired and humbled.

The book takes the form of a roughly chronological account of these women and their work. By the end, Showalter has traced a development through what she calls 'feminine' writing, which reflects already-established male traditions, succeeded by 'feminist' writing, which strives against the foregoing, then 'female' writing, which is specifically introverted and concerned with establishing identity, finally reaching 'free' writing, which is beyond restrictions of form, gender or subject matter, oblivious equally to the mouldered old monoliths of 'patriarchal norms' and the barbed prescriptions of extreme feminist scholarship. Showalter is not the first to declare this: Avital Ronell in a neat Nietzschean pun writes that we are now or ought to be thinking 'Jenseits von Mann und Frau' – not just beyond good and evil, but beyond man and woman. But it is impossible to criticise this book for its critical stances because it is so light on theory and so large with common sense and interesting facts.

The simple fact of course is that some women write and some don't, some need encouragement and some don't care; same with men I believe. But the huge question raised by the past is, how did they do it at all? We read of women struggling with disease, plague, revolution, dissolute or hostile husbands, endless childbearing, and jobs outside the home. In contrast to their English contemporaries, American women just got on with it. Few had servants, as even the poorest 19th century English writer did, and many valued domesticity even when they saw how it subverted writing. (And as for modern times, well, no less an authority than Betty Friedan has pointed out what I have always said, that labour-saving devices are in fact labour-intensive.)

Ideology and politics have been more important for American women writers than for their British counterparts. Many of these women were intensely involved in the struggles, defeats and occasional visionary glories of their times, willingly or unwittingly contributing to the grand canon of American literature, albeit so often and randomly forgotten. In 1883 Emma Lazarus wrote a sonnet for a fundraising enterprise. The object was the purchase of a pedestal for the Statue of Liberty Enlightening the World. At the dedication her poem was not read, but six years after her death, it was engraved on the pedestal. Many know of the huddled masses and wretched refuse who teem on the shores of the United States, but very few are aware of the author of these magnificent words. And all her other work is quite forgotten. Again and again in these pages, there are women who have written something of huge interest, even influence, for its time, and have then just disappeared. Showalter suggests this has happened because they lacked an informed readership who might have demonstrated their value to others and that this lacuna is a thing of the past. Her voice throughout is quiet and calm. She allows facts to speak for themselves but her great gift is to tell us what to think about these facts without making us object, or even be aware that she is slanting them. We enjoy her too much to disagree.

Chapters begin with a short overview of place and time followed by brief accounts of writers' lives and works. Even in the earliest writing, how various the women's voices are. In the 17th century the poet Anne Bradstreet writes of her home, her children, and her beloved husband while Mary Rowlandson describes her abduction by Indians who murdered 12 members of her family and friends; her six year old daughter died of her wounds and was left unburied. In the 1970s literary historians accused this woman of being 'pervasively racist' and failing to mention the suffering of Indians. Elaine Showalter ends the book with an acknowledgment to her own husband using Bradstreet's very words: 'If ever wife was happy in a man/Compare with me, ye women, if you can.'

What makes this book exceptional is its vigorous presentation of character and quotation, lives lived, and lives created. Willa Cather describes an old woman entranced by Wagner. She does not want to leave the concert.

For her, just outside the door of the concert hall lay the black pond with the cattle-tracked bluffs; the tall unpainted house, with weather-curled boards, naked as a tower; the crook-backed ash seedlings where the dishcloths hung to dry; the gaunt, molting turkeys picking up refuse about the kitchen door.

Showalter adds, 'It is Cather's vision of the wasteland, the nightmare landscape of failed quest, like Robert Browning's poem "Childe Roland to the Dark Tower Came"'. In one neat sentence we are given a parallel, an explanation, an interpretation and a judgement.

The aspirant hetaira Edith Wharton is easy enough to mock, but Showalter's picture of her with her Pomeranians and Pekinese is a tiny delight. 'Toward the end of the marriage, the dogs in the photographs sit snarling on her lap, shoulders and arms, totemic bodyguards of her erogenous zones.' Gertrude Stein earns opprobrium for her 'division of household labor between two women with one doing everything and the other doing nothing.' Of gladsome Pollyanna, the 1913 creation of

Eleanor H. Porter, who teaches everyone she meets to be glad, Showalter comments 'Despite her commitment to the power of positive thinking, Pollyanna is sorely tried when she is hit by a car and is presumed to be paralyzed for life.' Nevertheless, she informs us, 'Glad Clubs' were formed, even by prisoners, and 'the name has become emblematic of an American message of mindless optimism.' Mary McCarthy skewers an entire cultural myth with 'I've never noticed that women were less warlike than men,' and a paragraph on Dorothy Parker finely illustrates Showalter's method:

In the 1930s, Parker went to Hollywood, where she had a period of fame and wealth, but her alcoholism and a wretched marriage contributed to severe writing blocks. She went to France to work on a novel, to be called 'The Events Leading Up to the Tragedy'; but she never completed it. Her prayer at the time – 'Dear God, please make me stop writing like a woman. For Jesus Christ's sake, amen.' – may have had something to do with her inability to finish the book.

A work of selection must perforce have omissions. I would have liked to see Dawn Powell included, as well as the very witty Woman Who Shot Andy Warhol, Valerie Solanas, author of the sublime *SCUM Manifesto*. Few of us today want to be like either Powell or Solanas. Dorothy Parker 'saw a long parade of weary horses and shivering beggars and all beaten, driven, stumbling things. 'We don't want to be like that. We don't want the 'animal fatalism' noted by Edith Wharton. We may not want to be wise high priestesses in the Toni Morrison mode either. Nor need we be 'lush maternal gardens'. Among other things this book announces that the time of prescription and proscription for women writers is gone. With one bound we are free, and while this freedom presents new terrors, like those brave dead women, we must just get on with it.

THOUGHTS IN A GARDEN

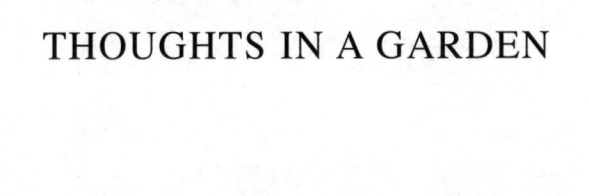

THOUGHTS IN A GARDEN

Mine is a riverine garden, and even indoors one is aware of this, not just by gazing through the window but by simply sitting still, committing words to paper in intense cold, while a great numbness seeps up through feet and lower limbs. Hemlock and the death of Socrates come forward in the mind. The tiled floor is laid straight on the earth in the manner of seventeenth century folk, and beneath this floor and a thin layer of earth lie the black sullen waters of an underground lake. This is true; I have seen those waters gleaming beneath a hole in the drawing room floor. Once the garden was fenland, embracing a much wider river, and Norsemen laboured up it in their long boats from the coast, intent on plunder and rapine. I am glad to have missed that.

Now time has modified the river bank, where bramble and hawthorn and snowberry and ivy tangle to forestall small children from a watery demise, and a high beech hedge divides it from the lawn's long slope. This hedge is a source of anger and grievance in postmen, rubbish men, delivery men of all sorts; they claim that its tentacular outreach damages their Vehicles, already woefully menaced by the muddy causeway which curves beside it, and mostly they refuse to come to the house. Which is fine by me, as I don't want to see them anyhow, except for the oil delivery man, who makes a ridiculous point of driving his colossal tanker backwards up the track.

Wet wet wet is the texture of the lawn, currently mounded by molehills of ever more ambitious scale. Wetter still is the stretch of wilderness leading to the pond and the graveyard of the important animals. Bog grasses are growing now, where once in more clement times my children played football or tried to hoist a sequence of angry ponies over jumps. I always chose the highest ground for the graves and I believe these noble beasts still sleep sound and dry; but even in the less sodden past the largest animal you could bury there would be a Labrador. Any deeper and it was standing water. Consequently, forty-one years on, space for final resting places is at a premium, and certain lesser creatures have had to be consigned to the edges of the lawn and peripheral nettly groves. Desdemona, the cat without character, lies here, and quite a few hens. I well recall beginning a new flowerbed and exhuming a dreadful pair of yellow legs complete with claws. 'That's Joanna,' observed a passing child, unmoved. Sombre, the trees gather about the upper graves, but in late winter their darkness is offset most exquisitely by the floating wanness of narcissi, and then wild primroses.

When we came here, all those years ago, the garden had ceased to exist. Nettles and brambles and ground elder and cow parsley and dock revelled luxuriantly through our first springtime. I had three children under three and was thus preoccupied; soon I had two more. My husband wrote his poetry in an upper room, looking out into trees, sky and river, happily removed from earthly concerns. When summer at last came we began to reclaim the lawn. Children need grass and trees first of all. Then their animals needed grass, and the hens, disdaining their run, claimed the trees. Albertine and Madame Alfred Carrière clambered cautiously up the house and early morning light, refracted from the river, flickered and shifted through shadowing rose leaves down our red bedroom walls and danced in the brass knobs of the bed. Albertine was vigorous and gorgeously pink but died abruptly after only three years. Madame Alfred, however, continues to thrive and even this December displayed a scatter of ghostly blooms, whirled to the sky's four quarters by the bitter Norfolk wind. And as the years have passed, at last there is the time and chance to give attention to the flowerbeds, time to alleviate the whelm of greenery.

My husband, the poet, died some years ago and I have tried to make a six foot garden on his grave; a rowan tree shades his stone and chequered fritillaries nod amid a profusion of forget-me-nots and foxgloves. In autumn there come the flaming arches of crocosmia. But the garden for the living is another matter. I am blessed in having married again and my husband, although eccentric and American, is a visionary gardener. I have seen him coax a rose, blighted and shrunk through wet and cold, furled tight in deathly pallor, into a perfumed ecstasy of splayed crimson, a performance so charged with eroticism that words must fail me. He has made a vast, overbalancing buddleia into an airy cavern of blue delight, underplanted by cranesbill and campanula; butterflies fold their wings along the silvery boughs and its haunting raspberry fragrance hangs in the air. I take intense pleasure in clambering up inside it and deadheading. There is an unearthly hush about the slow, gentle drift of the spent blooms to the ground, and through the branches I can see birds cross the wide sky, sometimes a swan, or a heron, or a flock of squabbling starlings, and I feel ethereal. But in truth I am a gardener manquée; I participate eagerly in the effect but do little to further the cause. Mostly I have the no-brain jobs, a little basic weeding, the wheelbarrow trundle to the unlightable bonfire, the gingerly poke at the compost heap. I am happy with these simple tasks; I believe myself useful but am without responsibility. Meanwhile, the paragon or paramour creates fabulous small vistas of colour, bells and spires; Saki's 'bewildering fragment of fairyland' glimmers in sudden surprise as you wander past a shrub or around a tree. Look, look, we cry.

He is, however, obsessed with turnips. He grows them everywhere, among cornflowers, and tulips, and beside the miraculous violet sculpture of sea holly. Where e'er your glance may linger, there rears a turnip. No other plant behaves like this. At all seasons they are conspicuous, in leaf, in flower, in white globular roots within whose deep recesses reptiles dwell. There are kindred disruptive elements in this garden; besides the molehills, a number of spiky dead trees present their barren limbs like amputees; still, they give pleasure to woodpeckers. Then there is the oil tank, behind which the junior dog has made a den, furnished by herself with stolen red cushions and Somerfield packaging; and we have the pathetic relic of the duck pen, containing an improvised and unused duck shelter fashioned from an abandoned azure plasterboard bookcase. Those ducks betrayed us. They sold us down the river.

Yet we can tell each other that the garden is beautiful, as the low white mist rises from the river and scarves the trees and we hear the sigh and rush of moving water, the toss of aspen leaves. The rainy sounding aspens, Sappho called them, nearly three thousand years ago; the same sound now. And other people tell us that the garden is beautiful as they sit round the lawn table beneath the ancient beech tree. For those summer moments none of us will notice that the great tree is dying from its crown; indeed, to save its life, it is to be pollarded this very month, cut across in half. I absolutely cannot bear to think of this, but I can see that it doesn't want to die. It has already put forth buds for spring and beneath its bark three new trunks are rising from its roots; slim and shining grey, they press with youthful urgency into the aged soft white wood.

At the bleak time of year how tempting it is to lie in bed, cosseted like bulbs; we are aware of the dawn beyond closed curtains and we may consider the virtue of 'maintaining a constant temperature in a dark place,' as recommended so cordially by gardeners and oenophiles. But then, like bulbs and bottles, we must be brought into the light. A garden is idea as much as it is terrain, and now it confers perhaps its greatest blessing; the knowledge that whatever has happened, here we have another chance. Here there will be renaissance. In a garden it is never too late.

A NATURAL HISTORY OF UNICORNS
Chris Lavers

This natural history of unicorns is not a work of dark and devious wit like *A Short History of Tractor Driving in the Ukraine*; it really does trace the unicorn, in many guises, from cuneiform script through the

Hebrew bible, Greek versions of travellers' tales, the Septuagint, the second century *Physiologos*, mediaeval bestiaries, religious and secular art, at last refining in the 14th century to the image now familiar to us, the prancing, white, fabulous palfrey with its single horn. These tangled threads resemble a page from a childrens' puzzle book, the dense web where you'll reach the end if you stick to the right line. But here you don't really reach the end. The author promises something disingenuous and it doesn't happen. Nonetheless the journey is enjoyable and you learn a vast deal of interesting and useless facts and lots of good words too, astragal, rhinocerine, alexipharm, osteodentine ('which has an attractive porridge-like appearance').

The very important thing about the unicorn would appear to be its single horn. Funny, that. Or not, for after all, that's what the Latinate word means, as does its Greek precedent, monoceros. Who or what was the unicorn, is the central question, and the contenders are countless and crazy, with the rhino and the mighty aurochs (a giant ox) crashing into the lead, despite the fact that they bear scant resemblance to the beast as described in numerous divergent accounts. And what of the onager, the musk-ox, the kiang or churu, the atti, or the okapi? Two horns may pass for one in a profile painting. Or anywhere, if you want them to. The book is studded with fetching pictures of creatures who may or may not have combined chimerically to create the mythic beast, described in early days at greatest length by Ctesias, a Greek physician at the Persian court in 398 BC. Its coat is red and white, its eyes dark blue, it is swifter than all beasts, impossible to capture. Its horn, crimson, black and white, confers immunity to disease and poison when carved into drinking vessels. And so the image recurs in varied forms through antiquity, endorsed by Aristotle, Pliny the Elder, and the Septuagint translation of the Bible from Hebrew to Greek. This Biblical authority derives from the arbitrary translation of the Hebrew re'em ('large, horned, domestically useless') as monoceros. Maybe it was the aurochs, maybe it wasn't. But from then on, it has one horn, and is a unicorn and in the Bible, so it must be true. Furthermore, it comes to represent first the glory of God, then Christ and his union with God. 'Who is the Unicorn, but God's only Son?' demanded Bishop Ambrose, one of the Latin fathers of the early Church. Dense symbolism and allegory accrued, thanks to Tertullian and other inventive theologians, and what is hard to follow in writing was transmuted into intricate beauty by illustrations deriving first from mediaeval bestiaries, which would describe the animal and then recount its mystic role in the life of the spirit. So the unicorn we recognise steps into tapestry and fresco, its horn symbolising salvation and divine union; humble and lowly, it is caught for us by the Virgin who is Mary. Hunters will come with spears and take it to the King in his palace as God's will took Christ back from us, and it will live again, perhaps bleeding pomegranate juice and seeds, triumphant symbols of rebirth. What sublime fusion of allegory and romance is worked into those tapestries of gardens enclosed, strewn with flowers and trees, beasts wild and gentle; what joy and what pain.

From this high point the book wanders into more digressive realms, medicinal properties, commercial products, further improbable identifications, allowing a very dear photograph of musk-oxen and a cuddly calf. Narwhals and walruses offer up their horns to the confusion of quack pharmacology.

The 18th century brought Newton, and nature's laws were harshly illuminated; Aristotle and the Bible were found wanting, and unicorns lost their interest, but not for long. Romantic excitement in travel, the supernatural and the noble savage sent scholarly explorers to India and to darkest Africk. No unicorns, as usual, but Lavers tells a wonderful true story of diplomacy, a pygmy city no higher than a dining table, a taxidermist and okapi, all set against a Congo background. This chapter is the finest in the book and could stand on its own, vivid, poignant and fraught with a dry and delicate wit.

Our times seem drab after such exploits, and there are odd lacunae – no mention of the wealth of unicorn-related art history, or the creature's prominent place in psychology; but one mustn't grumble. Why not instead hark back to the mighty auroch, most ancient and favoured contender for unicornity, and consider the closing lines of *Lolita*, where Nabokov writes, 'I am thinking of aurochs and angels, the secret of durable pigments, prophetic sonnets, the refuge of art. And this is the only immortality you and I may share, my Lolita.' A 20th century image of the unicorn and the maiden, Humbert and his Lo? Just a thought, but not without its charms. And now, as Lavers remarks, the mythic beast seems to have become the preserve of new age crystal keepers. In their pungent emporia one may find holographs of moonlit unicorns breasting the whelm of ocean. I bought one myself for my small granddaughter. Soon afterwards, she and I were wandering in a Maytime wood; a shaft of sunlight dazzled the glade before us, and a seemly virgin led a unicorn of my own devising through bluebells and campion into the shadowed beech trees and out of sight. I recounted this heavenly incident to a Cambridge psychologist. 'Of course you will tell her it wasn't true,' she said. I certainly will not. The child has seen a unicorn forever.

Unicorns don't exist, but we want them to exist. Why not? Thus have gods come into being. Meanwhile, in some remote *hortus conclusus* of the mind, the creature lingers yet, grazes and kicks up its heels. See it caracole.

APRIL

The countrywoman in the prolonged winter which is an East Anglian spring, spends more time slithering on the public highways than straying down nature's byways. She apprehends the world through a mud splattered windscreen. To some their Volvo, to others their Ford Cortina. While Volvo is a silly sort of name, meaning I roll something along, the Cortina is variously a cauldron, an Apollonian tripod, or, by poetic transference, the *vault of heaven*.

It's the one for me. Driving is not much fun round here because of the highways authority. Hospital wards are closed for lack of cash, little children are denied transport to school so that they, their mothers and infant siblings are obliged to walk two miles there and back along roads pounded by juggernauts. For the mother this means a daily trek of eight miles but it's spend, spend, spend with the highways authority.

Where'er one roams, be it ever so remote, there they are with their traffic lights and their bollards and their bulldozers and their proliferating notices couched in highwayspeak: 'Changed priorities ahead,' they proclaim, and a few yards further on, 'Cats eyes removed.' What's in a priority after all? Oaks planted by Humphrey Repton have been felled and dragged away in chains. But one must feel for the tormented souls of these planners, if they don't spend all their money now they won't get any more next year. What a very pleasant arrangement.

It is pleasant too, for the police, for they may lie in wait at the serial roadworks for the complacent motorist. Twice they have claimed they cannot see my tax disc. 'Haha,' saith the warhorse among the trumpets. There it is, dead centre of the windscreen, jammed into the middle of Kennedy's *Revised Latin Primer* and perfectly visible. It's bad enough to have to pay for a tax disc. But then to try to make it circular without tearing it, to spend a further 40p on one of those round containers which won't even stick to my windscreen, to insert disc into said round thing. *Non*. Kennedy is a comforting companion in the event of a breakdown. You may learn about the subjunctive of conditional futurity: *migrantes cernas*, 'One would see them leaving' (if one were there).

'Lovely job,' says the policeman, quashing disappointment. This sort of thing puts me in a bad mood when, eschewing the glittering wit of friends and family and the sullen charms of the Bulgarian vintage, I try to watch television. It is hard to rate this as an acceptable human pastime. The great god Car dominates the screen, there are the police again, then sex programmes and violence programmes. Only the two Clive men lighten the gloom, the hideous deadening vulgarity. And there has been the rugby which can be wildly exciting, an excitement enhanced for me by being in a warm room and remembering freezing afternoons at Murrayfield, the only girl in the schoolboys' enclosure. With pigtails. My parents would not agree. They would like to be at Murrayfield, and they would recreate the sub-zero conditions in their well-ventilated morning room. There they sit in their coats and travel rugs, oblivious to all but the game.

The only other good thing about television is that recently on separate occasions, two of my sons have appeared on it, one as an 18th century footman, the other playing his guitar.

A glimpse of Inspector Morse pretending to be Peter Mayle typing out of doors in the sunshine sends me in guilty retreat to my kitchen where I try to write pulling my sleeves down over my numbed hands.

Yet day by day spring advances and the view from my bedroom window each morning is pure delight. At first in the overcast world of dawn the grass is dull and glaucous with dew. Then a great red sun lifts through the mist and clouded blackthorn blossom and the day dazzles. Budding branches blur the blue sky.

In the bronzing cherry tree immediately under my window sits a fat bastard pigeon gorging himself. I hurl my cup of tea at him; he continues to sit there. Now I have no tea; now I will have to get up. Proceeding to work in my Apollonian tripod I pass banks starry with stitchwort and celandine primroses, violets, cowslips.

How lovely it is to make lists of flowers. Virgil has some good ones in the *Georgics*, and Shakespeare in *A Winter's Tale*, but my favourites appear in Milton's *Lycidas*. I have been trying to collect these and I have come upon small, surprising difficulties. Last year I planted the white pink and the pansy freaked with jet, only to find that on a second blooming the white pink became a dingy pink pink and the pansy unfreaked, never to freak again.

And what of that sanguine flower, inscribed with woe, which I take to be the hyacinth, imprinted with the letters AI, the ancient Greek cry of agony, in memory of the cruel death of the youth Hyacinthos? Where are these letters? Try asking a garden centre that one.

The awakening of nature has its drawbacks too; I fear the presence of a hornet's nest, for on five recent occasions, gigantic specimens have been droning unsteadily about my bedroom, according special attention to the bedside lamp. One of them missed the lamp completely and subsided into my hair. It would not come out. I shook my head into the freezing darkness but to no avail. At last I was obliged to wander about the house like Lady Macbeth, wailing for help. There are those who don't care (*sunt qui,* plus generic subjunctive, suggests Kennedy) to be asked to capture hornets at two in the frosty morning.

Which brings me back to the kitchen, where, although Inspector Morse may be warm and the cats, moored like barges around the Aga, are warm, I am not. I stamp about on the ancient tiled floor, which is laid straight on the earth in the simple mode of our forefathers, and I consider the icy black underground lake which stretches beneath the house. I indulge in some active smoking. Cough cough, purr purr. Hoot goes the owl. Somewhere across the river a swan is softly sighing.

AMPHIBIANS

Ten years ago a man came and dug me a pond. The pond was tear shaped, reflecting my lachrymose widowish ways, and when the garish orange digger raised its jaws for its final swoop, rills and trills and spills of water leapt joyously from the slick, slack mud. Within days, the pond brimmed full and trickled gently into a primrose-thronged ditch and thence into the river; days passed and miraculously it retained its level. The ancient Greeks had the beautiful notion that within the marble block the statue waits for release; so in that dull clay I like to think that until this moment the trapped spring had seethed and gurgled unbeknown, now to revel in crystalline liberation.

I had wanted a pond so that I might become acquainted with newts, and so that I might grow grey-blue irises; I would be seen by visitors, peering out at them, wearing a faded fisherman's smock and carrying a trug. The grey-blue irises have not happened, nor the smock, nor the trug. Instead nature has provided yellow flags and purple water mint. But newts arrived immediately, mysterious and magical as the spring itself.

It is important, when considering newts, to clear the mind of Ken Livingstone and pigeon culls and bendy buses. Red Ken has no place here. Newts are aquatic salamanders; they are ancient and wise and mythic; they are efts. An eft became a newt at some point in another mysterious process, linguistic this time. Other delightful creatures joined the newts. One morning in early spring I saw frogs dancing in courtship; they leapt high out of the water and dropped down in a great splash. Water voles sped across the lilypads, crossing the pond with the briefest of immersions, 'just like Jesus', observed my small grandson, his eyes bulging like lollipops. Toadlets loped through the grass and the horrifying and weirdly named nymphs of dragon flies patrolled the murky floor, grimly helmeted and murderous. It is not generally known that these exquisite and ephemeral beauties spend almost all their lives as underwater exterminators in hideous disguise. My family, too, appeared in the pond. We watched the total eclipse of the sun reflected there. The garden was silent, tranced in eerie dark green light; trees were suspended upside down in the water and among them gleamed the drowned images of my sons and daughters and grandchildren. I stood on the far side and thought of the underworld.

So for years the pond's life remained apart and intact, providing intrigue and excitement and otherness. But of late I have become aware of its impinging on my existence in unthought manner. Due to a sequence of ill-executed hip operations, I have taken to sleeping downstairs. So it was that I felt a flicker of movement in my slipper, and paused; out leapt a tiny black toad. What I had thought the skeleton of a leaf on the rug by my bed turned out to be a flattened newt. In the dark shadows of the hallway, creatures scuttled and lurked and compressed themselves under furniture or crouched motionless in corners. The invasion of the amphibians had begun.

Or, perhaps, it had always been there, coming and going, unnoticed, nocturnal. For ancient memories may persist in these infinitely delicate creatures, prompting them down the pathways of their ancestors, who have passed this way, variously leaping and loping and creeping, even from a time when this part of my old house did not exist. They make their inexorable passage under doors, they thrust themselves up between flagstones, if need be they will clamber. Like the ducal trains in Shakespeare's plays, a procession of newts may move side by side with one of toads. 'Did not I dance with you in Brabant, once?' enquires Berowne of Rosaline as she goes by in parallel procession. Headstrong and skittish the lass ripostes 'Did not *I* dance with you in Brabant, once?' Just so, I have seen a newt and a toadlette advance and retreat, swirl and sidestep, perform their sarabande along the hall. And all's well that ends well indeed, except it's *Love's Labours Lost*.

I have observed that people are sympathetic to newts, or at least to the idea of them. They watch newt television programs and subscribe to newt rescue funds. Toads in the house are quite another matter; they don't want to hear about them, and they don't want to see them. Few there are who are willing to pick them up and carry them out to safety, away from the crushing foot and the sadist cat. My pet pig Portia used to chase them too, but she has gone. Now I am the lucky legatee of a great quantity of gauntleted Marigold gloves, black and suggestive of fetishistic practice. Naturally I, as a Scottish gentlewoman, would never purchase such items; they are the gift of my American manservant who insists upon providing them out of his fast dwindling estate, but despite this alluring prophylaxis, help comes rarely. And toads should be lifted carefully, in bare hands, which are cupped, and closed. The exudation from their nubbly skin serves as a cure for warts and verruccae, and is of course totally wasted on black marigold gloves. Who would ever be rescued by a Black Marigold? Not I. Not Fay Wray. Why then a Toad? In Ireland, where toads are supposed to have been banned by St. Patrick, they are nonetheless known, along with poets, as warty boys. Once I was engaged to a poet who was walking before me up a muddy path when I saw a frog bound to confront him. 'Mind the frog!' I cried. 'Fuck the frog!' he responded, treading on it. That was the end of that, and I married another, and better, poet. I mention this incident only to show that I have a long rapport with amphibians who have at least in this instance shaped my life. Only thrice to my knowledge have I interfered with an amphibian's life – once the aforementioned flattened newt. And I brought back to life a tiny jewel froglet who had been paralysed by a floating and domed water spider, only to have it snatched from my finger tips and consumed by a passing hen. And once I transfixed an adult frog on the prong of a garden fork. This horrible moment was used by my heartless publishers on the cover of the paperback edition of my novel *O Caledonia*.

At this eftling time of year miniature frogs hiphop bright as dewdrops among the posies of heartsease and chamomile which adorn the stubble field. Dusk descends, then moon and stars. I sit in the darkness outside and listen to le transatlantique play Chopin's Barcarolle on his concert grand. A pinpoint of light gleams beside me; a newt is curved over a nasturtium leaf, its hands delicately splayed, its eyes reflecting the heavenly spheres; it is intent on its own secret life. When I go indoors it may follow, or it may not. And we may pass in the night, without signal, but on my part, with a poignant sense of privilege that our lives should ever cross.

PORTIA

It was on Christmas morning three years ago that I first met my pig. In a shadowed corner of the barn a heap of straw shuddered, was still, shuddered again. The children stood solemn and expectant. Motes of dust floated off the straw into the cold bright day and nothing happened. Then she was there. As a submarine surfaces, so a small black snout emerged, two blunt triangular ears, a cubic little creature, Medium Vietnamese with a snippet of Berkshire. She was quite wild then, and I spent many hours in the bleak January afternoons sitting on the barn floor, talking, coaxing, offering apples while she remained as far away as possible, always in profile, wearing an expression of intense cunning. It was cold and boring and I began to brood about my middle years and how very little I wanted to spend them like this. The daughter who provided the piglet had retreated to New York and central heating and glitzy urban life. Everyone else was in London doing grown-up things. I remembered that in childhood I could spend all day sitting about with animals, indulging in anthropomorphic fantasies. Not now, not any more. And a pig is for life, not just for Christmas. One afternoon, as I was wondering how long they live for anyway, she tiptoed towards me, seized the apple and reversed, chomping and champing and foaming at the mouth. Her little eyes glittered with triumph. I could see that she thought that she had outwitted me. So it was that our relationship began, on the strict understanding that she was cleverer than I was, and would do things her way only.

The pig's name was Portia and she was kind enough to respond to it, trotting nimbly from the bramble thickets and sere marsh grasses which represent my garden. More spectacular results could be gained by singing her special rather simple song: 'She's a pig, she's a wig, she's a piggy wig wig, she's a wiggy piggy girl.' Gruesome as this sounds, it was well worth it to see a gambolling pig, a pig fleet of foot, bucking and caracoling. She was free always to wander where she pleased and she showed a strong sense of territory, only twice ever straying beyond the bounds of my domain. It was on Easter Monday that she chose to visit the village and hold up the throng holiday traffic. Suffering from city dementia, motorists were crying: 'It's a wild boar.' Photographs were taken, people got out of their cars and daringly approached, but not too near. Portia was oblivious; she was licking a squashed hedgehog up off the tarmac. My sons, sallying forth to a drinking bout, were obliged to intervene; she would not move. The novelty had faded and the traffic jam wished to inch forwards. There was nothing for it but to sing her song. Alert, responsive, the pig raised her head, listened for a moment, and sped back up the drive. The boys cowered in the hedge, uncool for ever.

Her other excursion did not go so well. This time she was found uprooting shrubs in Mrs. Hooker's garden. Mrs. Hooker was absent, enjoying an afternoon at the Young at Hearts Club, but Will, her neighbour, tried to lure Portia homewards. This didn't work. He tried to shoo her; this worked even less. A pig at bay glowered from the splintered shards of the flowering currant bush. Summoned by a child, I ran down the drive to find that Will had just lassoed her. She somersaulted, she reared, she flung herself about like a dervish. And she screamed. I had never heard such screams; Jack the Ripper might have been doing all his victims simultaneously. They could be heard four miles away at the Young at Hearts Club. Then came silence. Will had pulled the lasso off but the pig knew nothing of it. She had passed into a catatonic trance; she was a stone pig, standing on her four short legs, breathing lightly but completely out of it.

I was distraught. I thought she would die. She must die at home. Just as one might move a statue, so we transported her up the drive, lifting, setting down, lifting. She did not flicker an eyelash. But as we reached the house the puppy came bounding out. The puppy was fond of Portia and Portia enjoyed his company. Together they would lie on the grass and snuff the breeze. Sometimes they and the nasty dwarf pony played chasing games, taking it in turn to pursue and be pursued, always skidding to a stop before collision. Now the puppy was licking Portia's terrible staring face. And now her snout trembled, and her ears flickered, her eyes focused. Very slowly she came back to life.

Another puppy, a terrier, had a less romantic encounter with the pig one windy summer afternoon. This I observed from a distance, helpless in my car. There stood the pig, gazing dreamily up at the shifting clouds and there, behind her, horribly attached, was the terrier, pumping vigorously. This monstrous incident did not produce any pogs or digs, and I believe that Portia was quite unaware of it, her personal geometry being such that she is unable to turn round except by executing a U-turn. Nonetheless she has been a trim and active pig, and she used to enjoy going for unambitious walks with me until some officious person pointed out the dangers and legal red tapes attached to the business of Pig Movement.

On one particular idyllic stroll through silent woodland she spotted a man in the distance and fled to the church for sanctuary. From infancy she has disliked most men, especially my son-in-law and my middle son, both of whom she has bitten. She bit them because they were in the kitchen where she liked to be. Her favourite upright position was leaning against my legs under the kitchen table. When she had done this for long enough, she would emerge and chuck a few chairs around, using her head as a battering ram and catapult. Like many pigs, she had a boisterous hooligan side to her nature, and a great relish for effect. Slamming doors was another satisfying pastime. Her extraordinarily acute sense of smell led her to go through handbags to extract an apple, to identify cartons containing fruit juice and on one occasion to steal a rustic wine box containing some fine Bulgarian vintage. She was furtive with the wine box, scuttling up the kitchen with it clamped in her jaws. Beneath the window she paused and set it on the floor; resting one trotter firmly on top she gashed the box with a single snap of those lethal incisors. A ruby fountain sprang towards the ceiling, falling back gracefully to rise again and play about the pig. Noisily she drank, catching the liquid as it leapt, catching the joy as it flies. Through the window the sun shone from the bright blue heaven; the pig stood ankle deep in her alcoholic lagoon and still the fountain played. Her fondness for wines does not extend to beer, a draught popular with many pigs of lesser sensibility, but on the evening when she had consumed a bowl of whisky trifle, a silent and balletic pig pranced beside me through the dusk towards the barn. Her tastes in food are demanding; not for her the bucket of pig slops, potato peel and vegetable trimmings. Salad is acceptable only if dressed with olive oil, carrots are too dull to contemplate, and you can keep your brassicas. But ratatouille and pumpkin pie provoke cries of ecstasy which I can only liken to sex noises on television.

While she is not an asset in the garden she is not destructive; she learnt quickly that she should not lie in flowerbeds, and she does not normally go rooting. She is addicted to geraniums, one tiny vice. In hot weather she will lie in the shade or wallow in a paddling pool or dig a shallow grave to serve as a dust bath. In all these activities she reveals a nature which is profoundly sensuous, mirroring the voluptuous curves of her swaying roseate belly and belying the staccato elegance of her small black feet. Certain members of my original Scottish Presbyterian family cannot bear to look at her. Not so the local Labour candidate, however. I spied him with his red rosette coming up the garden and shrank behind the curtains. The pig lay slumbering on the lawn. The candidate peered round and, feeling unobserved, bent down and kissed the sleeping beauty. She jerked into consciousness, saw the red rosette, saw the man and fled, doing her Jack the Ripper shrieking. Red as his rosette, the candidate knocked on the door. Neither he nor I mentioned the incident.

This hatred of men is a big nuisance when things go wrong. Portia's medical attendants have to be wooed from far-flung outlying areas where they have women vets. I had to try three different practices before I could find a vet (female) who was willing to cut her toenails – it is impossible for me to do this because she goes into Jack the Ripper mode immediately. Pigs die from stress, and they die from shock in anaesthesia. They are a nightmare to treat. I had tried unsuccessfully to obtain some anti-stress homeopathic pills to proof her against the toenail ordeal, and was startled when the homeopathic doctor advised me to have a police surgeon standing by since it seemed there might be an element of violence. After this disappointment I did find a female vet who refused to come because she had trimmed three of another man-hating pig's feet, carefully doing each foot on a different Wednesday, and after the third visit the pig had lain down and died. At last an intrepid young woman arrived, accompanied by a nurse, and sedated the pig with a blow dart in the manner of David Attenborough and the white rhino. Even this modest tranquiliser, she warned, was potentially lethal. It didn't seem to work, and a second dart was blown. The pig shrieked piteously, her whole being concentrated in one gaping set of jaws. The nurse and I cornered the pig with an old trampoline; the vet hung upside down from the barn wall, there being no space left in the improvised corner; the toenails were cut from the upside down position; and the screaming went on. I thought I too might die of stress.

Indian summer brought tranquillity to the pig; she winnowed the harvest field by moonlight, stately but agile on her smart new trotters. One late autumn afternoon I walked beneath a wild cobalt sky; seagulls planed on the wind high over the sepia oak trees, and long shafts of light shed random radiance. On a distant slope a huge pig stood, invested suddenly with unearthly glory. Beyond, his fellows rootled disconsolately in the mud, consigned to outer darkness. I mused then on fate's inconsistencies and thought that despite everything mine was a lucky pig. I should not have had that thought; or perhaps it was doom's harbinger.

For now, after a life so full of peril and pleasure, the pig has turned her face to the wall. Since October she has refused to leave her barn. She is in deep melancholia and she throws her water round her stall, flinging the bowl contemptuously out of the door. She eats, she sleeps and that's it. I have tried music, companionship, cats, toys, bunches of soothing herbs, mulled wine and rescue remedy. Nothing works. I don't know what to do. A wise woman called one day and she suggested that Portia might be pining for maternity. This could lead ultimately to 11 melancholy pigs facing the barn wall. I might become a latter day Circe. These pigs could never be for eating, but pigs are not popular now as pets; indeed I believe pig sanctuaries are opening. 'Their day has gone' someone said the other day. 'Like the alligators in New York.' *O tempora, O mores.*

DOG DAYS

Dogs are us in heart and soul, but better. How privileged we are to love them and know them and make guesses about them, and how painfully do we even as infants learn that the price of love is loss, but also that love and memory will outlive death. I feel that all my lifelong great loving of dogs has been threaded through with the fear of death, the unbearable knowledge that their days are so much fewer than ours. Only from earliest summers do I recall an untroubled love; the moment when the sea chills into dusk, the sands are suddenly cold, and you run from the water and fling yourself into the warm fur of the golden retriever, Rab the hero dog. His birthday was in May. Enthroned and robed in the scarlet gown of St Andrews University, he would preside graciously over the dining table. His festive tea included birthday cake, of course, and his favourite dog pies, available to this day in superior shops, and known to the English as Scotch pies.

It was said that he had saved our father's life and also that Polish airmen had kidnapped him and he had found his way over many months all the way back to the north of Scotland from a place called Aldershot. On his birthday we children read him poems we had composed commemorating these and other exploits, some, alas, involving sheep and hens, Rhode Island Reds and white Leghorns in particular. There were dark times when he and his assistant, the junior dog, an Irish terrier, wore the cumbrous corpses of these birds slung round their necks to teach them a lesson. They did not learn their lesson, and hen keeping was abandoned. Sheep harrying continued however, but somehow Rab eluded the police, the farmers, the gamekeepers and their guns. Often he was tethered on a very long and inconvenient rope which tripped everyone up at the bottom of the stairs. Or for weeks he would spend the hours of daylight brooding sombrely in his car, an abandoned 1915 Armstrong Siddeley which my brother had destroyed by reckless driving on the unmade hill roads. And, as often as not, on the twilight moment of release he would be off again, up to the moors and taking the more circumspect terrier with him. What wretched sleepless nights I endured, convinced that this time they would not return. Rab lived until he and I were both eighteen years old. More than going to university, or possessing a Hebe Sports tweed suit, or being offered a pink gin, his death marked for me the end of childhood. Eighteen years may seem a long while to be a child, but in those days there weren't teenagers and I certainly had no plans to be a grown up. I see him now, a golden dog running through a storm of seagulls at the water's edge, under the great clouds of summer.

How kind the dogs were all those long years. When they were not intent on nocturnal blood sports they slept like tombstones on our beds, their solid presence driving the ghouls far away. They were particularly helpful with the dreadful business of mealtimes, when you were expected to chew everything thirty times and leave nothing on your plate. Luckily we always used table napkins, in which a sly disgorgement might be ferried from lip to lap and thence to the silent canine jaws waiting beneath the table. Of course if we were not being watched, a quick flick of the wrist was all that was needed.

I employed this dexterous technique quite recently at a glum dinner party, where the host was drunk, the hostess was trembling and the food was grey. Grey mushroom soup gave way to grey risotto which gave way to grey pecan pie. I could eat no more, but I had spotted a handy terrier cruising by. I thought with John Keats 'This creature hath a purpose and its eye is bright with it'. Swift as lightning my pudding sped beneath the snowy reaches of the damask cloth, instantly triggering an almighty invisible dogfight. Everyone shot under the table, where not one but two identical terriers were up on their hind legs locked in mortal combat. Between them lay a great grey triangle of pie. Everyone saw this and no one knew it was mine. Indeed, there was some foolish speculation about how it could possibly have got there.

THOUGHTS IN A GARDEN

Whatever sort of dog one has at any given time, that sort will always be the best; this applies to the chief dog. The junior dog may be of a different breed, which will of course be favoured, but not to a dogmatic (ha) extent. So for nearly two decades my paragon was a golden retriever. Since then there have been other wonderful dogs. When first we moved from London to the country I presented my husband with a Doberman Pinscher whom he christened Matthew Arnold Revisited, Jockey of Norfolk. The rest of us called him Dobe. Dobe at once made it his business to ensure our social isolation. Adoring, docile, beloved and somnolent at home, he would sally forth from the end of our drive in an alert and independent frame of mind. Motorists would be startled and then enraged to find him slavering horribly, fangs embedded in their nearside front tyre, or pursuing them along the road barking in an excruciating high frequency. Bicyclists likewise had short shrift. Sometimes there was a tumble, sometimes there was a brief appearance before the magistrates. Villagers were not to leave their houses. If they ventured forth, just crossing the road, perhaps, to go to the shop, he would be there, rounding them up, leaping in circles and doing his crazy bark, driving them into the red telephone kiosk. There he would stalk back and forth on his hind legs, pressing his muzzle against the glass panes, dribbling and munching suggestively, while his prisoners, incoherent with fury, dialled our number to demand release, and repayment for the call, and punitive redress. He used to escort my minivan, attached to the wheel and barking, the four miles to the children's tiny primary school; there he would gallop joyously about the playground, indiscriminately licking little faces. 'Call him by his name, dear,' cried Miss Clark. Some hope. The whole tyre-chewing, slavering, barking business would be repeated as I drove home. He knew how to open doors and windows and so could let himself in and out of the house as he pleased. His greatest ambition was to bring down a plane. To this end he raced about the prairie field, his hind quarters displaying the rotary action so admired by connoisseurs of the breed. He hurled himself intermittently into the air, pawing at the sky. Fast living overtook him in the end. He returned one morning from seeing off a Fairchild A10, a low-flying war plane, flung the back door open, surged into the kitchen and dropped dead. It was very quiet after he had gone and I had to admit that it was nice to go to the village without his overweening company. I even painted his favourite room pink and hung up floral curtains, impossible hitherto because of his window opening. Then I felt guilty and took them down. The pink walls soon faded back to wood smoke and nicotine brown.

Oh what a gallimaufry of dogs memory brings, each one so loved and special. The deerhound steps his airy way towards me, his head tilted in gentle self-deprecation. He was bred by the late and great Anastasia Noble of Ardkinglas, whom I last saw in her quiet splendour at a gathering of deerhounds in the fens. The purpose of the meeting was said to be hare coursing, but the hares kept low in the dykes and the deerhounds, losing sight of them, so lost interest, and took to racing and leaping and caracoling. The spectral dogs, the freezing December skies and the vast empty landscape hang motionless before me, gathered all beneath Miss Noble's ghostly benediction. That is one aspect of heaven, in winter. A springtime glimpse reveals a haze of bluebells, shadowed by beech trees just coming into leaf. Two figures on grey horses pass among the silvery trunks; one of them might be me. Beyond, in a sunlit glade, the deerhound dances. There can be no heaven without dogs. I know this for a fact; our old vicar told me. In his seven churches dogs were always welcome.

Thinking of deerhounds makes me think of lurchers, dogs I may no longer keep due to problems with a nearby commercial enterprise involving pheasants. As one might put it. Graceful and loyal, lurchers are the most inward of dogs, in habit peripheral, delicate and fleeting as shadows. A brindled lurcher will fade into an old chintz sofa, or a gravel path, or dappled shade in the flicker of an eyelid; or again will dissolve into those great shafts of sunlight which move across the stubble in late summer. Lurchers are the most accomplished and elegant of all thieves; they run exquisitely through streams, their slender legs shimmering, beaded in silver droplets. They are swift, silent killers and unbelievably accident prone. They cost a bomb in vet's bills and they are worth every penny.

But now I can't have lurchers, not even on a visit, and I have wandered, by the chances that beset the dog lover, into the enchanted realms of the Labrador. Are Labradors not divine? The very word, delightful to enunciate, demands a capital letter. One of the Mitford sisters, employed in Spain during the Civil War as some sort of booking clerk, was relieved to find great numbers of Labradors leaving their warring land and always made sure they had the best travel accommodation possible. Eventually of course she was disillusioned; they were, not dogs, but dagoes (workers). Still, as a communist she could hold onto their preferential treatment. Our Labrador line began with Honey, given to us by a gamekeeper because she was gun shy. She changed her mind about this, and at the sound of shooting would slip off and join the fray with such tact and efficiency that people kept trying to buy her, and once someone stole her. She had a lifelong and fully requited illicit love affair with the farm collie down the road, producing one hundred and twelve puppies of great charm and distinction. We kept one of them, a delightful but caddish black and white hound. When Honey died he sat with proper solemnity by her grave, but as she was lowered in he realised it was lunchtime and left, returning in a few minutes to resume his vigil. He had cleared the kitchen table, but this was his last act of caddery, for now he was the senior dog, with family responsibilities. I am inclined to think that the early caddishness came from his collie side; in latter life he was the very soul of warmth and loving kindness, every inch a Labrador. Then there came Dido, rescued from a broken home, the fattest Labrador ever seen. 'With the owner's co-operation,' intoned the vet into his special recording machine for matters of importance 'Dido has now lost 26 kg.' She took to digging up radishes to cheer her tiny meals. A black Labrador puppy joined us. My son named him Hannibal after the Carthaginian general, not the serial killer, though now I think of it the general was even more of a serial killer.

Hannibal and Dido ran away into the woods. I stood wailing 'Hannibal, Dido,' over and over into the autumn wind and was surprised to hear another voice issuing from the beech trees. 'Cassiopeia, Cassiopeia,' it cried. We joined forces, agreeing that we were very stupid embarrassing people to give our dogs these silly names. Joggers were sneering at us. Joggers. Cassiopeia proved to be a flat coated retriever. On a similar occasion I encountered a woman shrieking for Horace; we discussed this name business while the dogs didn't come back, and she said she'd named him after the great Roman poet. 'I loved Latin at school,' she said. 'No one else did, except for one other girl. But she was very peculiar and chewed her pigtails and wouldn't speak.' In no time we discovered that we had been at school together, so long ago, in far off Scotland, and yes, I was that silent pigtail chewer. The dogs returned, she went back to London and we lost touch all over again. This I find is the way of coincidences. Nothing happens, they might as well not have been. Except that they were. Hannibal, for example, while browsing the grasses at the edge of the drive, makes a peculiar clonking sound with his jaws. My deceased husband used to make an identical sound eating an apple. I have never heard this noise otherwise. I had a moment of wild surmise; was it possible that George had returned to me in the form of a great black dog? But no, this was rapidly quashed. George would not have made a good Labrador. And goodness is what Hannibal is about, and wit and charm and resource and the genial engendering of unplanned litters on black Labrador bitches (only). He happens to have an astonishing pedigree so nobody minds too much. 'You've got a royal dog there,' said one doughty owner, instinctively removing his cap. Well, just a touch perhaps, but lots of other bloodlines too. Indeed Hannibal's state is kingly, and I could write a great deal about him, but I should keep it for another time. He is old now and stiff and can no longer climb onto my bed; he sleeps instead on a small sofa by the window. When I wake I watch him lying there, one ear draped most delicately over the sofa back; he breathes so lightly that I think he has gone, I almost hope it, rather than find myself once again colluding with the vet in that final act of treachery which is of course all for the best. Meanwhile my husband, who is jealous of Hannibal, has ghosted the junior dog Bluebell's autobiography, in a fabulous literary *jeu d'esprit*.

So September wanes and the early evenings are elegiac, still and scented with phlox and the straight plume of smoke going up from the bonfire. The dark shadow is there. I do not think Hannibal will see another summer. But now he is rolling on the mown grass, joyous as ever, joyous as a pup, and the sound of the piano floats from the open window. He walks towards me down the green slope with the low sun behind him; he is limned in golden light and his eyes are shining. He is a paradisaical Labrador. I would not myself mind dying if I was certain we might meet like this, in a place where Labradors swim with seals and angels.

HENS I HAVE KNOWN

Literature, legend and art honour the cock, potent symbol of masculinity, plumed and gleaming life force, harbinger of doom. Thrice he crew at Gethsemane and through the millennia his voice shrieks warning time and again:

The cocks are crowing on merry middle earth.
The channering worm doth chide . . .

And due homage has been paid to his pride, his arrogance, his colours and his spurs. Not so the hen.

No need to dwell on the crass brutalities inflicted upon these creatures in the name of human greed. Hens dwell apart, invisible to all but their assassins, debeaked, desexed, suspended upside down on conveyor belts and finally beheaded to become pallid neo-natal objects known as 'chickens', with no sentient past.

And so for most of us, our earliest intimations of the hen derive from ancient illustrations to nursery rhymes or, most especially, from the idyllic England of Victory jigsaw puzzles, a land of green and gold and blue, where rust-coloured rustic birds scratch comfortably about. How helpful they are, and how pleasingly their plumage tones with the aged bricks and tiles. 'She lays eggs for gentlemen.' This is her task.

Sometimes she deviates into motherhood, a wondrous sight, couched on her nest with a myriad little heads poking out of her feathers. But in this role she is not admired. 'Mother hen' is a term of derision, implying pointless clucking, ungainly fussiness. Even to glorious Milton they are but 'tame villatic fowls'.

Well, mighty organ voice, I disagree, although I, too, once saw them only as a hospitable adjunct to the breakfast table, uneasily quelling a very early memory of a dog grinning ingratiatingly and wearing a large, bloody and dead hen slung around its neck (a folk remedy for hen killing).

So hens came to us, and idyllic indeed were the early days; little children gathered dark brown eggs in straw-lined baskets, and sometimes, most magically, found a single stray egg laid among the ivy tendrils which smothered the oak tree's roots. But soon nature was out; hens let it be known that they were romantic, racist, cruel, heroic beings.

So many incidents, lives, deaths. There was the enchanting silkie bantam, clad in white Cossack trousers and matching tam-o'shanter, who was so horribly persecuted by the rest of the flock (American puritans in sober black) that she fled and took up with a handsome cock pheasant. Over the stubble into the autumn sunset they strayed together, and in the spring she returned, with a following of shadow-coloured birds, a clutch of phantoms. Meanwhile those same puritans huddled malevolently along the kitchen dresser shelves, beady eyes fixed in triumph on the egg cups smashed below.

More noble is the memory of the tiny bantam Badminton (B is for Badminton, bird of the year) and her daughter Emerald, who died on their feet, wings outspread to shield their infants, in a terrible canine massacre.

Conversely, one heaven-sent summer morning, in the children's pond, the first tadpole had become an exquisite jewel of a frog, scarcely larger than a drop of water. But over the surface of the little pond came floating, mekonlike, a spider with a bubble-shaped air chamber and it stung the frog, who drifted lifeless and flattened in its eddy. Wild tears of grief and outrage; so, 39 weeks pregnant and beyond belief rotund, I lay on the grass and stroked the tiny corpse with a fingertip. Astonishingly, it began to pulsate, feebly and then more strongly, until we were able to place it, gleaming and live again, on its rock in the water. A beldame hen strolled by and whipped it down her throat.

On a more tender level was the triumph of a hybrid bird, programmed never to reproduce, who managed to hatch a strange, damp, grey, long-necked creature of her own.

All our hens refused outright to live in their own run and consequently, over the years, having multiplied exceedingly, they formed three separate flocks, roosting with open scorn in the winter trees (bare ruin'd choirs where now the grim hens sit).

Many guerrilla raids were made upon the kitchen and on picnic rugs and tables, until we returned one weekend from a visit to a household not blessed with hens, and looking at our ravaged habitat decided: these birds must go. Forthwith they were rounded up for market.

All, that is, except for two cocks, a father and son, whom we couldn't catch, and one hen who emerged days later from a clump of catmint. And hereby hangs a tale for our times. For this hen's life now became a torment to her. Whenever she stopped to peck, a cock would leap vigorously on to her. Soon she would run when she saw them coming; but they ran faster. She became exhausted and emaciated, unable to eat or drink, to browse or rest. But the cocks, accustomed formerly to a vast harem apiece, were now inflamed with insatiable lust and had a fearful battle in which one slaughtered the other. Blood-boultered, a scarlet lacquer bird, he stood on his son's corpse and crowed.

And the hen continued to decline; her feathers fell out, bald patches appeared, her eye was dull and her comb shrivelled. At the slightest sound or movement she was off. But one morning as she scuttled nervously across the grass, she paused, stretched her neck upwards, and she CROWED; this was not a crow in its full range of arpeggios, systole and diastole, but it was unmistakably a half crow, and an intended crow.

On following days the crow grew louder and more authentic, until it was as richly resonant as Harvey the cock's own cry. And now her comb became pinkly elastic, upstanding, then red and splendidly serrated; her stubby tail feathers curved out in glossy black and green plumes. The hen had become a cock; perforce. So, no longer an anorexic concubine, nor yet a lustful rival cock, the metamorphosed and hastily renamed Hennery high stepped it round the midnight house, crowing reproof to late-night revellers, anticipating dawn by many hours, accompanied and abetted by the former rapist Harvey. A prodigy indeed.

But from a dictionary of superstition, under the heading 'Hen' a chilling warning came; if you have a hen which has changed into a cock you must destroy it at once, for it will bring death to your family.

Impossible to harm Hennery, but what a burden of knowledge, responsibility. Surely no one deliberately courts the fates. The dilemma was resolved by the milkman who collided with the bird of woe one icy morning.

This story has oracular meanings which I cannot yet interpret. Late in the day as it is, therefore, I make my plea for the respect due to the magical, reckless, random and august ovipositor.

FRIENDLY FIRE

'There is a shift in the wind.' Oracular utterance, betokening woe. It was brought regularly by a kilted runner to my mother in her tower, from the far and dark recesses of the kitchen, the very shrine of the Aga, the household god, and its grim priestess, Cook. My mother would wring her hands and commence her customary smooth-running six-minute speech which treated with the injustice, inconstancy, and rigour of a life passed largely in an *abnormal* house, a vast stone castle crowned by battlements toppled regularly by this same wind, whose dominance extended even to the provision of life's basic necessities. A shift in the wind meant that the Aga was dormant; it meant that dinner would be late, or that dinner would not happen. Good news, however, for us children, cosy by the nursery fire and looking forward to supper of Heinz Tomato Soup (sometimes Celery) heated on Nanny's Primus stove. Sometimes a jackdaw would provide diversion by crashing down the chimney into the fire, always to be saved, messily and energetically, by my brother. Otherwise this was a peaceful time, with the wind soughing and sighing through the pine trees far below and our mother's militant voice fading into the downward maze which led to the kitchen.

Even better if the wind was wayward still in the morning. These days people speak highly of porridge, cooked slowly, all night long, in an Aga. Ha! Year in, year out, there it was on the breakfast table, a grey, lumpy quagmire, every spoonful to be eaten up, impossible to flick under the table to a helpful dog. Lucky the little ones at their Midlothian Oat Food in the nursery. I wondered often if the porridge was kept in a zinc-lined drawer in great rectangular slabs for daily reheating, as in Stevenson's *Kidnapped*, but this I could never confirm, for children were not welcome in that kitchen. Nor was our mother, come to that.

It was a long, pale blue room, with a vaulted ceiling and a flagstone floor. A plain wooden table stretched from one end to the other, where the mighty triple-width Aga reigned from its raised dais.

On the hot plates Aga kettles boiled continuously so that the air was hazed and steamy, and through the steam you might glimpse the white-clad forms of the irascible Cook and her acolytes, red of face, mighty of forearm. On the wall, usually askew, hung a Bateman print 'Cook Doesn't Feel Like It', depicting a drunken cook with her feet up on the table and an empty bottle rolling floorwards. But there were worse sights in the real and sober kitchen; bald, earless rabbits lay soaking in bowls of blood-tinged salted water, or brains or sweetbreads in gleaming coils. My mother's terrier removed the sweetbreads once and carried them all the way upstairs and laid them by my bed so that my bare feet sank into them first thing in the morning. Other cheerless sights included the amputated dusty stumps of twenty-four geraniums, kept in their pots forever in the hope that one day they might live again. These had been eaten by the Shetland pony I had taught to come into the house. My husband – an American – asked why I taught the Shetland pony to come into the house. Because, of course, as any reader will understand, that is what you want a pony to do, just as you want a duck to sit on your lap and watch television. Just once a year, in early winter, we were encouraged into the kitchen and lifted onto chairs to stir the Christmas Pudding, black, unctuous, bejewelled with silver threepenny bits, and a single mother of pearl button, the bachelor's button it was called.

Such were the offerings fed to the Aga, who sometimes looked kindly upon them, and sometimes not. Its disfavour, usually expressed in sullen sulphurous darkness, occasionally took strength from another shift of the wind; then the hot plates and the simmering plates would glow in a brilliant, translucent red and the mighty altar would shudder convulsively and the chimney would roar not only like the wind but like the ocean. Years later I read in *Wuthering Heights* of Heathcliff's eyes 'like the clouded windows of Hell' and thought at once of those raging metal surfaces.

There was an interregnum of some years, when Esperanza and her sisters came from Spain and ousted the resident tyrant, to rule the kitchen. They placated the Aga and coaxed it to provide perfect paella and most exquisite meringues. The family moved freely in and out of the kitchen. Our mother sang some of the happier Scottish hymns to herself and gave dinner parties. At night I and my older siblings sat on the Aga lids smoking cigarettes and swinging our legs in a devil-may-care manner. The Aga did not scorch us, and Esperanza did not tell on us, for she carried a deep anger in her heart that left no room for other resentments: when letters came from Spain in envelopes whose stamps bore Franco's image, she would seize the great black chopping knife and stab him again and again; then her sisters took their turn; how their eyes flashed and their bosoms heaved; how heavy the air grew, dense with imprecation and the swirl of long black plaited hair.

In my own years of motherhood, a condition from which I now wish to abdicate, I too became the custodian, or should I say guardian, of an Aga. I concluded then that the Aga of my early life had been a household god of extreme temperament; but time had passed and doubtless things had improved. Wasn't that what happened with time? I can only suppose I thought this because I was bemused by the enchanted mirage of one's children's early infancy; five of them, so various, so beautiful, so new. I made rice puddings and stone-age loaves. I even made porridge. I thought I was an Earth Mother. The baby goat jumped on the hot plate and scorched his tiny hooves. My husband remarked that Hell would smell like this. Heedless, I brought dying kittens to life in the bottom oven, and hatched chicks. Only once did the Aga play me false. A downward swoop in temperature produced a clutch of stillborn Marans. 'Marrons glacés' observed the family wit. The rack above the Aga dried baby clothes, then football socks, then rugby shirts and teen frills, poignantly recording the passage of time. The chief cat lay there, golden limbs extended; occasionally a paw curved down to claw the scalp of a passing punk or poet. The junior cats squabbled and copulated on the back ledge and the dogs snored against the warm façade. Guests jostled companionable hips in the traditional winter position of leaning on the Aga rail. If you do this too vigorously, you slide with surprising momentum sideways to the floor. My pig enjoyed observing this ritual, but resented the presence of men; a swift nip in the Achilles tendon ruined a relaxing moment for my son-in-law.

'It's the heart of the house, the Aga,' people would say, always with that air of being the first to think up this bon mot. 'It is, it really is,' I would respond. Well, the heart grows older and the heart grows colder. One day I caught sight of my reflection in a friend's long mirror and upon that minute I ceased to be an Earth Mother. Away with the billows and bosoms, and on with the clinging black silk.

The Aga sensed my treachery; it sulked, it fumed. I propitiated, fed, riddled, dug its very expensive nuts out of the frozen earth floor of the midwinter coal shed, breaking all my new long lacquered temptress fingernails, and to no avail. As I crawled about, desperately riddling, in a last ditch effort to make it hot enough to produce Christmas dinner, and the fuel remained opaquely black and not the tiniest chink of red appeared, the cover of the Scottish Church Hymnary came to my mind, with its bas-relief emblem of the Burning Bush and the inexorable legend 'Nec tamen consumebatur', 'Nor yet was it consumed'. Once you get that into your head, it doesn't go away. I became inured to festive occasions, Christmas most specially, being marked by car journeys transporting the raw materials of dinner to friends' gas or electric ovens at tactful times of day, suited to them and not to me. More than once the turkey reached the table at 11 pm. And the fumes grew worse. Aga engineers came and went, expressing gloom. Usually they said they'd never seen one like it. However, this was what professionals invariably said about my domestic appliances. These experts curiously all bore the names of geological features. There was Craig and Dale, there was Glen and Cliff, and there was Ridgway ('no e'). It was Glen who said 'This is a no wake up situation. And the dogs will go first.' I hadn't really been listening to the first sentence, but the second reached me all right, and it shook me.

Has not the Aga a heart? Is it not a household god, an icon, a status symbol? Had I not heard a nine-year-old schoolboy ask another, 'Do you have an Aga? Ours is the old-fashioned cream sort, they're the best.' And had I not heard a lady of uncertain age, and provenance, say to an astonished country gent, 'I'm more gentry than you. I have an Aga!'

No, no, no. The Aga had turned murderous. The Aga or the dogs? The Aga had to go. And why? 'Well, the chimney's in the wrong place. So the wind's been blowing the rain straight down the chimney. And now it's all rotten inside and you're getting carbon monoxide.'

Ah, yes. It was dragged away in chains and beneath it I found a solitary wishbone and a pair of baby shoes in softest pink kid leather. I did not lament its passing, but it left a substantial gap in the kitchen. After a decent interval, my thoughts strayed towards a Rayburn. People told me they were much better than Agas because they would burn everything. The Aga professional Ridgway now revealed that he was also a Rayburn man. 'They're all good. Except the Nouvelle,' he told me. 'Don't get a Nouvelle, whatever you do.'

Within a few months, an earthenware OH pot had been hand crafted for the chimney by loinclothed potters in the Gobi Desert and transported by dromedary, camel and mule to wildest Norfolk. Now, at last, I could be the very proud owner of a racing green Rayburn. My grown-up children came back from the real world and we all stood gazing at it, silent with admiration, and a sense of triumph, too. We had outwitted the Aga. Admittedly the Rayburn didn't burn everything; only oil, in fact. But it worked. Time sped by in this easeful, happy, modern way of life, involving constant warmth, cooperative cooking, no fumes, no filth, no effort.

One day as I was standing there admiring it, I noticed an embossed word flowing attractively across its front. How had I never before noticed this? How indeed? The word was terrible; the word was Nouvelle. And upon that moment the tryst was broken. In no time at all, I became aware of small malaises, and then the Rayburn ceased to heat the adventurous radiators, it rejected the water system; it refused even to cook. That was it. Finito. Kaput.

Craig, or was it Cliff, was summoned.

'There's really nothing to be done. The chimney's in the wrong place. The wind's in the wrong place. And the relay's gone bad – I doubt they make replacements and you couldn't afford one anyway.'

'What if there was a shift in the wind?' I ventured.

'There won't be,' he said.

I heard my mother's voice wail down the wind and I smelt the burning of goat feet. Huge angry faces peered at me through shifting vapours, great floury arms wielded cleavers. My children appeared and receded like the unborn sons of Banquo; then came the scent of meringues and Gauloises, a vision of warmth, a home with a heart, all fading, impossible, gone now, illusions lost.

It will just have to stay there. I can't go through this again. The Nouvelle and I will grow Vieille together, equally useless. Bye-bye happiness, hallo Baby Belling.

SPRING

'And so, at last, we have come through' declared D. H. Lawrence on a first, joyous morning of spring. 'For lo, the winter is past, the rain is over and gone: the flowers appear on the earth, the time of the singing of birds is come, and the voice of the turtle is heard in our land' is Solomon's less concise, but sublime, celebration, with its extra little unplanned frisson of making quite a few people think that he is talking about tortoises coming out of hibernation. After the drab skies and unrelenting cold, how sharply the natural world impinges on our senses in April. Each morning I wake to a jubilation of geese across the river, clamorously welcoming their infants and stomping to and fro as though in jack boots. Once again the heart trembles over little lambs and all this renewal speaks treacherously of a second chance, and forgiveness of the past, which is far more beguiling than the grim and lost intentions of New Year. But it's not all bird song and lambkins. The bright air stirs ancient dust through houses, windows are dingy, insects bestir themselves, spiders leap from taps. Nettles are suddenly everywhere, and ground elder too. Ivy twines through an upstairs window and nesting birds crash down chimneys. It's a time of ambivalence, advancing and retreating. In one poem Gerard Manley Hopkins wrote ecstatically 'Nothing is quite so beautifully as spring'; in another he sees its abundance as a cruel taunt 'See, banks and brakes/Now, leaved how thick! laced they are again with fretty chervil, look, and fresh wind shakes them; birds build – but not I build; no, but strain Time's eunuch, and not breed one work that wakes.' So much depends on one's well being, physical or mental.

For myself, my apprehension of the natural world has been and still is unrepentantly anthropomorphic. A post-war childhood of Beatrix Potter, *The Secret Garden*, Bambi, Arthur Rackham's glowering trees, Woodland Happy Families, the singing sands and beasts that talk – I don't really see how it could be otherwise, although I have outgrown wanting to dress rabbits in blue shorts and pugs in tutus.

Recently I watched an old home movie. There I am, whispering complicitly into my pony's ear and careering off along the glen. She understood everything that I said, and we were more or less one creature. Oh sorrow. The film reveals that she is bored and sullen, longing for the peace of her stable; grudgingly she transports a lopsided rag doll with flailing pigtails. But nothing can warp the memory of my jackdaw, who lived unconfined in my bedroom, free to come and go as he pleased. Outdoors I would call his name three times, and he would appear, a tiny speck in the shifting clouds, zigzagging through chasms of light and wind down to my shoulder. He tried to entice me into my pocket to build a nest, and he hopped beside me up the great staircase, when he might have flown. I was lucky to grow up in a landscape of great beauty, pine forest and moorland, which fed the imagination with wild romance. I live now in another beautiful place, marsh and river, ivy hung oak trees and the floating white owl who at dawn, from my chimney, shrieks defiance at all the valley's other owls as they return from hunting. Lying awake and listening to this confusion of hoots and squawks and whoops, I will switch on my lamp and be joined immediately by a dozy winter wasp who must be caught and tipped out into the cold, fatal air. This is my territory, and the wasps have their own, in the attic above. For years they have nested there and mysteriously lived on into winter. Different wasps built a nest on the tip of a beech bough, at the edge of a small wood. One day it had blown to the ground and split open. Inside the tiny creatures lay profoundly still, densely packed in their hexagonal cells, and it seemed profane to be looking at them. And then they made me think of that cult of shaven headed, purple shrouded people who committed mass suicide in the belief that thus they would enter eternity with the comet Haile-Bopp. What a dreadful name for a comet. One thing leads to another in the natural world and its influence on the wandering mind. Susan Sontag once defined camp as an oak tree in winter. I have thought that a cormorant, cruciform, drying its wings would do as well. You may imagine my rapture when I came upon *fifteen* cormorants perched about a dead and isolated oak tree. I have lurked there, hoping for some wing drying, but so far it hasn't happened. Heavy horse foals on parade might also qualify, for the glorious way they raise their hooves.

Nature and mankind have contrived intriguing mysteries. The hyacinth in Greek Mythology springs from the blood drops of the dying youth Hyacinthus, slain by a jealous god. It is said to bear the letters Alpha and Iota, commemorating his cries of agony – Where are these letters? The bluebell is described as *non scriptus* – *not* written on, to differentiate, so someone (Linnaeus?) has taken this seriously. Also in ancient Greece, at the time of Pan's festival, people liked to thrash their statues of the god with bunches of hyacinths. Bizarre and clearly impossible. Or is the hyacinth not the hyacinth, and why not? Why is there no classical Latin word for rat? There is no rat in Virgil's list of farmyard pests in the *Georgics*, no rat in Juvenal's description of the vileness of city life. Speaking of Virgil, who liked to present himself as a countryman, son of a beekeeper, how did he get away with claiming that baby bees are found under flower petals and borne to the hive in the jaws of a heroic leader bee (over oceans if required). Why do beech woods in spring at once make one think of cathedrals – rather than the other way round? But these are questions that may remain enjoyably unanswered, just as one may take pleasure in nature's triumphs and anomalies. From the security of indoors, it is a fine thing to watch, beyond a friend's clifftop garden wall, the cagouled upper torsos of ramblers in silhouette against the evening sky; as darkness falls, at one stroke of Mother Nature's wand they are transformed into a column of rats moving one by one in stealth along the wall. Later the rats will move to the window sill and peer in; their eyes glitter in the candlelight. The writer Colette was distressed, almost afraid, when she saw her mother exultant over a blackbird who had outwitted their scarecrow and continued to ravage their cherry tree. This lady shared her evening bowl of chocolate with a spider who would descend promptly on its thread of gossamer, reeling itself back to the ceiling when sated.

Civilisation's curious balance of retreat from and exploitation of the natural world is what makes it possible for us to indulge in such pleasures. No one would wish to experience hurricanes and typhoons directly. Contrasts are needed. The freezing beauty of a starlit night is complemented by a house that is warm. Nature is neither friendly, nor hostile, but as Housman said, heartless and witless: the relationship is one-sided. Always remember that just as you can eat every bit of a pig, so it can eat every bit of you.

THE DRIVER'S SEAT

My first driving lesson took place 24 years before I passed my driving test. My capacity for cowardice, irresolution and day-dreaming thus enabled me to experience, though not enjoy, lessons and tests throughout the late Fifties, the Sixties, the Seventies, and on into the early Eighties. As I lurched and stalled from decade to decade two constancies went with me: the certain failure of the test and the heart-rending optimism of my ever changing instructors. This time, they promised, things would be different; this time I would be calm, alert and competent. Alertness, however, is not given to us all, and optimism soon faded to stoic resignation, clenched knuckles, despondency and madness. It was just like learning Maths all over again.

However, on the bright December morn of that first lesson, I knew nothing of this. Soon, I imagined, I might be motoring southwards, down the pale dusty roads of Provence, some demon lover stashed silently and admiringly beside me.

So it was that with modest hope I clambered into the small grey Austin parked outside our house. It was difficult to get in because I was wearing my only pair of high heels in case my legs looked fat, and I was conscious of my siblings' jeering faces plastered against an upstairs window. Mr Methven's bald pate dazzled in the frosty sunlight. He looked at my shoes. 'Ye'll need to take those off,' he said. I kicked them insouciantly in front of me. One lodged under the accelerator pedal. Sighing, he leaned over and chucked them into the back. He told me about the gears. My mind was racing. What was wrong with my shoes? Could I drive in slippery nylons? Why were there three pedals when you only had two feet? Slippery nylon feet. Would the pedals ladder my nylons? 'Look in the mirror,' he commanded. What now? I looked and saw only a stretch of icy empty road. I twisted it sideways and peered at my pallid freckled face. It didn't look much worse than usual. What was the matter with him? He yanked the mirror back into position. 'Thon is for the *road*, for *oncoming traffic*. Ye're no in the boudoir now, Madame.'

I realised I hadn't been listening to what he said about the gears. He went through it all again. Eventually, after a number of false starts, we moved off, veering erratically about the village street. 'Look in the mirror,' he yelled again. I looked. There was a car behind us. Shaking with fear I slammed on the brake. We both shot forwards. The car behind drove past, its driver making the V for Victory sign. All was well. I ventured to look at Mr Methven. His face was contorted and his scalp was no longer dazzling, more a rosy pink; its texture too seemed changed, velours, perhaps, I thought. 'What the hell did ye do that for?' 'Well, just to let him past. That's all right isn't it? He seemed pleased.' 'No it is not. No he was not.'

On we went through the village. The legions of the damned were out, determined that I should run them over. People, bicycles, dogs, parked cars, moving cars. Had they no sense? Why weren't they indoors? How I hated them. The motorist requires an empty road. At last we reached the open country. What a relief. But now there were bends. Bends are dangerous. You can't see round them. Mr Methven was getting angry again. 'Will ye kindly go into top gear. And stay there.' Top gear was far too fast, anyone could see that. And how could I possibly concentrate on driving when he wouldn't stop talking, on and on about eye, hand, foot co-ordination. Wasn't there a disease like that, something caught off rats in the trenches? Had Mr Methven been in the trenches? Round another bend we sped in demoniac fourth gear. Ahead was a vertical drop, a glacier snaking to St Andrews Bay and certain death. I braked violently, the car skidded sideways, stalled and fell silent with its nose embedded in the bank. A storm of lapwings rose from the kale field, crowding the sky with omen. In silence Mr Methven got out and fetched his spade from the boot. In silence we heaved and shoved and shoved and heaved. At last we had the car facing homewards. My shoeless feet were frozen and lacerated, coated in mud and grit. As I drove back I felt a warm trickle of blood ooze from my big toe, down the clutch pedal, onto the dove-grey carpet. The pain was almost pleasant.

In the village street, the thought of Mr Methven and my parents and my future in driving caused me to shake again. 'Change down, change down,' he yelled. The schoolchildren were waiting for their bus. We passed them in a series of convulsive lurches, jerking back and forth like a pair of marionettes, heads grotesquely nodding. 'Go into neutral. Put the brake on.' I grabbed the gear stick, yanked. Out it came into my desperate fist, meek as a flower. I pulled on the handbrake, switched off the engine and handed the gear stick to its owner.

'I think I'll no be seeing you again next Tuesday,' he said. In the event we never met again, for a couple of weeks later, returning from Hogmanay revelries, Mr Methven was killed on that self same glacier above the sea.

AUF WIEDERSEHEN PETS

In the years of maturity, poised like parasitic mistletoe midway between earth and heaven, one may find that certain long held assumptions have become invalid; one may indeed find everything is pretty questionable, and most of all oneself. In the years of immaturity one was busy creating a persona with which to deceive everyone else. Later, in the years of motherhood, one had forgotten one ever had a self.

Now, saith received wisdom, is the time for a thorough investigation. Many secrets lie beneath the sands, so go and dig them up. Know yourself, be true to yourself, be *comfortable* with yourself.

Some people in America undergo marriage ceremonies to themselves, as seen on television. Mr and Mrs Me. How lovely. Personally, the last thing I want to be is myself. It is bad enough looking in the mirror. Say no more, leave the secrets in the sand, look away and forget the sad psyche. Thus the odd little self-related aperçu will come as a fresh surprise, or of course a nasty shock, but salutary in its sudden revelation, a tiny apocalypse.

One evening not so long ago I was selflessly unpinning sheets from the line in archaic rustic manner. The customary Force 8 East Anglian gale was blasting away and the sheets engulfed me, wrapping themselves round my head and shoulders, billowing and somersaulting.

So it was that I failed to notice a sly skateboard lurking beneath the washing line, so it was that I stepped on it. Joyously it sped off, bearing my mummified form into a headlong hurtle on the concrete yard. Speechless, bombinating agony, then a feeble little flicker of a thought. At least no one could see me.

Wrong as usual. On my left there was a gurgling, gargling noise and a tugging movement; on my right a high-pitched silvery screaming. There stood my pig and there stood my terrier, both staring hard at me, not with concern or sympathy, but with beady-eyed cupidity. I knew then that if I had been killed they would have eaten me. The pig had recently sampled the delights of human flesh with a mouthful of my son-in-law; she was ready for more.

That unhappy incident has affected me physically and mentally. I have an arm that aches like hell whenever I am bored, most poignantly when people are going on about income tax, the benefits of the computer or their cat.

And I have found myself brooding over Piero di Cosimo's wonderful painting, The Death of Procris. Procris who has not bothered too much about getting dressed, occupies the foreground, lying in much the same position as myself, post-skateboard. She is a woman with a chequered past, but she has always meant well and does not deserve her cruel fate. However, she has done some dim things, like giving her unfaithful husband her very own unerring spear. So in the end, in the painting, there she lies, pierced by that same spear, expiring among the small bright flowers of mythic spring.

At her head crouches Pan, attentive and priapic; at her feet is her hunting dog, Lailaps. Beyond the shore swerves and, on the strand, hounds hold a boar at bay. It is an estuary scene and a dwindling rivulet wanders its way towards the sea.

Down by the water the hounds are half-hearted, one sitting down, one approaching the boar shyly, tail half-drooping, ears flopped. A number of large birds are paying absolutely no attention. Distant headlands merge into haze and the blank indifferent sky.

The ancient Greeks had a notion that the image lay waiting to be discovered and released. So, it seems to me that images deliberately lurk about in the effluvium of our lives until such time as we recognise them. They have always been there waiting for this moment.

I have loved this painting for more than 30 years, but it is only now that suddenly it speaks to me of an end to supernatural leanings, a farewell to the sympathetic fallacy. Pan's tenderness is fleeting; he has his purposes. The dog Lailaps is profoundly courteous but he is just waiting for it all to be over and then he will be down on the shore with the others. Lailaps has his own doom to fulfil; he must always catch his prey.

Looking at those figures, I realise that I have outgrown half a century's misguided involvement with animals, an exhausting series of pulsating one-sided relationships. I wish them well, but they will no longer dominate my life. When the cats go they will not be replaced. Well, I might have one but I certainly won't have six again. And a kindly detachment will be the order of the day. Ha!

What I am having, contrary to all my expectations and prejudices, is computer classes. If I try very hard my daughter may, just may, give me her discarded Mac. Then, instead of droning on about cats and dogs and pigs, I can join the queue for the e mail monologue.

Foreword to
EAST ANGLIA: *A Literary Pilgrimage*
Peter Tolhurst (1996)

The fusion of literature and landscape offers peculiar joys, great and small. Who could look unmoved upon the links at Cromer where Arthur Conan Doyle, inspired by his golfing partner's tale of Black Shuck, conceived the notion of *The Hound of The Baskervilles*? In a certain Norfolk cliff-top cafe one may encounter Miss Havisham dispensing tea and cake with a remote and icy dignity appropriate to one who has unaccountably wandered out of *Great Expectations* and into *David Copperfield*. There is a brand of metal corkscrew with lifting arms which never fails to conjure up for me that terrifying, spectral figure which comes bobbing over the groynes in M R James' *Whistle And I'll Come To You My Lad*. Such correspondences bring delight to the daily round. On a wider scale one's whole life is enriched by the knowledge of those who have gone before us, who have recorded our landscape through their own unique sensibilities.

East Anglia has a long and proud tradition of tolerance and Non-Conformism which has extended to the motley throng of writers who have lived here, a lineage so various that their only common denominator is their sense of place. Some, like Anna Sewell or George Crabbe were born to this landscape and grew up with a sense not only of its beauty but of the inexorably desolate lives of its impoverished inhabitants: 'There pigs and chickens quarrel for a meal / There dropsied infants wail without redress /And all is want and woe and wretchedness'. Others came on holidays, or to visit friends or relatives and returned again and again. The great houses, parklands, sprawling rectories and shadowy rook-haunted trees entranced the childhood imaginations of L P Hartley, M R James and Osbert Lancaster. Conversely, for the adolescent Brendan Behan, East Anglia was a borstal on the Suffolk coast; for Arnold Wesker it was the kitchen sink of the Bell Hotel in Norwich. Over a drink or two Captain Marryat swapped his London house for one in Langham, where he wrote *Children of the New Forest*.

Other writers came to research, to escape from London, or simply by chance. Some were drawn by literary obsession; Benjamin Britten by Crabbe, W H Hudson by Bloomfield. Once here, not everyone wished to stay. Sabine Baring-Gould, redoubtable author of 'Onward Christian Soldiers', found Essex a litter of warped minds and sealed fates overcast by a miasma of sewage and sprats and mosquitoes. At the seaside Virginia Woolf predictably displayed her talent for snobbery, while Henry Williamson struggled miserably with his unyielding land. Of the dissenters here, most poignant is the poet Cowper, melancholic and ill at Mundesley, brooding on a solitary pillar of rock at the highwater mark: 'I have visited it twice and found it an emblem to myself. Torn from my natural connections, I stand alone and expect the storm that shall displace me'. Most comical is George Orwell, resentfully writing *Down and Out in Paris and London* amid the bourgeois comforts of genteel Southwold.

A writer's landscape is both factual and imaginary, cast and then rearranged in the mind's eye. The desolation which overwhelmed Cowper was a thrilling delight to Sylvia Townsend Warner: 'The east wind sobs and whimpers like a Brontë in the kitchen'. The fluctuations of those coastal, marginal lands, transient and treacherous, 'ambiguous territory', have brought solace to unquiet spirits. The solitary, anxious, self-questioning task of the writer may assume perspective amid such constant metamorphosis, a literal rendering of Villon's *Autant en emporte le vent*. Where there is loss and displacement there is also freedom.

Not everyone is bound by wind and water. Inland affords its own pleasures. Lytton Strachey found transcendence in the Suffolk grasslands; Angus Wilson's garden, cleared from the wild wood, became for him a practical realisation of 'the symbols underlying my novels'. Ronald Blythe remarked on the invisibility of farm workers 'slipping back into the earth they had toiled for thousands of years', but it was George Ewart Evans who, in his unsentimental oral histories, gave their recollections a voice and a lasting validity. A surprising number of writers here have also farmed their land. How curious it is to learn that Sir Rider Haggard, author of some sixty novels, was knighted for his work on agriculture and smallholdings.

While East Anglia is famous for its painters, it has been poorly served by compilers of Literary Companions. Peter Tolhurst's wonderful book, a true labour of love, is a timely avenger. The diversity of the landscape is mirrored by those who celebrate or disparage it. No one is indifferent. It is impossible not to be profoundly moved and exhilarated by these fragments of other lives. Here are two estuarine experiences. For Richard Mabey 'the mud slid out of the ebbing water with the moist shine of a new-born animal'. Sylvia

Townsend Warner meanwhile, and elsewhere, is simply 'socketed into the universe, passionately quiescent'. This is a book which urges the reader on to authors unvisited, unknown even. If some of their landscapes have been altered or destroyed, we may recreate them, pass there ourselves like ghosts, knowing them with an older familiarity.

Much has not changed. The lime tree avenue where Dorothy and William Wordsworth walked still stands. Rider Haggard noted road rage long since, tormented by coveys of bicycling clergymen: 'Thrice have I nearly fallen victim to their rage!' And Edward Fitzgerald, translator of *Omar Khayam* and one of my very favourite people here, – by his own modest declaration 'a very lazy person who do nothing' – 140 years ago was lamenting that 'the petty race of squires who have succeeded only use the earth for an investment'. Turning away from felled trees and levelled violet banks he found content on the water 'where friends are not buried nor parkways stopt up; but all is as the poets say, as Creation's Dawn beheld'.

To read this book is to attend an impossibly perfect millennial party. Radicals, dissenters, monks, mystics, farmers, fascists, free-lovers, poets and novelists mingle and time is suspended. Outside, forgotten, the equinoctial gales wail in off the marshes, and a great black dog pads silently along the cliff path.

THREE NORFOLK ARTISTS
Introduction to an exhibition at King's Lynn Arts Centre

I know very little about painting and drawing and I don't know what I like, so it was with great trepidation that I set off on this project. On all occasions I revealed my lack of credentials, a declared ignoramus (curious that there is no female form of this word. Makes one wonder, if one has the time.)

Derrick Greaves was my first port of call. He lives inland; in an old school house flooded with sunlight. It is marooned in a long green garden where purple ribbed cabbages droop langorous leaves like elephants' ears. In the trance of afternoon dewdrops still linger on them. I tried to think of a word for their colour. 'Nacreous' materialised, silent and stealthy, in the dim recesses of my skull. I kept quiet about this and asked Derrick how he would describe them. A moment's pause. 'Nacreous' he said.

Indoors the house feels like a ship, shining white and orderly: the steep angles of roof timbers suggest rigging and mast. Maritime, a stranded ship beneath a tree. And it is the sea which draws these very disparate artists together. I had expected talk of the great skies of East Anglia, the lure or grand illusion for so many generations of painters, but not one of them mentioned the sky; they all spoke of the sea. Furthermore each had come more or less randomly to Norfolk and found himself settling here with surprise, then slowly gathering delight. In Derrick's studio sea images proliferate. Pebbles and flints lock in a solemn watery embrace: the tattered outlines of *North Sea*, thunderous black and mauve criss-crossed by iridescence, heave like the perilous waters or form storm clouds, anchored by the steady clear line of the horizon. Conversely *Beach Fragments* is all childhood, a memory of sandy caves and starfish, beachball and shells, the curve of a leg flipping through the waves, a flounder which might be a whale or a whale which might be a flounder; you never know what will turn up at the seaside. Other drawings are dreamily erotic; lyres, flowers, corollae sway and drift in a haze of aquamarine; budding tendrils stretch hungrily towards each other. A musing on present happiness and a memory of the amniotic waters whence we came?

Angela Carter, in one of her last essays asks 'Where was I before I was born?' She goes on to speculate that this is the primal question of life. The sea conjures such thoughts, and thoughts of death too, 'So do our minutes hasten to their end.' Derrick Greaves spent childhood holidays on beaches in the West of England and remembers with nostalgic warmth. Now he takes pleasure in the desolation of the winter shore, the giving and taking and treachery of the tides as they wash in broken ships and human detritus, but also scour and bleach before withdrawing. He told me with delight of his little son's comment when first he saw the sea, 'It's clean.' Clean seems to me a good word for Derrick's work. 'Every inch is considered' says Anthony Benjamin. Yet there is no fuss, no clutter, instead a bold clarity which perhaps mirrors his life. 'I've decided to finish with having problems' he announces. But this enviable state has not been achieved lightly and the apparent simplicity of the drawings likewise masks complexity of image and of intention. He challenges himself to 'pull it off'; as he challenges viewers to unravel their own interpretations. He does not believe that this should be easy; although he describes his work as figurative, it has passed through a crucible, a melting process which removes it from representation and transforms it into art. Without pretension, and with wit.

Wit is something else all these artists have in common, wit and forbearance and generosity. I was late when I went to see Derrick Greaves, even later for Roger Ackling, latest of all for Anthony Benjamin, having lost my way yet again in an ever increasing derangement. Feeling hotter and older and fatter every minute, I drive in circles, cursing the Highways Authority who have so much money that they are re-laying almost every road in North Norfolk but cease to signpost villages from three miles off. On each occasion I was received with courtesy and warmth and quantities of wine. Roger Ackling lives immediately above the sea, in a cliff top coastguard's cottage. That summer day the landscape shimmered in primary colours, crayon blue sea, golden sand, scarlet poppies in the green green grass, the sky a shade paler than the sea, idle winds softly murmuring. A bit different in winter. Roger made some inscrutable remarks about his work, chortling gently: 'It's something to do with something, unless one's a liar.' 'If you put a stick through a spider's web what do you catch?' 'I've always wanted to be a baldheaded Buddist bowman.' I was becoming apprehensive. He added that some found his stuff utterly impenetrable, while others told him that it wasn't very demanding. This always pleased him. For himself he found it best not to think.

'Maybe I'm a hippy, maybe I'm a bullshitter.' In fact of course he is neither, but he enjoys these peripheral skirmishes. At the cottage he leads a life of extreme simplicity, without electricity or material concerns. He gathers pieces of driftwood and crouched on the shore he burns tight gridworks of lines on to them, slanting the sun's rays through a magnifying glass. As the wind shifts there are infinitesimal variations in the patterns. He occasionally uses card instead of wood. The end result is extraordinarily beautiful, strange silver or golden tablets which appear to bear the dark and enigmatic script of some ancient, vanished civilisation, voices long silenced pleading to be heard. He describes the dots with which he composes his grid lines as 'over exposed and merging photo images of the sun.' Looking closely at them it is easy to capture the excitement generated by the wind's breath. If you stare long enough you can become mesmerised, so that when you look away the image seems still stamped on your retina. He claims that they are not representational, not dramatic, purely geometric. However I have always had rather big problems with abstraction and the mathematical, and I had no difficulty in transposing Roger's work into the figurative, ranging from the pre-Mesopotamian tablets to a homely Tiger Tim jersey. The great horizon which he overlooks is echoed in these tiny horizontals, the smaller the better as far as their creator is concerned. It is said that he can transport an entire exhibition in his pockets. His desire is to bring out 'the smallest instance of something'. Down on the storm beach, under the wind, he has the sense of being alone on the surface of the earth, a flicker in the gaze of eternity, an atom of dust dancing in the winds before the eye of Buddha. Earth, air, fire and water; an elemental economy.

As I was leaving, an elderly gentlemen appeared at the garden gate. He had made his way painfully down the long, uneven track to arrange a game of bowls with Roger, 'Friday then' they agreed. He stumbled off, back up the track. The wind was rising and little puffs of sand bombasted him. For the last five years, said Roger, this laborious assignation had been made twice a week. 'But it's never happened. It never will.'

Inland I drove through the poppies, in search of Anthony Benjamin, who had in fact been kind enough to send me a detailed map of his whereabouts. His studio is in a green Wordsworthian dell, within sound but not sight of the sea, and only four minutes by car from Roger Ackling. But I was coming from a different direction, and it was an hour later, after many a three point turn in unchartered hinterlands and an unpleasant encounter with a youth who was eking out his disaffected day by lopping branches from a blooming buddleia bedecked with butterflies, that I found Anthony's solitary working abode. It is a large barn, whose interior, as in Derrick Greaves's house, is white, orderly and filled with light. I never cease to be astounded by the meticulous neatness of those who paint and draw. I can see how necessary this is, but how do they do it? All the writers I know live in a hideous shifting necropolis of skyscraper piles of books and papers regularly toppled by cats. They can never find anything, not even their special pen that Eliot once borrowed, or Ginsberg scratched his head with.

Anthony Benjamin clearly possesses the secret of eternal youth. Although he was born in 1931 he looks about 38 years old. There is no point in asking him about this because it wouldn't interest him and he is reserved about the past; he asked me not to write about such parts of it as he was prepared to disclose. Suffice it to say that his battered but youthful exterior is a testament to his spirit's survival against great odds, and not to self preservation. He has lived through turbulence and travelled far, in every sense. Now, he says, he is imposing some order on that past. He has painted, sculpted, drawn, with and without colour. At present he is working mostly in tones of grey, but colour is reappearing. His studio is impersonal, a cool, efficient working area. The light comes from glazed sections of the roof; his door is closed and he has no windows; he cannot see out. This is deliberate. He sees his work as an ongoing process, delving through genes and memory into his own expended life. His present life exists outside the studio door, separate and fresh as the trees he cannot see until he crosses the threshold. His verbal reticence is transmuted into images, abstract or figurative. 'Art is always autobiographical' he says, 'but also hidden, indirect.' Like Roger Ackling and Derrick Greaves he has no patience with the instant image, implicit with its packaged history, which is the currency now of much of Europe, retailed obviously by advertising and television but also in Britain by the demise of education, by Thatcherism and the cult of art as investment. Time spent in Cornwall years ago gave him a lasting appetite for landscape, now refined into landscape deployed as a philosophical outlook. I think this may be what poets do with landscape and I was not surprised to discover, at the end of the afternoon, that Anthony Benjamin reads a great deal of poetry. Both Derrick and Roger seemed to have reached a point of some peace in their lives, however transitory. I felt that Anthony had a quantity of unresolved energy and anger in him, miles to go before he sleeps. But Norfolk has perhaps offered him a respite. He watches minute by minute the changing seasons, and again the sea, surging in, brings its strange appeasement, fragments of other lives, seaweed, fossils, the enormous past. He says he will make maps of this, but not representations. I saw some reproductions of his soft grey drawings and I loved the vase of irises beside a skull. The skull is pursued by a whooshing nimbus of arcs, as though some malevolent god has just flung it down. One of the irises drops into darkness, into destruction. The others stand delicate, some scarcely delineated in their gentle glass, aloof; soon they will die. Sharp light illuminates the surface on which the vase stands perilously near the edge. Beneath is darkness, a tomb, a repository. The skull glares unforgiving from one eye socket, helpless; hopeless. Anthony showed me a poem by Wallace Stevens:

The exceeding brightness of this early sun
Makes me conceive how dark I have become.

And reillumines things that used to turn
To gold in broadest blue, and be a part

Of a turning spirit in an earlier self.

THOUGHTS IN A GARDEN

I think that's it really. And the season changes.

So here they are, the three of them, proud, difficult, all men of integrity, a quality not much visible these days. And I do mean visible, for the work reflects the life. By their works shall ye know them. A farewell for each of them: for Derrick, a childhood memory of his own; a lonely estuary, the sands shining in early evening. And then the tide is there, the castle collapsed, gone, and the Dragon flag of Wales floating out to sea. For Roger I leave an old fashioned wooden boule so that he may adorn the turning world with air and fire. And for Anthony the Ode of Horace which begins 'Diffugere nives' and is also wonderfully translated by A. E. Housman. Nothing should ever be easy.

TELLING TALES

CATULLUS
Charles Martin (1992)

With characteristic perversity, Gaius Valerius Catullus has left us a grand profusion of vivid glimpses into his life, but no overall account. The known facts are few. He was born in 84 BC to a wealthy family in Verona. At the age of fourteen or so he moved to Rome to further his education; there he remained. Although he made regular visits to his family's properties in the north, the city was his element:

Illa domus.
Illa mihi sedes, illic mea carpitur aetas.

He began to write poetry under the patronage of Memmius and circulated at least one collection of poems. His beloved elder brother died in Bithynia, and in 57 he visited his grave while on a year's diplomatic service in Asia Minor. He had a long and turbulent affair with a woman whom he called Lesbia. In 54 he died. One hundred and sixteen poems survive.

Catullus is generally regarded as the most accessible of Latin poets. His language is simple, his voice direct, his imagery colourful and often lurid. He and his fellow spirits, rich, dandified and hedonistic young men, were innovators, *neoteroi*, reacting against the old Roman epic tradition and mocking it where it persisted: *cacata charta*. Their models were the poets of Alexandria, whose work was characterised by extreme sophistication of technique, experimental rhythms, erudite allusion and word play lurking under a veneer of concise simplicity. To this Catullus added a powerfully personal element. The majority of his poems directly address friends, enemies, places, himself, even a door. Any subject was fit for versifying; only the didactic incitement to civic or martial duty was rejected. So he created an effect of effortless colloquialism and spontaneity which belies its own artistry.

Charles Martin's handsome book seeks to emphasise the modernity of Catullus's poetry and examines the relationships of individual poems to each other with a view to proving that they were arranged by Catullus himself, and not, as is often claimed, by some unknown posthumous editor. They are set out in three groups, according to length and metre. The first 60 poems, which are fairly short, are written in a variety of metres and generally described as the polymetrics. In the centre of the book is a series of long poems, followed by 47 more short ones in elegiacs. The very first poem offers the book in dedication to Cornelius Nepos; the final one seeks a worthy recipient for the poems of Callimachus. This is the sort of formulaic evidence on which Martin makes his case for Catullus as editor; it is unconvincing, to say the least. What of the fragments? The poems which may have been lost? Catullus's works disappeared at some point in the late Classical period and were undiscovered until a parchment codex was found by Dante's patron (putative but pleasing) at Verona in 1300. This copy could not have been made until (at the earliest) the third century AD when the codex form began to replace papyrus scrolls. Why should the first poem addressed to Lesbia be the 51st in the book, and the last be number 11?

According to Martin, the long poems, which consist of four poems in different metres, followed by four in elegiacs, are a single entity with eight sections, 'linked by chiastic inversion'. This claim is illustrated by a diagram and a discussion of the poems' themes – sanctified married love and unsanctified passion. It is all quite interesting and quite fun, but one can't but feel that it just doesn't matter. And it really is very hard to believe that Catullus, iconoclast as he was, would have intended his address to a door to be regarded as part of the Peleus and Thetis poem, or indeed the Attis and Cybele. You can dwell too much on a fondness for chiasmus.

This said, Martin does provide an excellent chapter on the Peleus and Thetis taken in isolation, explaining the apparent lack of unity between the description of the wedding feast and the description of the coverlet in terms of a series of wall paintings. This is a device which Catullus also uses in his celebration of his boat, her life and times. Here Martin is at his best, writing with vigour and enthusiasm, tracing the repetition of images, the convergence and dispersal, the elegance of structure with the vanishing mast of Theseus's ship as its axis. He illustrates his points, as he does throughout, with his own competent and conscientious translations. In the case of Catullus, this is a rare achievement. And, while on the subject of translation, let me add that it is more than time that a new Loeb Classical Library version appeared. The current one was first printed in 1913, is remarkably vapid and archaic – 'O filth, O beastliness!' – and is so prudish that it simply ignores the existence of any lines it deems improper. This means that a lot is left out.

Catullus's most celebrated poems are the twenty-five which deal with his relationship with 'Lesbia', a pseudonym chosen, not, of course, to suggest that she was a homosexual, but as a compliment, implying that she was a *puella docta* of Sappho's calibre. As Martin points out, it also has the same metric weight as Clodia, thought to be her real name. Propertius said that Lesbia was more famous than Helen of Troy, while Clodia herself was notorious for her profligate behaviour. Ironically, the poem which comes nearest to identifying her is one in which Catullus refers to Lesbia's incestuous relations with her brother, complaining that she prefers him: *Lesbius est pulcher*. Clodia's brother (described in court by Cicero as Clodia's husband) was known as Clodius Pulcher. Martin discusses the Lesbia poems with a certain literal-mindedness: 'What Catullus wants is nothing less than sole and exclusive possession – given all those thousands of kisses, when would she have time for anything else?' I don't feel we need this. What he fails to mention is that this poem, 'Vivamus', contains some of the most marvellous lines ever written.

Connecting the lament for the sparrow with 'Vivamus', he remarks: 'The conclusion to the logical syllogism we expect is overwhelmed by the conclusion to the poetic syllogism. This is a syllogism of pure intentionality.' What can he mean? Every now and then such grim turgidities occlude his normally lucid style, perhaps his vision too. He takes the famous last lines of the final Lesbia poem, with the image of the flower broken by the passing plough, as indicating a role reversal, with Catullus playing the flower and Lesbia the plough. Certainly the poem discusses Lesbia's brutal behaviour, but the flower is not Catullus – it is his love for her. And he discovers the anagram *Lesbi* in the phrase *at tu dolebis*. This is absurd.

Turning to the other shorter poems, both polymetric and elegiac, Martin points to the differences between the poet's trade then and now: notably, the social nature of Roman poetry, which was written to be read aloud, in the colonnades of forums, at organised readings, at dinner parties. Thus Catullus is able not only to single out his friends and enemies for abuse, but also to render this abuse immediately public. There is none of the isolation which attends the modern poet. But the expectations of audiences were different too: few, even now, could publicly bandy the obscenities which flow so easily from Catullus, conjuring up images of a sultry city seething with twined male bodies, prostitutes lurking by bath houses, incest and pederasty. But just as Catullus can combine intellectual and technical virtuosity with marvellous lyricism, so he infuses his scatological poems with a saturnine merriment and meticulous structure. Even in the notorious

Pedicabo ego vos et irrumabo
Aureli pathice et cinaede Furi.

which as a delicate Scotswoman, I don't propose to translate, there is the crisscross of chiasmus; even in the most obscene of all, to Aemelius, where there is the pissing mule (to put it very, very mildly), the language is chosen with deliberate artistry.

Martin makes much of Catullus's poems of invitation and threat as aspects of his 'modernity', evanescent in that they are specific, offering no generality. Sometimes they are in monologue, sometimes in dialogue, but are set by their nature in the present, with an implied future, and in this respect they do, of course, differ from the old poetry of Rome. They exist in themselves, for themselves. But ultimately they are simply elegant *jeux d'esprit*. The same, I feel, goes for the poems on present-giving. Martin gets carried away on the fusion of death, dinner and desire.

The best part of the book, to my mind, are the pages which discuss poem 65, to Ortalus. This was written at a time of profound grief, after the death of Catullus's brother. Ortalus has asked for a poem. Catullus cannot write; he addresses his brother in lines of great beauty:

at certe semper amabo
semper maesta tua carmina morte canam.

The poem passes from acute pain and sorrow, through the legend of Procne and Itylus, into a promise to send some verses, and then an image of renewal, an apple or pomegranate rolling across the floor. The poem is wonderful, and so is Martin's exposition. For us, latter day readers, that is. I doubt whether Catullus would have cared too much. But he would have been delighted to find his poems read two thousand years on, fulfilling his gleeful prediction:

at non effugies meos iambos

AMERICAN GHOSTS AND OLD WORLD WONDERS
Angela Carter (1993)

This volume contains seven stories which Angela Carter had completed before her death last year, one unfinished draft for a screenplay, and 'Ghostship', a defiant celebration of the ancient rituals of the Winter solstice and the 12 days of Christmas in the face of puritan New England.

Celebration is the keystone of the book – the 'carnival of the unacknowledged and the fiesta of the repressed'. Things are seldom as they seem, boundaries are there to be crossed, there shall be mirth and anarchy, experiment and excess. A winged pot of mustard traverses the wintery heavens. 'Imagine,' urges Carter, and her Circean presence haunts every page, dazzling and disturbing, bestowing an aftermath of lurid, kaleidoscopic dreams.

The four stories which make up the first part of the book are all set in America. In 'Lizzie's Tiger' the squat, square infant, Lizzie Borden, who will one day take an axe to her parents, slips out illicitly to the circus, and is almost consumed by a tiger. Carter writes in the round, in three dimensions, so that we see the scene simultaneously through the eyes of the child, the tiger and the author.

I cannot tell you how much she loved the tiger . . . It was the power of her love that forced it to come to her on its knees, like a penitent. It dragged its pale belly across the dirty straw towards the bars where the little soft creature hung by its hooked fingers. Behind it followed the serpentine length of its ceaselessly twitching tail.

The crowded darkness and rich detail of that circus evening is in stark contrast to the great empty prairie and windswept skies of the beautiful, elegiac 'John Ford's *Tis a Pity She's a Whore*', a melding of Jacobean dramatist John and American filmmaker John, part story, part screenplay, all tragedy: 'The dusk bird went chink-chink-chink with the sound of a chisel on a gravestone.' Here the language is as spare and pruned as Hemingway, and there is only the faintest touch of irony, perfectly judged. 'Gun for the Devil' likewise reworks the stuff of legend, a Faustian drama set in the sleaze of Mexican borderland. But it is unfinished, at times confusing and the least satisfying of these stories. This section is rounded off by the wildly funny 'Merchant of Dreams', where a living Hollywood legend, attended by the ancient MGM lion, undergoes a strange metamorphosis, within sound of the Pacific's 'foamy peripheries'.

In the second part, Carter largely abandons straightforward narrative for a series of giddy, mind-blowing frolics. Here there are disquisitions on pantomime, mandrakes and asceticism, gender and motherhood, Cinderella and silence. The setting is Europe but a Europe of the past, a fairy-tale realm of forest and swamp, steep gabled houses and cobbled streets, where 'everything is excessive and gender is variable'. The breathtaking accumulation of images and objects is perhaps at its most spectacular in 'Alice in Prague, or the Curious Room', where Dr Dee sits beneath a stuffed flying turtle and tries to coax angels from his crystal sphere while the deranged Archduke Rudolf copulates with a fruit woman created by the painter Arcimboldo. 'Poor Tom's-a-cold' calls the melancholy raven from its snow-bound tower. Into this place comes Lewis Carroll's Alice, who is desperate to ask a question or two. No one can answer her: she has strayed from a world of logical deduction into an age 'in love with wonders'.

The wonders are there in every piece: a ship's mast becomes a laden cherry tree, another ship is a Christmas pie, Cinderella's mother becomes a cat, a cow, a bleeding bird, Mary Magdalene passes into sainthood in the trance of a candle flame. The Principal Boy and the Dame gleefully transcend their gender; nor will the principal boy be a New Man – 'she's gone to the bother of turning herself into a Principal Boy to get away from the washing-up in the first place.'

Mary Magdalene also transcends gender to reach 'the radiant, enlightened sinlessness of the animals . . . now she has no option but virtue'. For Angela Carter virtue is one thing, but penitence, mortification of the flesh, rejection of pleasure is another: 'penitence becomes sado-masochism. Self-punishment is its own reward.' Her essay on the 'Wrightsman Magdalene', Georges de la Tour's 17th century painting of Mary Magdalene, is yet another wonderful piece of writing; she passes from image to image of this Mary, blackbrowed Palestinian, 'gaunt as famine, hairy as a dog', or young and adulterous, or withered and eremitic; she ends with the mirror and the candle flame and a profoundly moving account of birth.

Those who already know Angela Carter's work will need no

encouragement to read these stories (she is the only late 20th-century writer I know who can use an exclamation mark and get away with it); for others they offer a joyous introduction. Susannah Clapp, editor of this volume, promises more to come.

THE INFINITE PLAN
Isabel Allende (1993)

Isabel Allende's fourth book is set in California, 'the last frontier, the goal of adventurers, desperadoes, non-conformists, fugitives from justice, undiscovered geniuses, impenitent sinners and hopeless lunatics, a place where even today every possible formula for avoiding the anguish of living proliferates'. She traces the fortunes and fugitive devices of a huge cast of characters over the last 50 years, weaving a brilliant and violently coloured tapestry around her central figure, Gregory Reeves.

Gregory's father is an itinerant preacher and a painter, wildly eclectic in both disciplines, but charismatic and eloquent. Beneath a suspended orange, which represents the soul, he stands entwined by a boa constrictor and preaches the Infinite Plan, God's creation, in which nothing is random and salvation follows on observance of clear-cut rules. Urinating on a hilltop at sunset, the infant Gregory exults in his sense of being part of this world of wonders, of unending possibility. Fifty years later he will recognise that there is no Infinite Plan, 'just the strife of living'.

When Gregory's father dies, the family settles in the *barrio*, the Hispanic immigrant area of Los Angeles. His mother, who has withdrawn from the world in horror at the bombing of Hiroshima, ignores her children, concerned only with opera, Bahaism and the weekly visits of her husband's ghost. Gregory and his sister learn to survive, outsiders in a Latin world, but sustained by the friendships of the Mexican Morales family and the wondrous Olga, a midwife, fortune-teller and magician, a woman of 'visceral talent'.

At high school Gregory becomes a scholar, reading everything from Aristotle to Zoroaster under the tutelage of Cyrus, the communist liftman. Gregory is obsessed by women and money. Olga relieves his hormonal torment and the rest of his life is taken up with earning. His confidence increases to the point where he can confront the worst bully of the *barrio* in a duel; protected by the Virgin of Guadeloup, he wins: 'pieces of Martinez were scattered across the landscape'. Thus ends the first of the book's four parts.

Gregory leaves the *barrio*, goes to university in Berkeley, then law school in San Francisco. Longing for the warmth of a family life of his own, he marries. However, his dream of a rose garden enclosing a pie-baking wife is at sad variance with the times. Promiscuity and transcendent experiences have become life's ordinants. Sick at heart, betrayed by his wife, he joins the army and goes to Vietnam. The third section of the book deals with the hallucinatory horrors of that war and its aftermath, the fourth with Gregory's subsequent career as a lawyer, his disillusionment with his target of wealth and fame, and his redemption through psychotherapy. At the end he is returning to the *barrio* and a new woman and the suggestion that at last he will have a little happiness.

This is so nearly a great novel. The characters, maimed and heroic, all displaced, all searching for the indefinable, both convince and fascinate, the sense of place is stunning, lyrical and passionate. Allende describes with equal vividness women preparing a feast in a slum back yard, a small town breathless in the heat of summer, or a battalion slaughtered by night on a mountainside. This last scene, dominated by Gregory's screaming figure, is the dreadful polar twin of his moment of childhood happiness on the sunset hill. Allende's writing is supremely elegant, dense yet economical, and her effortless disposition of vast hosts of troubled humanity against their random historical circumstances, her courtesy and tenderness towards them, reminded me of the Pasternak of *Dr Zhivago*.

But alas and alack, during the final section of the book, in the 'Bacchanal of conspicuous consumption and noisy patriotism' which disguises the humiliation of the defeat of Vietnam, it is as if Allende loses heart. The writing becomes two-dimensional, characters are allotted success and happy endings in a manner which seems quite arbitrary, and Gregory wrecks his credibility by making remarks like 'they say that the first five or six years are very important in our formation', or, worse, 'I needed to revise that aspect of my personality.' He concludes that the most important thing is to find one's own soul, be reconciled with oneself, be self-aware. This drab solipsism, as much as greed, was one of the unpleasant characteristics of the Eighties, and it is sad indeed to see it spoil a work of such potential splendour.

LOVE AND SUMMER
William Trevor (2009)

This is William Trevor's first novel since *The Story of Lucy Gault*. Like much of his writing it is set in rural Ireland and like much of his writing it is a flawless work of art. The spare, beautiful language, meticulously judged sentences and paragraphs, each word in its only possible place, the rhythms and cadences, inversions and spaces, create a litany of bereavement as surely as they may describe an abandoned garden or the final packing of a suitcase. And Trevor accords the same respectful impartiality to his characters, dignifying the smallest rituals of their daily lives, the stuff of things.

The time is the late 1950s. A sultry summer unravels through a dusty small town and its surrounding hills, strewn with rocks and gorse. Much goes on in people's heads and hearts, but externally there is little change, so the inhabitants may say with modest complacency that in Rathmoyne nothing happens. For it is all too late. The long tentacular shadows of the past enclose endeavour and aspiration.

No one is much concerned with the future. Florian, in his twenties and planning departure forever, imagines the rest of his life passed in obscurity, a single room in a far country, where he will be alone, reading and remembering. He has dabbled in painting, writing and photography, and not found a way. 'And did it matter, now that so much was over for him, and his disappointment's sting had long been drawn?' He is selling his childhood home, a large decaying house; he thinks of his loving parents in their graves, so close but unable to touch. He dreams of his absent cousin Isabella, a piano playing Schubert, a heron. And he encounters Ellie, childless wife of a hill farmer, neither happy nor unhappy in a marriage of mutual kindness. As a foundling, raised by nuns, she is glad to have her place in life, her appointed tasks and her decent hard-working husband: 'He wasn't sentimental, but he respected sheep.' He is also silently consumed by the grief and guilt of a terrible accident years before. Florian is attracted to Ellie and the gentlest of summer dalliances, but Ellie's susceptible heart leaps to the inkling of high romance and she cannot let it go. Her bicycle and her parcels of shopping are made numinous by his presence. Her quiet evenings at the farm are fractured now with guilt and terror. She and Florian meet in secret places, a graveyard, a lost garden. Florian reads Dostoevsky as he waits for her. There are powerful echoes here of Trevor's masterpiece *Reading Turgenev*; characters spring living from the pages of a book or from a faded watercolour. A scarlet skirt swirls, a couple converse in an empty theatre. Colours are extraordinarily vivid because he uses them so seldom.

Small joys and small cruelties abound and although the prevailing mood is elegiac, there are moments of wild wit. While Florian and Ellie are the central figures, other tragedies are revealed and other complex, intensely realised characters pursue their bitter pleasures. One or two of them actually lead lives of modest content, in a numb sort of way, and you want to keep them safe.

Ellie, rightly, is given the raison d'être of it all: 'The past he talked about himself became another part of her . . . Being with him in the woods at Lyre, where the air was cold and the trees imposed a gloomy darkness, or walking among the monks' graves, or being with him anywhere, telling or listening, was for Ellie more than friendship or living had ever been before.' This is the miraculous essence, the consummate artistry, the telling of it.

ELECTRICITY
Victoria Glendinning (1995)

Victoria Glendinning's fine novel displays many of the qualities of her biographies, which in turn are often glowingly described as reading like novels. *Electricity* describes the coming-of-age of Charlotte, spirited, intelligent and educated beyond her social position. 'Knock and it shall be opened unto you', Miss Paulina has taught her. But now in the mid-1880s she sees no future beyond a job in a haberdasher's, and no escape from the mean trappings of respectable poverty in a house where her parents exist 'locked forever into petty routines and rivalries in a stuffiness of personal odours and unspoken discontents'.

Charlotte has an eye for a metaphor. She looks at her mother and recalls a lost puppy, still jaunty, questing and absorbed; then she remembers its bewildered desolation as the alien world encloses it. She is ready to knock on almost any door. When her hand brushes the hand of the new lodger, Peter Fisher, electrical engineer, she feels the tingle of connection which will change her world. She loves Peter for himself but also for his metaphoric value, the world beyond the closed door, the intellectual excitement, the limitless glory of his obsession. 'God is electricity. Electricity is God,' he says.

The electrification of London has begun; at King's Cross the courting pair gaze up at the new platform lights: '"Four hundred thousand candle-power there", breathed Peter.' For Charlotte it is all romance and crusade. They marry and go to Hertfordshire, where Peter is to wire up Lord Godwin's huge country house. The affable but amorous Godwin is happy to open more doors for Charlotte. She discovers botany, geology and adultery, enduring them alike in a 'calm and prosaic' spirit of inquiry. She sees Godwin and Peter as 'two electrified rods and myself as a filament between them, binding them together and holding them apart'. She believes she can control her life, loving Peter, in love with Godwin. Peter defines control as the task of civilisation, the setting of order on chaos, light upon darkness. But Charlotte has gone too far; she has lost control. With the illumination of the great house comes a series of hideous disasters; the leisurely idyll darkens into tragedy. Back in London Charlotte tries to make a living as a medium, persuading herself that spiritualism, like electricity, is a medium of communications, a mirror image of science which seeks effect rather than cause. It doesn't work. Her own energy seeps away; she is short-circuited. The electric metaphor has run its course. Armed now by painful self-knowledge she confronts a life of self-determinism.

Charlotte is an attractive heroine, resourceful, witty and intelligent, despite her admiration for Peter's intellect she acts on instinct and survives. Peter's pure spirit and clarity of mind cannot preserve him from fatal human error. The fourth main character, Aunt Susannah, a robust Yorkshire widow, is the most vital of them all. She dispenses good sense, clad in jet-encrusted bombazine, or a hessian tent tied by a drawstring at the neck for modest moments. She has 'such long growing and bushy eyebrows that she appeared to have hairy eyes'. And, unlike the others, she does achieve control over her life.

But the great virtues of this novel lie beyond the plot and even the characters. The background becomes the foreground, crowding into the arguments over power, religion and science, choice and heredity. Clothing, rooms, furnishings, garden tools, bicycles, food and drink are minutely described. Glendinning's gift for lyric exactitude dazzles. Gas brackets are 'fizzing blue fishtails of flame', flints become the 'shoulder blades and knee joints of prehistoric animals'. There is a vast trove of information on female education, gemstones, class distinctions, fungi, housework, hat-making, the treatment of women committed to mental asylums. A dead horse plugs a gaping pothole. Metaphors and images layer the narrative with a dreamlike texture, and there is a strange proliferation of the semi-globular, appearing as melon, brain, amethyst geode, pregnant stomach, crystal lightshade, apple or raspberry.

So much colour and sensuousness, such a feeling for time and place would be overwhelming if it were not balanced by Glendinning's spare limpid prose and economy of style. But rather in the manner of a Renaissance painting, the gaze is drawn away from the drama in the foreground to wander in the further landscape or linger on the incidental brightness of fruit or flower. Unless of course it can all be put down to the heroine's relish for facts; or perhaps, as her gnomic spiritualist mentor would say: 'It's the same difference.'

THE INFERNO OF DANTE
A New Verse Translation
Robert Pinsky (1994)

It is almost 700 years since Dante, exiled forever from his loved Florence, wrote the *Commedia* (it did not become divine until the 16th century). The first part, the *Inferno*, is set through Thursday night to early Sunday morning of Easter in 1300 and it tells of the poet's journey to the depths of Hell, guided by his mentor Virgil. The passage through the infernal circles is fraught with ambiguities. Dante the pilgrim, mortal and vulnerable, moved by pity and sorrow, is also Dante the narrator, recorder of moral justice and retribution, the irreversible torment of souls who chose sin.

Hell's depths offer the pilgrim spiritual attrition; through his vision of choice and consequence he will attain salvation. Every temptation is delineated; the narrowing infernal pit contains all the potential evil of the individual soul; it also represents a contemporary world without hope. It is the story of a chimerical, nightmare journey and it is an allegory of Christian revelation. Classical myths, medieval theology, the corrupt politics of the city state, the internecine strife of Guelf and Ghibelline, combine to create a background text dense with allusion and ironic hindsight. Like the pilgrim, we need a guide.

In this handsome volume with closely matched parallel texts, Robert Pinsky, a poet highly respected in the US, proposes a Dante for our times; this is a gallant and justifiable enterprise and one can only admire his energy and scholarship. The 'eloquent vernacular' of the *Commedia* had a profound influence on the language of European literature; Dante addressed his audience in the living speech of his time and the faithful translator must do likewise. Already Dorothy Sayers's admirable rendering (Penguin Classics 1949) seems a trifle dated and tarnished.

There have been many translations in prose and assorted metrics, but Pinsky, like Sayers, has boldly ventured into terza rima. This is the form Dante created for his epic, a sequence of interlocking three-line stanzas with an intricate rhyme scheme – aba, bcb, cdc and so onwards. Even in Italian terza rima has been little used, apart from Petrarch and Boccaccio, and despite attempts in English by Wyatt, Byron, Browning, Auden and others, only Shelley's 'Ode to the West Wind' does real justice to its forward leaping movement, its enchanting fusion of sinuous power and fragile delicacy.

Pinsky claims that English just doesn't have enough rhymes; he is fearful of sounding funny or of being forced into tortuous, contrived sequences by the exigencies of his line endings. (Other poets have coped perfectly with the sad deficiencies of our enormously rich and beautiful language, but never mind that.) Accordingly, he has chosen to use oblique rhymes, consonantal or echoing, as employed rather differently by W B Yeats. Applied to terza rima this method doesn't always work too well, often involving him in the very contortions he had hoped to avoid and wrecking the urgent striving of the rhythm:

'And at its end the sheet it's shrouded in / Is essence of nard and myrrh. As one who falls / and knows not how – if a demon pulled him down / or another blockage human life entails –'. Here the juxtaposition of 'blockage' and 'human' is a little unfortunate. Elsewhere we read 'I found among those there for thieving / Five of your citizens, which carries shame / For me – and you gain no high honour thereby'. He is very partial to enjambement (as indeed was Dante). Sometimes this works to great effect – 'Now I am where the noise of lamentation / comes at me in blasts of sorrow. I am where / All light is mute, with a bellowing like the ocean / Turbulent in a storm of warring winds' – but as often, more often, it is anticlimactic, weakening the force of a line end-stopped in the original.

There are other infelicities. Virgil, introducing himself, begins the first line of a stanza 'Poeta fui', a proud statement which Pinsky moves into a mere aside, tucked towards the end of the line. The fallen angels 'piovuti', 'rained' from heaven are 'spat / Like rain' for Pinsky. Not only is 'spat' discordant and ugly, it introduces a secondary image. Dante's small flowers, bowed and closed in the night frost, are described as 'shrunken' while the frost goes unremarked. Spirits are 'crowded in a herd', hands are pawing. The wondrous word *rimbombo* is feebly translated as 'noise' and all the onomatopoeia of this tercet is lost. 'Quando la brina in su la terra assempra / L'imagine di sua sorella bianca' has a texture and a music absent from 'when the hoarfrost mimes / the image of her white sister upon the ground'. 'Mimes' is not right for frost; besides it has too forced an air of doing its consonantal work with the line-endings before and after it, 'beams' and 'seems'.

Pinsky is especially ill at ease with Dante's sudden bursts of the colloquial. 'But let your conversation not be long / till you return I'll parley with this beast / so we may borrow his shoulders'. Half a century ago Dorothy Sayers primly rendered a grand guignol moment: 'He promptly made a bugle of his breech'. Says Pinsky: 'And the leader made a trumpet of his ass'. Not much linguistic advancement there; and really that ass takes the biscuit.

Where Pinsky does excel is in passages of sombre simplicity. His inscription over the gates of hell is magnificent, the best I have seen. He handles the famous meeting with Paolo and Francesca with great delicacy, his language intense, melodious and anguished as the original, only stumbling at last over 'Nessun maggior Dolore . . .' His birds are marvellous, too. 'As winter starlings riding on their wings / form crowded flocks, so spirits dip and veer / foundering in the wind's rough buffetings / upward and downwards, driven here and there / with never ease from pain nor hope of rest / as chanting cranes will form a line in air / so I saw souls come uttering cries – wind tossed / and lofted by the storm'. One can forgive much for those chanting cranes.

There are other fine passages, notably Ulysses' sorrowing apologia, and plenty of competent if unremarkable writing, slumping now and then into the deeply laboured. Nicole Pinsky supplies concise and lucid notes and Michael Mazur's doomy monotypes may or may not enhance one's reading. I could do without them.

The real and very great pleasure of this fresh translation derives from the parallel texts. With the assistance of a modest dictionary and very little Italian we may each make a Dante for our own time, wandering through the infernal circles, dazed by that extraordinary vision, the swoops from the supernatural to grim farce, tenderness and pathos to brutality and inexorable retribution. The darkness of hell is shot with earthly images, a dog's teeth grinding his bone, wet hands steaming in the winter air, a frog's snout surfacing in a pond, a tower swaying against passing clouds. And again and again the plangent cry of the dead: 'Conforti la memoria mia'. Remote we may be from Guelf and Ghibelline, but the *Inferno* remains immediate, poignant and ferocious, with places well appointed for us all. No one should miss this trip.

BABEL TOWER
A S Byatt (1996)

This massive novel is Antonia Byatt's first full-length work since *Possession*, which won the Booker Prize in 1990. *Babel Tower*, the third volume in a planned quartet, continues the story of Frederica Potter and her family, the central characters of *The Virgin in the Garden* and *Still Life*. Here we find Frederica, in her late twenties, unhappily married and now fleeing from rural seclusion and a violent husband. With her small son she arrives in London. Old friends provide generous support, finding her a place to live, jobs, a GP and a solicitor. They cook her delicious little meals, admire her fortitude and welcome her back to the world of the thinking man (or woman, but as Frederica says, 'The kind of woman I am is not quite sure she is a woman').

Frederica, never an attractive character, has not improved with age. Initially she is suffering from shock, an axe wound, VD and anxiety about her son; even so, her acceptance of people's kindness as her natural due seems graceless, and her self-absorption is breathtaking. She learns that her husband has beaten up her brother-in-law and attacked her elderly father. 'Help me,' she cries. Without any apparent irony, she assures a social worker that she loves her child 'more than anything else, including my books'. She hates to write 'I' because: '"I" is a character I am inventing who/which in some sense drains life from ME into artifice and enclosedness.'

She teaches a fiction course, reads for a publisher and agonises over language and meaning, for it is the early Sixties and the educational assumptions of her past are being cast aside. She shares a house with equally high-minded Agatha, who quotes from 'Lycidas' one morning. 'They grin. The quotation makes them both feel better. They do not question why this should be so; they are women who share a certain culture.' This culture, shared indeed by most of their friends and colleagues, exhales a fatal miasma of complacency and self-righteousness. The spirit flags, becomes torpid and sullen as it is guided through the labyrinths of Frederica's search for the truth about herself.

'I am not thinking clearly. I am accusing Forster and Lawrence of making me marry Nigel, out of some desire for a Union of Opposites, of Only Connecting the Prose and the Passion. Whereas in fact, at least in part, I married him for exactly the opposite reason, because I wanted to keep things separate. I thought the sex was good, was satisfactory, which is better than good, and I think I thought that because he was rich, I wouldn't have to be a housewife like my mother.' And so on. Frederica provides us with a Burroughs-inspired collage of quotations and anecdotes which gives her intense pleasure but is tedious for anyone else; we must also read her lectures, her reports on books, and her friend Agatha's Tolkienish children's serial, with bumper dramatic episodes on Sundays: 'the requirement of the Sunday Shock is formally very satisfying, no doubt like constructing episodes of novels like *The Idiot* or *Dombey and Son*.' Ah yes, no doubt. But how one yearns for a spot of frivolity, for kitsch and ketchup, for warmth and humour.

There are even greater inducements to narcolepsy in the endless small-type pages of *Babble-tower*, the novel within the novel. In allegorical and chivalric prose this describes the creation and self-destruction of a Utopia in a towery mountain fastness. Not only must we read this sub-novel, we must also endure discussions, eulogies, reviews and finally a court trial, held to determine whether the sub-novel is obscene or of mitigating literary merit. I can tell you now that it is neither; it is just annoying and boring and I was delighted when the Lady Roseace was chopped up by a sex machine and the infant Felicitas fell off a tower.

In the novel proper there are many towers. The central image of the Tower of Babel represents the intellectual, social and moral confusions of the Sixties, the collapse of old, received wisdoms into the welter of opportunism, or into well-intentioned liberal theory. In contrast are the tiny spiralling towers of snail shells, the twisting of certain branches, the coil of an ammonite, all representative of pure form, immutable order, the harmonious truthfulness of numbers. In the enlightened primary school, children create cardboard towers, the concrete heights of a new university shadow an Elizabethan garden, the ziggurats of

Babylon vie with Kafka's castle, Frederica's spine twists into a helter-skelter of desire, a madman burns toppling piles of books. Towers of presumption, towers of aspiration, towers of folly.

This is a profoundly didactic book; each tower is implicit with questions and answers and argument. Byatt moves expertly among her structures, discoursing, debating, on language, the teaching of English, education, sexual freedom, television, the legal system, pollution and the genetics of snails. Her versatility and parodic skills are dazzling. She assembles a government committee of academics and writers to study the teaching of English, and peppers it with vignettes of recognisable characters bearing half-familiar names, mischievously deployed – Roger Magog, Naomi Lurie, Mickey Impey, Hans Richter. Here, away from the mainstream of the narrative, there are some genuinely funny scenes and satisfyingly sharp glimpses of group interaction.

The scene shifts between London and the Yorkshire Moors, where we come upon Frederica and some people with names that just go too far – John Ottokar, Jacqueline Winwar and Dr Luk Lysgaard-Peacock. Byatt's descriptions of landscape are ravishing, underpinned always by some small surprising comment or parallel. Here, as Dr Luk Lysgaard-Peacock and the others chat about radiation and genetic polymorphism, Byatt describes the early warning system, three vast white spheres. 'Their size is incommensurate with the moorland, their scale is in another world. They are beautiful and sinister. They are so beautiful and simple it is not easy to see them as man-made, and thus they do not seem to spoil the wild landscape as they might be expected to. They are huge yet unobtrusive.'

Such descriptions, truthful and resonant, stand out distinctly in a book where one is often unable to suspend disbelief. Yet there is an energy behind this restless, striving and unwieldy novel which makes one read on, makes one want to know what happens next to Frederica, tiresome as she is and tiresome as Byatt's continuous use of the present tense is. Much is demanded of the reader, but much too is given, even if it is often concealed to an oracular degree in analogy or metaphor. 'Is a naked prancing man a mask for a brain and a pair of eyes watching and watching and trying to make sense?' Well, is he?

A BOTTLE IN THE SHADE
A Journey in the Western Peloponnese
Peter Levi (1996)

This amiable book describes Peter Levi's visit last year to Greece, a journey into his past, a reunion with a beloved friend, a pilgrimage to a grave. Levi intended a series of poems addressed to the poet Nikos Gatsos, who died in 1994; but 'memory disturbs purpose', and the diaries and notebooks of that visit have resolved into a series of musing recollections and disquisitions, a look before and after, an acknowledgement of renewal and change, so that the tone is both elegiac and celebratory.

Levi travelled out in early spring and spent four weeks based in Pyrgos, in the house of his friend and fellow poet Giorgis Pavlopoulos. Day by day they made forays out into Arcadia, Triphylia and Zakynthos. They met friends, gave readings and interviews on radio and television, explored ancient sites; they ate and drank and they talked. It is the talk which is the very essence of *A Bottle in the Shade*, for although they sustained a demanding month of travel and conviviality, ill health dictated that this must be an elderly adventure. At times Levi had a sense that 'I found myself in a new stanza of a very old poem whose lines were laid down long ago', and at times he was fearful that he might not be capable of climbing the mountain paths or seeing the brilliance of the stars. Despite all misgivings, they discovered old and new delights in the lowering landscape of Arcadia, overhung by Mount Lykaion 'like a wolf's pelt and skeleton hung out to dry'. As recently as 1965, wolves slunk among these boulders; they consumed a peripatetic musician, leaving a hand which still grasped its fiddle.

Levi found Olympia hideously changed in the thirty years since his last visit. The old hotel was looted and locked; fences and bus parks overwhelmed the ancient sites. As a true philhellene, a scholar in Greek, ancient and modern, he wastes little time on this vandalism, commenting with weary clarity, 'The Greeks do love ugliness if they can afford it; they have a passion for it', and 'Only with the death of education and religion does the ministry of tourism get to work, making roads to the remotest convents and the most inaccessible antiquities.' As for the terrible fate of the temple at Bassai, which is shrouded in a flapping three-gabled *tent*, weighted by lengths of old drain-pipe, its pillars fettered and chained to keep them upright, its floor waterlogged, he says simply, 'The general effect is more pitiable than I can easily express.' Other trips were happier. They spent idyllic days in Zakynthos, seeking out painted balcony screens, ikons and the spirit of the nineteenth-century poet Solomos in his dandified gloves. A visit to Patrick and Joan Leigh Fermor was 'the refreshment of a dream'. Indeed, wherever Pavlopoulos and Levi went, they were cherished and fêted. Giddy with wine and hospitality, he noted that at Easter his hostess contrived to spend £600 on paschal lambs, lambs which represented Christian sacrifice, but were also symbolic of the freedom of the mountains.

Levi puzzles over the nature of memory, architectural enigmas, pleasure and oddities. Flinging up questions and abandoning them. Is there a distinction between ancient and modern blasphemy? Why do contemporary poets tend to be known for a body of work rather than individual poems, stanzas, lines? Why was the image of Pan threshed with squills, and was this a graven image or a human representative? I am suspicious of this squill business. Squills are liliaceous bluebells; you couldn't flog anything with them. The ancients were often very unsound on botany; notably so, in fact, in the bluebell area. Consider the hyacinth and its cry of woe. Levi laments the corruption of the Greek water-melon, moves on to Victor Hugo and Dickens, bestows bouquets of loving recollections on the gifted dead, Bruce Chatwin, Philip Sherrard, the poet Takis Sinopoulos, and Maurice Bowra, who sends a *bon mot*, turned out of Horace, from beyond the grave: 'Pelvis et umbra sumus.' Especially Levi honours Nikos Gatsos, including translations of his poems and the elegy he wrote for him.

The author's restless and eclectic mind ranges, focuses and moves on, sometimes too swiftly, so that one is left with a tantalising half-story. Why was he imprisoned? What traumatised the eight-year-old Pavlopoulos as he fired a gun into a rosebush? Why were the colossal wine-barrels, 'like elephants grazing in the cool grass', named Mississippi, Orinoco and Thames? Why is Levi sympathetic to Pausanias' description of singing trout, but unimpressed by Aristotle's mention of the mice of Lousoi who can swim? 'So can the chickens of Hook Norton'.

The modest, conversational prose at times reads a little eccentrically, as if it had been taken down verbatim over that bottle in the shade. But it is layered with enchanting allusion – 'the sea was as calm as if we had been carrying the dead body of Arthur Hallam' – and it is shot with the sudden insight of a poet. Sailing out of wintry Ancona he saw no seagulls, only the 'sun like a crystallised apricot in a sky of ice'.

The book concludes with an unresolved search for the Falls of the River Styx, the ancient river of death, which flowed through a region of marsh and fog on the western limit of the world. 'I had attained complete peace of mind as to whether we found the place or not . . .' And perhaps there is poetic justice in this abandoned quest. Peter Levi has more landscapes to cross before he passes into the ninefold coils of those black waters. And more conversations to hold with Giorgis Pavlopoulos. 'It is Baudelaire we must talk about when we meet again.' One sees the two of them, like the Trojan elders in the *Iliad*, 'excellent speakers, sitting there in the tower, like cicadas perched on a tree in the woods, chirping delightfully'.

THE WITCH OF EXMOOR
Margaret Drabble (1996)

'Once upon a time there were two little girls, and their names were Everhilda and Frieda Haxby.' Oh God, surely not. Well, as it turns out, yes and no, for the author has confessed: 'There were so many versions and all of them were false.' So much for the suspension of disbelief.

From the beginning it is clear that we are in some never-never land, subject to the whims of an invisible group leader. 'Let them have everything that is pleasant,' she proposes, wafting us to an idyllic country kitchen. Hairy Nathan, freckled Dennis, pin-up David, 'the Imran Khan of politics', and their assorted wives and children, have enjoyed dinner; now 'they are taking their ease and eating slice after slice of solid brown bread'. In between mouthfuls they discuss the Veil of Ignorance, the impossibility of social justice, and the antics of Frieda, matriarch and saboteuse of their own small social constructs. They are decent, intelligent, affluent professionals; they are also selfish, complacent, greedy and insincere. There is Gogo 'smiling her sardonic smile', there is David 'smiling his civil, engaging, disarming smile', there is David again 'smiling his charming televisual smile'. These people are recognisable and I don't want to meet them.

Our spectral leader treats them with a faintly patronising detachment. Her intention is satirical, but she expects us to be concerned with them and they do not engage sympathy. Besides, there is too strong an authorial presence, a sense of manipulation. 'Imagine David D'Anger,' she commands. 'You say he is an impossibility, and you cannot imagine him.' I have said no such thing; I can imagine him all too well. 'But you are wrong,' she resumes. 'The truth is that you, for David D'Anger, are the impossibility ... .Look at him carefully ...' I have little inclination now to imagine the dusky charmer. Nor do I care about his vision of the just society. I will not collude with his creator. As David and Daniel wander through the rose garden discussing cultural appropriation and communitarianism, a tide of resentment slowly rises.

Frieda, however, is well worth meeting. Hers is a strong, convincing presence. She burns with gleeful malevolence and dispenses sharp good sense about disease, survival, consumer societies, ring roads and beefburgers, 'food that smells of hot vomit'. Balefully she works on her family's pretensions. Finally she will leave them floundering, half-submerged, choked in the undertow of enlightened self-interest. Meanwhile she cherishes her solitude and squalor, prising mussels from the rocks and offering the occasional visitor a slab of soggy Ryvita.

Frieda's wilful reclusiveness in her derelict Exmoor mansion is a source of anger and anxiety to her offspring. While this is an issue central to the book, it sadly lacks credibility. There is no reason why she should not live as she chooses in this beautiful and uncomfortable place. She is active, intelligent and articulate; she has never 'had much truck with comfort and she didn't see why she should seek it out now'. She is not even very old; she is in her sixties. Her eventual come-uppance could happen to anyone of any age.

Throughout the book there is a scatter of infuriating rhetorical questions, in the manner of another distinguished female novelist. Surveying the house, someone ponders 'Whoever could have built such a thing here, and how, and why?' A knitting needle pokes through an orange: 'Now who would wish to torture an orange?' The writing is often over-explanatory; we are told what to think, but we may not agree. There are endless sequences of short sentences in the present tense: 'The days are long. The light glimmers on the water. The moon is on the wane. And so is she. She has had her supper of tuna and brine . . .'

This is a nobly intended novel which contains haunting imagery and some powerful polemic. But it cannot sustain its own weight. While Drabble takes issue with the manifold evils of our lives, her characters belie her humanity and weaken her argument. Their disintegration, when it comes, seems arbitrary and unbelievable in its scale. There is sound, there is fury, but the just society remains as nebulous as ever, fading into the struggle for individual survival. Can there be any hope? The moral stands, bleakly reductive: 'Everything dwindles, everything shrinks. A blue ballgown hangs limp on a brass rail in the Oxfam shop.'

EVERY MAN FOR HIMSELF
Beryl Bainbridge (1997)

Beryl Bainbridge's marvellous new novel chronicles the *Titanic*'s fatal maiden voyage in April 1912. This colossal floating palace, the biggest vessel in the world, was deemed unsinkable. Morgan, the 22-year-old narrator, nephew of the owner of the shipping line, is no stranger to splendour: 'For us there was nothing new under the sun, nothing, that is, in the way of opulence.' But the ship's engines are another matter, inspiring hubristic speculation: 'If the fate of man was connected to the order of the universe, and if one could equate the scientific workings of the engines with just such a reciprocal universe, why then, nothing could go wrong with my world.' When the *Titanic* hit an iceberg four days out into the Atlantic, 1,500 people drowned. Morgan survived to know unease, guilt and a sense of dishonour at his very survival.

The novel opens deceptively, presenting what seems a pastiche of Conan Doyle or even Buchan. On a spring morning in Manchester Square, an unknown man dies in the narrator's arms, passing onto him a photograph of an oriental lady. A couple of days later, and Morgan is breakfasting by Southampton Docks. Across the room are three people only, a swarthy foreigner, a beautiful distraught woman and a scar-faced, smooth-talking fellow. On board they meet, mingle and are party to alarming coincidences; clues are thinly scattered and mysteries unravel with the logic of dreams. Indeed, the whole book has a chimerical effect. Half a dozen characters occupy the foreground; others shift in and out of focus, flirting, gossiping, linked in a *danse macabre* against their glittering backdrop.

Morgan joins in the manic conviviality. He is often drunk. His head hurts. Snatches of conversation, remembered precepts, prefigured cries of terror bombinate about his skull. He is looking for a direction in life, questioning his uncle's maxim that 'a man has two reasons for the thing he does, a good one and the real one'. He has brushed with Marxism and has a wavering sympathy for the under-privileged, derived partly from his own, only half-revealed, origins. None the less the passengers in steerage remain faceless, huddled masses and he has no qualms in insulting members of the crew who may seem to step out of line.

Bainbridge's last book, *The Birthday Boys*, celebrated and lamented an ideal of masculinity, a way of being and seeing, which ended with the First World War. Here she examines another side of that society, the entrenched social attitudes of the upper classes, the snobbery of the wealthy, their small excoriating unkindnesses. The great ship itself forms a metaphor for society, with its reserved upper decks, its rejection of the steerage class who may be viewed with condescension from above as they whoop and swoop through Highland reels. Just after the collision comes an especially Breughelian glimpse of the rabble: 'Coming to the starboard rail I looked down on to the well of the third class recreation area; there were chunks of ice spilling and sliding in every direction, all shapes and sizes, glittering under the light of the foremast. Steerage passengers, most in their ragged night-clothes, were chucking it at each other as though playing snowballs'. Very soon, the rich young Englishman with 'nothing to do save ride round the family estate with a gun under his arm, waiting for his father to die' and the black-faced stoker and the young mother 'carrying an infant, a shawl over her breast, the tiny fingers of the child caught like a brooch in the wool' are in the same boat for good and all.

Bainbridge does not attempt to assign blame for the catastrophe and its aftermath. 'We was just going too fast and not heeding the ice warnings,' says one of the crew. The ship should not have been allowed to sail in the first place; one of its bunkers was on fire in Southampton and continued to blaze throughout the voyage, diverting manpower from other tasks. The technicalities of releasing the lifeboats led to delay and the immense drop meant that some of them could only be partly occupied for fear of rupture. The size of the ship also made for communication problems, so that many people were unaware of their acute danger until too late. There are no conclusions beyond those which speak for themselves.

Despite its lavish setting, its sharp and satisfying dialogue and its decent, youthful narrator, this is a much bleaker book than *The Birthday Boys*. There Bainbridge presented heroism, gallantry, aspiration and comradeship. Here too there is heroism, but there is also complacency, greed and cynicism; every man for himself in a Ship of Fools. The exquisite pacing of the narrative, the hints of foreboding, the stunning descriptions of the cataclysm itself build up a tragedy, not of the individual, but of warped, muddled, perverse humanity. The sense of desolation is so great that the eventual approach of the rescuing ship *Carpathia* seems almost an irrelevance, jauntily corporeal in the hallucinatory world of the ice floes, the flotsam and the tiny boats of the survivors.

THE UNTOUCHABLE
John Banville (1997)

John Banville's new novel is the memoir and self-portrait of a disgraced former spy, who has been Keeper of the Queen's pictures, Director of the Institute (Art) and an eminence in the Department (Foreign Affairs). He is not called Anthony Blunt; his name is Victor Maskell.

In old age Maskell broods and muses over a life of treachery and seeks his own betrayer. He discovers that he was never trusted, that his leaked information was of little value, that he was a pawn in the game he thought he controlled. Now he has lost everything; even his treasured Poussin, the one constant love of his life, may not be authentic. There is nothing to do but gratify his children by dying: 'Why do the young always think it better that the old should be dead?'

Like many scholars he had a vague yearning for a life of action; after Cambridge and the Apostles the spy business seemed an amusing pastime, blending harmoniously with his other activities. His friends of course were all doing it too. But unlike his friends Maskell has no political allegiance. Accused of having betrayed everything, he is able to reply: 'What you mean by everything is nothing to me. To be capable of betraying someone you must first believe in it.' At the moment of his recruitment, certainly, he is aware of a 'brief tumescence in the air'; he is also aware that this is a game, exciting but ludicrous. When a Russian comrade describes atrocities in the war against the Whites, Maskell nods in grim complicity, but 'just below the lid of my sobriety there was squeezed a cackle of disgraceful laughter, as if there were a merry little elf curled up inside me, hand clapped to mouth and cheeks bulging and weasel eyes malignantly aglitter'.

For him, the fall of Barcelona in the Spanish Civil War and Poussin's 'Capture of Jerusalem' have the same significance; they are both 'remote, complete. All frozen cry and rampant steed and stylised, gorgeous cruelty'. Cruelty has appealed to him from infancy; his brother, born with brain damage, was his first silent, defenceless victim. His native Ireland, his father, his stepmother, his home are all shrugged off; so too his wife and children, his only continuing relationships are with fellow spies and dissenters. He is seduced by Danny, his friend Boy's lover ('Welcome to the Homintern,' cries Boy) and he pursues his new sexual career with unflagging appetite, later he wonders if women realise 'how deeply, viscerally, *sorrowfully* men hate them.'

The world of Queerdom and the world of espionage converge; by night he goes 'prowling in mad excitement, with his dark desires and his country's secrets clutched to his breast'. By day, for order and silence and tranquillity he turns to art, to his monograph on Poussin (20 years in the writing), to the great collections at Windsor and at the Institute. For these he cares as he cares not and will not care for people.

Cold, snobbish, cruel, fastidious, Maskell is a horror. One might entirely weary of him were it not for his occasional inklings, bewildered apprehensions of another world from which he is excluded. Catching sight of his wife's engorged breasts beneath her bedjacket he is consumed by anguished pity; just twice he finds himself weeping silently, uncontrollably. And at a lover's sleepy smile, 'something opened in me, briefly, as if a little window had been thrown open on to a vast, far, dark, deserted plain.'

Banville excels and exults in such moments, when 'something snags and stops, turning and turning, like a leaf on a stream.' Wind and weather, sunlight and the great passing clouds shadow, illuminate and overlay the grim and acerbic narrative. The prose is stunning; every sentence is perfectly judged in length and weight, every simile is piercingly apposite; a faint, familiar shock is 'like a sootfall in a chimney'.

There are occasional oddities – a curious number of comparisons involving dead animals, an excess of descriptions of poor, kind, Hettie the stepmother – as beast of burden, as big old bag of bones, as sorrowing old buffalo, and as settling into a car with a 'henlike subsidence'. On the other hand, they are too good to waste. The language is formal and dense, intoxicating in its precision. 'A thick drop of sunlight seethed in a glass paperweight on a low table.' Words like flocculent, oneiric, brumous and umbrage shed a sombre glow.

Like the earlier *Dr Copernicus, Kepler* and *The Newton Letter*, *The Untouchable* mixes fictional and historical truth. The accumulated detail of characters and situation makes for a strange sense of half-recognition, of *déjà vu*. There are echoes of Conrad, of Waugh, of Patrick Hamilton and of Graham Greene (who appears, disguised, in various outfits, but notable in a high-shouldered dark brown suit which reminds the narrator of an HP sauce bottle).

Fog shrouds the streetlamps, inscrutable figures move into doorways, coat collars turned up, hat brims lowered. There is a great deal of drinking and a charming disquisition on smoking as a Watteau-esque activity.

While at the core of the book, at the heart of Maskell, there is a desolation, an icy vacuum, its literary delights are overwhelming, a verbal demonstration of Poussin's requirements of a painting: 'It is an imitation of anything that is to be seen under the sun, done with lines and colour. Its end is delectation.'

GRACE NOTES
Bernard MacLaverty (1997)

After five years of wilful absence, Catherine is home for her father's funeral in a small town near Belfast. She finds the buildings sheeted in polythene, bristling with scaffolding, bombed out by the IRA. She remembers from childhood the Orangemen and their drumming contests up on the high cross-roads, the drums so huge that it took two men to harness each drummer; she remembers the overwhelming noise. 'They practise out here above the town to let the Catholics know they're in charge. This is their way of saying the Prods rule the roost,' says her father. 'You're looking at a crowd whose highest ambition, this year and every year, is to march down streets where they're not wanted. Nothing to do with the betterment of mankind or the raising of the human spirit.' Catherine is not attending. She is distinguishing the left beat from the right, her body and soul vibrating, filled and thrilled by the sound.

This is not a book about the Irish Question. Nor is it, as the blurb suggests, a book about coming to terms with the past. In clear, simple prose, sometimes modestly colloquial, sometimes sombre and elegiac, MacLaverty examines abstraction and paradox, the simplicity of the complex, the collective voice which may extinguish or confirm the importance of the individual, the possibility of transubstantiation through art. So many anxieties and speculations jostle with memory and reflection in Catherine's weary head. Now she is in her twenties and gaining recognition as a composer. She has a baby daughter and a discarded lover. She lives in Glasgow, suffering from post-natal depression. Recently and against many odds she has seen her first symphony performed in triumph.

The first part of this beautifully structured book deals with Catherine's three days in Ireland; the second moves back a couple of years to cover the baby's birth, the developing depression and the writing of the symphony. The account of Catherine's state is awry and shocking: her heartbeat muffled between her ear and her pillow, her mind racing into the abyss. 'Inside a boiled egg there was a skin. Thin as tracing paper. If you cracked and crazypaved the shell and peeled it off then beneath that was the skin. You could tear it. A membrane. Like the fontanel . . . .Think of something else. Leave yourself alone. You're worrying about worrying. I am thinking about what I do not want to think about.'

Music, the mirror of her life, will be her salvation. Remembered images reform as incidents, metamorphose into musical phrases. The hundreds and thousands sprinkled on cakes for the funeral tea become the lights of Glasgow seen from the night sky. A group of monks moves singing out of a great empty workroom in Kiev; their voices fade into silence. Four Orangemen drum their way down the side aisles of a church in Scotland; and slowly the drum-beats die away. A school experiment with candle flames quenched by carbon dioxide serves as a metaphor of her depression: 'She felt the darkness of the bright days descending on her, step by step.' Everything is woven into the symphony, and like the symphony the book has the symmetry of a hinged scallop shell.

Catherine can no longer believe in the Catholic dogma of her girlhood; but if substance is more important than form, then music may take its place. 'I can see music as the grace of God,' says Melnichuck, her Russian mentor: 'Through all the communist times they did not allow religion. For us music was a way of praying, music was a way of receiving God's grace.' At last, listening to her symphony, she finds herself filled with the knowledge of that grace.

Although this is an inward novel, the external world is vividly presented. MacLaverty bestows the same grave courtesy upon the hot-water bottle and tea-caddy as on the dark night of the soul or the nature of composition. There is something of Dante here, in his effortless movement from the plangent to the domestic or bizarre. A friend's husband is a quantity surveyor. 'Catherine asked her what exactly a quantity surveyor did. "He surveys quantities."' MacLaverty's ear for dialogue is impeccable – and for the gaps between the words.

There are no facile conclusions. Although the ending is triumphant, we know from the beginning that Catherine's depression will continue, that music cannot alter the catalogue of man's inhumanity. But we do also believe in the power of creation to transmute suffering into celebration, 'a joy that celebrates being human. A joy that celebrates its own reflection, its own ability to make joy, to reproduce.' Catherine calls her symphony 'Vernicle'. A vernicle is worn by a pilgrim, testimony to his journeyings. 'I have been there,' it proclaims. 'I have done this.' In the same way, Catherine sees her work as a token of her living; she has made something exist; it was not there before. She remembers too 'the childish awe of stepping on fresh snow, of marking it with her small foot'.

I have to say it. This is a marvellous book.

VITA BREVIS
A letter to St Augustine
Jostein Gaarder (1997)

'I went to Carthage where I found myself in the midst of a hissing cauldron of lust.' So begins the third book of the Confessions of St Augustine, with an opening sentence as memorable as any. As an 18-year-old student Augustine plunged vigorously into 'rank depravity'; at last however he fell in love with an unnamed young woman of limited means. For 12 years they and their son lived together, in Africa and in Italy, until Augustine, now professor of rhetoric in Milan, conceived an ambitious marriage and renounced his mistress. He claimed that his choice was forced upon him and it was 'a blow which crushed my heart to bleeding for I loved her dearly'.

She returned to Africa, leaving her son behind. Augustine, frustrated by the prospect of a two-year wait before his wedding, took another mistress. In the event he never married: after so many years of agonising over the nature of God, faith and doubt, original sin, worldliness and the senses, he underwent conversion and was baptised. He returned to Africa, became Bishop of Hippo and devoted his long life to pastoral duties, writing his extraordinary books and fiercely campaigning against heresy and enemies of the Church. In 430 he died, in the midst of the Vandals' siege of Hippo, 20 years after Rome had fallen to Alaric.

Jostein Gaarder offers us this *Vita Brevis* in a cheerful, take-it-or-leave-it spirit. He purports to have found a bundle of papers in a secondhand bookshop in Buenos Aires and to have recognised them as the possible transcript of a letter to St Augustine from his discarded mistress, here called Floria Aemilia. He claims that he took the documents to the Vatican, who later denied all knowledge of them. 'I had naturally taken care to make a copy of the MS,' but, less naturally, 'it was incredibly naive of me not to ask the Vatican Library for a receipt at least!' I think the exclamation mark gives the avuncular game away. But what's in a game, from the author of *Sophie's World*?

The epistle is arranged in 10 sections, roughly corresponding to the first 10 books of the Confessions; which Floria has been reading. She reproaches Augustine, violently at times, for rejecting her in favour of his own salvation. She questions his precepts, especially the redemptive power of abstinence, and defends the pleasures of the senses, pleasures given by God, who may or may not exist. She will not be baptised so long as she sees theology triumph over earthly love, repressing the physical joys of the world, tarnishing the infant with original sin.

So far, so good. Initially one feels for her and her cruel dismissal, and the absolute loss of her son who died when he was 15. But Floria makes the same points over and again and she is too fond of citing Horace, who as a self-confessed 'sleek pig from an Epicurean sty' makes an inappropriate ally. Gradually she alienates the reader by her patronising tone and her arch, cutesy turns of phrase. Up flashes the exclamation mark again, casting a creepy negative glow. 'So many heads, Aurel, so many opinions!' 'Poor Aurel! How ashamed you are of being a man, you who were my little stallion.' And, most gruesomely: 'Do you think some parts of the human body are less worthy of God than others? for instance, is your middle finger more neutral than your tongue? You did use your finger too!' You begin to feel that he was well out of it.

Augustine was deeply moved by the fourth book of the Aeneid, which tells the tragic story of Aeneas's entanglement with Dido, Queen of Carthage. Floria makes much of herself as a latter-day Dido, and there are parallels. They both spent time in Carthage, fell in love with men who were in search of a higher destiny and were abandoned. But there the resemblance ends. Dido is a tragic heroine of raw, desperate truthfulness. Floria is smug and self-regarding; her undoubted suffering does not impinge. Bad luck, have another fig.

Still, this short book is lively, readable and prettily produced, with an abundance of very explanatory footnotes which occasionally run into prime lunacy. This is my favourite:

'The expression "hen-pecked" (*tøffelhelt*: "slipper hero" in Norwegian) existed as far back as late antiquity. However, I have been unable to find any occurrence of the word either in dictionaries or in any text from late antiquity. Here Floria uses the word "crepundia" which should probably be translated as "rattle" (a child's toy) or "bangles" or "baubles", from "crepo", rattle, jangle or clatter. But cf also "crepida", a Greek sandal, a derivative of the same verb! Directly translated then, Floria describes Aurel as Abstinence's "bauble". I have chosen a freer translation, the Norwegian "slipper hero", for Floria's "crepundia". [I have rendered the Norwegian as English "hen-pecked". Translator].'

Conceivably, *Vita Brevis* might direct a few readers towards St Augustine's Confessions, if not, alas, to Gaarder's objective, 'a renewal of interest in the Latin language and in classical culture as a whole'. It remains a pleasant *jeu d'esprit*, even if Floria isn't up to the game.

CASANOVA
Andrew Miller (1998)

In this glittering confection of 18th century *moeurs*, Andrew Miller focuses on a few months in the life of the fabled seducer who, in 1763, came somewhat whimsically to England in search of rest and reflection while in exile from his native Venice. Miller tells us that the story is in part based on Casanova's own memoirs, but is mainly an invention.

The Casanova presented here is a vain, amiable hedonist who at 39 is suffering from intimations of mortality; bored and fearful, he must seek new conquests and confirm past triumphs, for he has glimpsed himself 'sitting with his make up smudged, waiting for the next performance'. But his prey eludes him and it is in the ensuing dark night of the soul that humiliation and mortification drive him first to the doubtful joys of honest toil, then to a flirtation with writing and then to an unpleasant sample of country life. After a not very long time he is back in London, gaming and whoring and still pursuing the scornful and combative object of his desire. No change.

Once upon a time he did re-create himself, changing from illegitimate street child to 'exactly what the silk-wearing classes had needed: a truly accommodating fellow with a scrap of genius who, like a Venetian canal, was all the more charming on account of his corruption, the shimmer of his pollution'. This first invention and work of artifice have exhausted his resources.

The Hogarthian background is vividly drawn and spotlit by tiny details: a ferryman smoking his pipe upside down in the rain; Dr

Johnson's cat, 'a creature about the size of a pedlar's knapsack'; prophylactics made from sheep-gut which, when in use, smelt of roast lamb; four blind musicians, each carrying an instrument in one hand and resting the other on the shoulder of the man in front. There are descriptive passages of extraordinary power and beauty: the city drowned in a mighty flood, the construction of Blackfriars Bridge, an outdoor coupling performed as 'gods and sparrows did it, clenched under the public sky, racked by the moment'.

Yet, despite such piercing joys, or even because of them, this is a disappointing and unsatisfying book. Casanova himself is a two-dimensional creature, too shallow and self-absorbed to engage sympathy. His night of tortured self-examination and its sequel just don't convince; his actions and the actions of those around him often seem merely arbitrary, and one doesn't care what happens to any of them. It is hard to accept that the Casanova depicted here could have caught the interest of Dr Johnson, or indeed achieved his own haunted notoriety. His observations on life and love are banal and his twinkly-old-roué tone of voice is acutely irritating. 'Munich! Where every card had been a losing card and that little dancer, La Renaud, had stolen his clothes and his jewels and infected him with a vile disease. Exquisite pain.' There is a lot of this sort of stuff. Casanova does not speak English although it is his voice which dominates the book; perhaps this is why some of the prose is oddly awkward and laboured, tipped off balance by clumsy relative clauses. Then beyond every dazzling image or comparison lurks some far-fetched, unworkable simile: dawn 'showing one by one, like an auctioneer, the things . . . of the world' or an old clavichord which grins 'gap toothed, like some man's mistress put out to grass when he could no longer bear the sight of her'. Meanwhile the phrase 'ate gratefully' and the adverb 'grimly' bode no good. And yet, so much must be forgiven of an author who can see a pink gloved hand as a glamorous piglet or describe Casanova's mind 'anaesthetised by drink, by gambling, curled inside his head like a dog in dreamless sleep'.

Is it possible that this book has been written too swiftly? If so, *porca miseria*, as its hero would say. For despite its flaws, at its best it confirms the unshakeable certainty which possesses anyone who has read Miller's marvellous *Ingenious Pain*: that here is a writer of very rare and outstanding gifts, no matter what.

LAVINIA
Ursula Le Guin (2009)

Virgil's women are fabulous, both literally and colloquially. Throughout the Aeneid, they bring about confusion, high drama, tenderness and tragedy, a shining counterpoint and interruption to the background of war and travail, past, present and to come, and the immutable forces of destiny which of course engulf them too, struggle as they may to thwart them. In the earlier books we encounter Venus, on one occasion clad in high scarlet leather boots, ghostly Creusa, towering, tragic Dido; later come the enchantress Circe, Camilla the warrior Princess, so fleet of foot that she can pass through a cornfield and not disturb a single blade, assorted Nereids, nurses, mothers, and female personifications of vileness. And in that throng someone scarcely visible, Lavinia, in the words of the great Gilbert Highet, 'a quiet, dutiful, passive little girl.'

This is Ursula Le Guin's heartfelt offering to Virgil, a *munus* in the Roman tradition of a gift to the honoured dead. She has dispensed with 'the literary machinery of the Pantheon,' and using Virgil as her guide to setting and events has brought Lavinia out of her strange obscurity, strange because Lavinia's destiny, confirmed by oracles and supernatural events, was to be an unwilling cause of war in her native Latium, to marry Aeneas himself and to bear him a son; their descendants would be the founders of Rome. Yet Virgil gives her scant mention; she has rosy cheeks and blonde hair. She has suitors but she must marry Aeneas. And that's it. He gives ten lines to the ominous swarm of bees that sags black through the palace laurel tree but just five to the one dramatic moment of her youthful life, when her hair catches fire. Dryden's translation likewise makes little of it, 'and lambent Glories danced about her head.' Her nasty mother Amata receives more attention; there is a marvellous scene in Aeneid Seven when Allecto, the Fury most hated by other Furies, gaily flings one of the snakes that drip and drop from her metallic blue locks into Amata's bosom where it writhes into the gold torque on her neck, into her headbands, driving her to Bacchanalian frenzy and ultimately suicide by hanging. Le Guin gives us the madness, the drinking and the death but not the Fury, an opportunity sadly missed, albeit by choice. But she provides poor overshadowed Lavinia with a life in a normal girlish world, enhanced by trips at twilight to the oracle's shrine in the forest of Albunea. There she meets the ghost of Virgil, who has not yet been born but is about to die, and she comes to realize that her existence depends entirely on her acknowledgement by others especially by the vatic poet. She is simply contingent. The good side of this is that she cannot die, presumably so long as Virgil is read. But her importance will never be personal; she has a tiny part only in the great scheme of others. Virgil tells her of the past and the future and noble, pious Aeneas, and he says quite a few other, less helpful things, like 'Maybe I am a bat that has flown here from Hades. A dream that has flown into a dream. Into my poem.' Lavinia is given to this sort of talk too. 'I am a fleck of light on the surface of the sea, a glint of light from the evening star.' Occasionally she accosts the bemused reader 'I know who I was, I can tell you who I may have been, but I am, now, only in this line of words I write' or 'I am not the feminine voice you may have expected.' The shade of Toni Morrison hovers hard by. For instance Virgil and Lavinia have some dreadful conversations: 'He looked across the dark air at me and I could tell he was smiling. "Oh my dear," he said, still very softly, "My unfinished, my incomplete, my unfulfilled. Child I never had."' Equally calamitous are later glimpses of happy married life with Aeneas (untold by the Aeneid which stops abruptly with the death of Lavinia's cousin and suitor Turnus); here the couple are enjoying warm milk and white figs, here they admire the cutesy lisping of baby Silvius who is helping to prepare a sacred offering, '"Only the beans, Silvius" she whispered, and he, very solemn, said "Ony bees"'.

This is a maddening novel of opportunity wasted, and not merely over the snake in the bosom. It is extraordinary that a writer of Le Guin's intelligence and strength of voice, as witnessed by her recent review of Stefan Zweig in these very pages, should produce so nebulous a book. Lavinia, while pleasant enough, just doesn't have normal reactions; perhaps it's because of her contingency. The opening scene, when the huge alien ships turn up the river from the sea, should be freighted with fear, the knowledge of what is to come, but it is simply lyrical. And certainly Le Guin writes most beautiful descriptive prose. But the huge issues of *fas* and *nefas*, sacrilegious right and wrong, of conflicting piety, destiny and choice, the blind horrors of war, the nature of blood lust, *furor*, are touched upon but not moved into the central positions they demand. Wonderful sentences lead to nothing: 'What is left after death? Everything else. The sun a man saw rise goes down though he does not see it set. A woman sits down to the weaving another woman left in the loom.' This is immediately followed by a passage of typical Lavinian maundering; over and over, nothing impinges, nothing save one recurring image: a dove is tethered to a pole on a rope long enough for her to strive and stretch her wings to flutter upward only to be jerked back, over and again until she is fatally pierced by the arrows of the archers below. Target practice.

In the pessimistic afterword Le Guin speaks of the demise of Latin and thus of Virgil. I do not believe this to be so; a slow but discernible revival of interest in this most beautiful of languages is apparent here in England. Latin lives yet, and Virgil; Lavinia shall not die! Even though she has, in a manner unexplained either by Virgil or Ursula Le Guin, mutated into a little owl.

COUNTING THE STARS
Helen Dunmore (2008)

Latinity is in vogue, with an abundance of classically situated novels for children, novels for adults, historical constructions, feminist deconstructions, historical re-appraisals, horticultural treatises, and even, whisper it, do-it-yourself language manuals, drawn up in colourful array along the bookshop shelves, although that language remains sadly absent from the nation's classrooms.

And so, timely and pleasurable it is, in bleak midwinter, to drift through a couple of Roman summers half a century before Christ, and revisit Catullus's doomed romance with the woman he called Lesbia. The known facts are few. Catullus was born about 84 BC to a landowning family from Verona. He died about 54 BC and spent most of his life in Rome, where under the patronage of Memmius he developed a reputation as a poetic innovator, renouncing the old epic tradition and circulating verses of dazzling immediacy and extreme sophistication, addressed to friends, enemies, places and a door. Their most perfect expression is found in his poems for Lesbia.

Lesbia's real name was Clodia Metelli: Catullus chose her literary name to protect her identity and to compliment her as a *puella docta*, a young woman of wit, education and literary ability, to be compared, albeit distantly, with the great and legendary Sappho, whose works shaped and inspired Catullus's own. His very first poem to Lesbia is a version of a poem of Sappho's, and the name Lesbia has the same metric quantity as Clodia. Clodia Metelli, the woman Catullus declared he loved more than any woman ever had been loved, the woman who inspired the famous 'Odi et Amo' and some of the most beautiful love lyrics ever written, was a married woman from a patrician family, ten years his senior, and the possibly incestuous sister of Clodius Pulcher, a notorious aristocratic gangster.

Clodia was notorious too: Cicero, that pillar of republican probity, defending one of her former lovers in court, refers to her with elegant obliquity as 'a woman who has always been widely regarded as having no enemies since she so readily offers intimacy in all directions'. And Clodius, 'the woman's husband – sorry, I mean brother, I always make that slip – is my personal enemy'. In the end of course she was too much for everyone, most of all Catullus.

Helen Dunmore's poetic sensibility is well suited to presenting the vivid background to this volatile affair. Rome's sultry, stinking alleyways, cool courts and fountains, bitter winters and glaring summer light form the backdrop to a jittery society where there is no certitude, and love, truth, and loyalty are as much commodities as slaves. Her narrative, strung lightly across a framework made from the poems, moves in sensuous leisure. There are glittering set pieces, most notably a boating picnic and a patrician funeral; the landscape is exquisitely realised – 'his fear grows like the evening shadow of an umbrella pine, sprawling until it swallows a field'. There are casual horrors, torture and murder, familial affection, dead dogs, and phallocentric afternoons – just your everyday life in ancient Rome.

It is tempting to find parallels here with our own world and inevitably there are common joys and sorrows, but the difference of aspiration and expectation is enormous. They really weren't, and aren't, just like us, despite Catullus's immediacies. How could they be? Their otherness is inadvertently pointed up by the perennial difficulty of rendering historical dialogue convincingly. Senators are clichéd old buffers with lines like 'no doubt she's a damned fine woman'. Our hero dismisses a rival poet with 'that bastard is enough to make tradition cower like a slave before a beating'. Oh, please. And there's an awful lot of tiresome quasi-foul mouthery: 'Shafted, both of them. A right royal shafting they've had.' There are ghastly phrases like 'serious party animals' and a most tedious and unrelenting play on people's nicknames or cognomens, 'Pretty Boy' for Pulcher, 'Old Chick Pea' for Cicero and so forth. Most citizens' cognomens involved some form of the personal (Naso – The Nose; Calvus – Bald, etc) and would not be worth harping on about. The unvarying translation of *mea puella* as 'my girl' also becomes irksome, as, most seriously, do the improper renderings of certain famous lines and phrases: *nox est perpetua una dormienda* ('there is one endless night for sleeping') is given as 'night is forever sleep'. The fabulously beautiful lines

>   *lingua sed torpet, tenuis sub artus*
>   *flamma demanat, sonitu suopte*
>   *tintinant aures ...*

are translated:

>   *I can't speak,*
>   *thin fire runs over me,*
>   *my ears pound*
>   *with the thunder of my blood ...*

This rendering ignores the original nouns lingua and artus, the phrase sonitu suopte, and the verb torpet, and introduces words which simply aren't there – thunder and blood. This should not be happening and it happens several times; once is too often.

If one sees the book as a wall painting, executed in the serial manner beloved of the Romans, moving along to its highly effective and darkling end, in two-dimensional colour and imagery, it works pleasantly enough. But the characters are stereotypes: they do not develop, their voices are distorted; they are forced into anachronism, the sum is anodyne. As MacNeice observed, 'It was all so unimaginably different / And all so long ago.' Catullus says everything that needs to be said with such power, economy, grace and wit that other versions of his story may be redundant. His is the triumphant last word:

>   *At non effugies meos iambos.*

And by the way, Roman make-up was not water-soluble.

A MERCY
Toni Morrison (2008)

'Ordinary people in an extraordinary time' proclaims the back cover in block capitals. This tale of everyday folk in late 17th century Virginia and Maryland may surprise those who have not previously read Toni Morrison. 'Don't be afraid', it opens. 'My telling can't hurt you in spite of what I have done and I promise to lie quietly in the dark – weeping perhaps or occasionally seeing the blood once more – but I will never again unfold my limbs to rise up and bare teeth.' Others, familiar with this writer, may find the first page of *A Mercy* rich in self-parody, while aficionados will abandon themselves joyfully to its weird, inconsequent stream of consciousness, imagery and oddity. Visual oddity – 'when a dog's profile plays in the steam of a kettle'; linguistic oddity – 'the wicked of how it got there' or 'if a peahen refuses to brood I read it quickly'. Who is this giddy narrator talking to? What is going on? We are none the wiser until page 97, which is too long to wait. By then, some will have put the book aside in dudgeon. It is insulting for a reader to be dragged into a threatening and fathomless quagmire and left to sink or swim. The phrase 'a minha mae' occurs from time to time; one assumes some sort of witch. At last one deduces it is Portuguese for 'my mother' but it's not even printed in italics. Did you know 'a' is the Portuguese for 'the'? Well, I didn't.

The second chapter initially bodes better. The third person narrative comes as a relief, as it describes one Jakob Vaark wading ashore. 'Fog, Atlantic and reeking of plant life, blanketed the bay and slowed him.' Fabulous. But as Jakob continues his complex journey to a luncheon engagement, hiring a horse, considering the turbulent history of the times, freeing a trapped racoon, reflecting on the offensiveness of Popery and the vileness of the slave trade, it becomes clear that Morrison is ill at ease. She cannot handle straight narrative. The writing is stiff, over-explanatory, often clumsy and astonishingly amateur. 'Upon entering this privately-owned country, his feelings fought one another to a draw.' He is dazzled by his host's mansion: 'He had heard how grand it was, but could not have been prepared for what lay before him.' A decent man, an independent farmer and entrepreneur, he returns to his wife and home in the North fired by ambition for a great house of his own, to be financed by dubious dabbling in the sugar trade. 'A remote labor force in Barbados' need not trouble his conscience. With him travels a young child, part payment for a debt, the slave-born Florens, entrusted to him by her anguished mother.

Time moves on, the house is built, but Jakob cannot live in it for suddenly he is dead, taken by smallpox. His wife too lies stricken and she sends 16-year-old Florens to fetch a mysterious blacksmith who once healed the crazed slave Sorrow from a plague of boils. Florens loves the blacksmith, who is a free man, with all that phrase implies. No good can come of it. But her journey and return form the thread which binds the loose ends of the novel, woven from stories of each member of the household, Rebekka, the mistress, outcast from England, Lina, a native American servant or slave (I don't know which; nothing is clear in this book), wild Sorrow with her silver eyes, red hair, and black skin, flung up by the sea, Florens herself, rejected, as she sees it, by her mother. We have the story of Jakob too, and of a couple of casual white male labourers. But the real substance is the experiences of the women, whose lives are lived in terms of and for men so entirely that Rebekka can reflect that her strict Baptist neighbours and her former louche and criminal shipmates have 'everything in common, with one thing; the promise and threat of men.' Yet with Jakob and Rebekka the three slave girls know safety and kindness. Florens's mother had seen Jakob's decency, his willingness to take her child, as a near-miraculous chance, the mercy of the book's title. After Jakob's death, the women realise that their illusory family, forged by companionship and isolation, is lost. Greater than that sense of familial loss and yearning is their common 'Mother-hunger – to be one or have one.' This, more than time, place, or circumstance, is the driving force of all their lives. They seek and find and lose mothers and children, calling up memory and ghosts and the unborn, in language that is powerful and poetic, reminiscent of *Beloved*, Morrison's great novel, which is set 200 years later, but which treats with many of the same themes – slavery and its 'pathless and terrible terrain', familial yearning, women's need for men despite themselves, babies lost and saved, desires unfulfilled and questions unanswered.

But in *Beloved* there is a consistency of narrative voice beyond the testaments of individuals, which sweeps the reader along, at times overwhelming, but never bewildering. *A Mercy* reads almost like notes for this earlier work, matching it now and then in power and lyric beauty: 'Sudden a sheet of sparrows fall from the sky and settle in the trees. So many the trees seem to sprout birds, not leaves at all.' Or 'What about the boneless bears in the valley? Remember? How when they move their pelts sway as though there is nothing underneath?' Such images abound but these marvels only offset the turgid discomforts of the narrative, the indulgent babbling, the weird modernisms. Sorrow has 'unbelievable and slightly threatening hair.' Florens, who speaks in inscrutable idiolect – 'I know the claws of the feathered thing did break out on you because I cannot stop them wanting to tear you open the way you tear me' – suddenly remarks in the tone of a millennial social worker, 'I like her devotion to her baby girl.' Most maddening of all is the technique which Morrison uses also in *Beloved*; she sets up a scene or a tiny incident and then abandons it, so that the reader is left baffled, plodding trustfully on, referring back, made to feel stupid, then cross, then insensitive for feeling cross. For example, we are suddenly told that Sorrow often goes to the river to talk to her dead baby. There has been absolutely no word of this dead baby and there is no further mention of it for another 60 pages. Morrison of course does this on purpose. In a new foreword to *Beloved* she has written 'I wanted the reader to be kidnapped, thrown ruthlessly into an alien environment as the first step into a shared experience with the book's population – just as the characters were snatched from one place to another, from any place to another, without preparation or defense.' This works in *Beloved* where the narrative, natural and supernatural, flows in its grand tidal sweep, but it doesn't work here in this much shorter book. To make sense of *A Mercy* you must read it twice; you may not wish to do this. It is a muddle, and despite all its discordant striving its real theme seems to me to hark back again to *Beloved* and another definition of mercy: 'Softly, suddenly, it began to snow, like a present come down from the sky. Sethe opened her eyes to it and said "Mercy." And it seemed to Paul D that it was – a little mercy – something given to them on purpose to mark what they were feeling so that they would remember it later on when they needed to.' There is the simplicity and the truthfulness, wilfully lost in this new book.

THE GOOD PARENTS
Joan London (2009)

The title may seem foreboding. Does it suggest that this is just a phrase, decorative, like Christmas cheer, but lacking in practical application and moral truth? This fine novel examines familial relationships from every point of view, uncritically exposing the devouring needs of visceral love and the guile, indifference and resource deployed by its objects in their necessary bids for escape, set against backgrounds of cosmopolitan Melbourne, a small country town, a beach-house, a forest, a tea-plantation in Ceylon, all wonderfully realised.

The story begins in 2000. Young Maya, newly come from semi-rural life to Melbourne, is in love with her middle-aged boss. His wife dies and he persuades her to leave with him and his business associate, the mysterious, half-seen Mr T, to some unspecified destination. Off she goes on her adventure, vanishing without trace. Her parents, Jacob and Toni, arrive on the Melbourne visit they have all planned. Maya's housemate, Cecile, insists that they stay on with her in the hope that Maya will soon return. She does not return. Weeks pass; the police are unhelpful, desperation and terror possess the parents. Day by day, they search the city to no avail. Jacob wrenches his foot in a grating and is confined to the house. This is a masterly touch. How often does someone closely involved in a family disaster suddenly disable himself. And I say himself advisedly. Jacob passes the time in considering his past, questioning his assumptions and illusions. He drinks red wine and conceives a modest infatuation for Cecile. Toni likewise on her lonely perambulations looks back to her own life, beginning at the moment in her schooldays when she stepped into a stranger's black Citroen and everything changed. At Maya's age she herself disappeared, to marry her enigmatic stranger, and only met her mother very occasionally for lunch in a department store. 'I keep thinking I see you,' her mother would say. This meant nothing to Toni.

Back then, Jacob had been reading Tolstoy instead of swotting for his exams, telling himself that he preferred art to life. He moved on into the 70s, grew his hair, rolled joints, tried to write. Now he is aware that what he still calls 'the Tolstoy factor', and others would call work displacement, may have brought him an artistic vision but it had also made him distrust himself. Unable to do anything practical about his missing daughter, he smokes dope with Cecile's nasty friend Dieter whom he has recognised as his natural born enemy, a member of Generation X. He admires the stars. Dieter sneers, 'You guys are so cosmic with your drugs.' 'Why do you smoke then?' asks Jacob. 'To relax, to watch porn on the Internet. Get into music.' There is much reference here to the importance of generation. Magnus, Maya's younger brother, makes a compilation tape to further a middle-aged romance, 'Leonard always sent that generation wild.' Toni, in her wretchedness, goes off to an ashram outside Melbourne, a truly 70s enterprise. She returns shaven-headed with a nebulous desire for 'a lightness on the face of the earth' and a life apart from Jacob. She admits she still doesn't know what she means by 'good'. And they both have always intended to be good. Jacob, too, has inklings of a new life where he will shed the parental role, and show his real self. But the moment Maya is found (by the unconvincing intervention of a very bad but very efficient character whom we have met and feared earlier), they are swept back into their familial maelstrom, joyfully abandoning all lessons learnt, in favour of the compelling present and the definition which parenthood bestows on them. The story's ending is open, but tiresome Maya is already makng a telephone call which will lead to a lot more trouble.

London introduces a vivid range of characters and treats every one, no matter how minor, with detailed respect, sympathy and never condescension. These are people one wants to go on knowing, in places one wants to revisit. The narrative focus shifts from person to person and is studded with sharp and eccentric observation. Jacob's penchant for feeling like a character in a film strengthens him when he elopes dangerously with Toni. Road movies always come out right. 'We're not parents like your parents,' he says later. 'From the start this was an article of faith between them.' But also from Maya's birth, Toni has been aware of tension, 'Your girl child, your stony watchdog.' Not many authors have treated the excruciating pain which children, often randomly and equally often with deadly intent, inflict on their parents.

Most marvellous, in a book crammed with delights, is London's descriptive writing: 'The old-fashioned chortling of magpies in an empty playground' or this, of convent girls at prayer, 'The clap of their skirts, as they fell to their knees, like birds landing.' She writes often of birds, one way or another, flying about gorgeously presented landscapes. Her prose here is sumptuous, beautifully balanced with the controlled spare elegance of her narrative voice. The final message, if you can call it that, is bleak. Love won't make you a good parent. You can't be a good parent, but you might try to be a good person, or you could try to disengage. Otherwise, you might aspire to be efficient.

Joan London is a writer hugely admired in her native Australia and in America, but despite having been long listed a few years ago for the Orange Prize with her novel *Gilgamesh*, she is scarcely known here. This splendid book deserves to be blazoned forth. We may not all be parents, but we are all elderly children.

COLLECTED STORIES
William Trevor (2010)

William Trevor's genius is to make the bleak alluring. His characters crowd one's memory in the manner of people one knows or used to know. With delicacy and consideration and gentleness, but no mercy, he presents portly murderers, weasly children, drunken priests, drunken couples, drunken farmers, and best of all drunken middle-aged women, who are often widows, svelte, and ready to scheme. Embittered unmarried sisters, some, but not all, on the way to sainthood, eke out life with their pale thin brothers in decrepit houses: 'he and his sister might alone have attended the mouldering of the place, urging it back to the clay.'

Arm in arm, death and decay stalk the draughty upstairs corridors. Bramble and nettle encroach from beyond the lake. Beloved dogs die; their graves are dug up by young unmarried mothers growing vegetables for the nuns. They chuck the bones about.

In the small towns of rural Ireland, where nothing much happens, everything really is happening, particularly love and desperate renunciation, and a great deal of drinking in the hotel bar, and weekly dances in the roadhouse Ballroom of Romance, where the hill farmers come down on bicycles to seek their brides; time passes, the maidens themselves grow on into early middle age, still unmarried. They accept at last that if they can't have love, the next best thing is a decent man. They too arrive on bicycles and when the lights go down in the

Ballroom, and they make their reluctant way home, the moon shines fondly over pairs of bikes propped against field gates.

It's not all poverty, but the owners of the big houses are equally unfortunate. They make small mistakes – Trevor's small mistakes are always life-changing small mistakes – they are misunderstood, find themselves shunned, or fearful for their lives. They may sell their estates to the wrong people, who in turn will be shunned for yet other reasons.

Enterprising children report the death of their teacher's mother; slyly explaining 'a man interfered with her.' They then pour concrete into their father's golf-bag. Another child dwells in happy familial innocence which is undermined by the sorrow of a noble old woman; the knowledge not of good but of cruelty is unwittingly imparted to the child. Circumstance sets it to work. Circumstances, small or large, usually small, activate the moral dilemmas at the core of Trevor's work. So often tragedy develops from the merest chance, acts and incidents of no significance. Two schoolboys meet in a boilerhouse to toast bread painfully and ineffectually on a length of wire thrust into the boiler's embers. A third boy joins them and they smoke a single thin cigar. The fates are listless, waiting. Randomly but inexorably they seize this quiet hour and nurture it into long-drawn nightmare.

When happiness occurs it is fragile and short-lived. The afternoon radio, cups of tea, familiar china, a silver mustard pot lined with dark blue glass, domestic routines, are shored against ruin and chaos. I am sorry not to have encountered a Goblin Teasmaid here. I feel it is a particularly Trevorine device. Meanwhile, a car mechanic is substantiated by the contents of his father's garage shelves. The physical world, past and present, is most beautifully and sparely realised. Colours stand out, for they are seldom used. The concrete building which is the Ballroom of Romance is pink outside and blue within. You wouldn't forget that. Memory is hugely important. The past constantly informs and reforms the present. Memory flickers and focuses, sometimes on a single isolated image: 'Again the playing cards fall. Again he picks them up. She wins and then is happy, not knowing why.' She doesn't know because she has Alzheimer's. There are often surprises and clues in Trevor's stories – the heritage of the thrillers and detective stories that paradoxically nurtured his post-Jamesian art. Or there might be a whole episode, a parallel imagining of times gone. You might be married to a memory and the honouring of memory might be as strong as love. Or it might come and go through your life and wreck you with unresolved guilt.

Trevor presents these spare materials in fastidious prose, spiked by gorgeous contrasting rhythms, and patterns of speech intrinsically Irish. And he is extremely funny. Through the vast range of these stories, written over more than forty years, the narrative voice and eye remain constant. Almost uniquely in a great career, there are no youthful follies, perhaps because he started writing in what was then considered middle age. These two splendid volumes extend to nearly two thousand pages; by the time you have finished reading, you will be ready to start again. Thus out of sorrow cometh forth joy. Happy days.

THE ARABIAN NIGHTS: TALES OF 1001 NIGHTS
trs Malcolm C Lyons (2011)

In his witty essay on the translators of the *1001 Nights*, Borges celebrates a hostile dynasty, each scion striving to annihilate his predecessor. There are so many manuscripts to choose from, none definitive, representing a fantastical melange of tales preserved, embroidered, lost and re-invented by countless oral storytellers, Arabic, Persian, Indian – and French. Antoine Galland, the first European translator, in the 18th century, is thought to have created two of the most famous stories, *Aladdin* and *Ali Baba*, himself. J C Mardrus's French version of 1899 (meticulously translated into English by Powys Mathers in 1937) has been hugely criticised for its delightful additional details – a dish of rice cream comes from him 'powdered with sugar and cinnamon', while the Arabic 'girl' may become 'an enchanting child.' Why not? This is the tradition of the storyteller. A contemporary translator, Hussain Haddawy, recalls stories from his childhood in Baghdad: 'as the embers glowed in the dim light . . . she would spin the yarn leisurely, amplifying here and interpolating there, episodes I recognised from other stories.' So it goes on. Everything is an aide-memoire for something else.

This new version of the *Nights* by Malcolm C Lyons is the first direct translation into English of the Calcutta II recension since Sir Richard Burton's famous 19th-century version. The three volumes bear introductions by Robert Irwin, who rises to Borges's prescription and does indeed cast scorn on earlier translations, though Lyons himself notes debts to Haddawy and to Enno Littmann, the German scholar derided by Borges for his literalism: 'Like Washington, he cannot tell a lie.'

If one were to find fault with Lyons's monumental achievement, it would be in the painstaking plainness of his diction. Like Haddawy, Lyons falls often into linguistic traps that are avoided by the exuberant Mardrus and Mathers. Instead of 'cripple' or 'lame' (traditional fairy tale adjectives), Haddawy writes 'paraplegic' while Lyons has 'semi-paralysed'. Lyons also consistently translates the common Arabic *zib* and *kis* as penis and vagina. The cumulative effect is clinical, jarringly out of place in the perfumed chambers and ghostly gardens of the *Nights*. In the tale of the second barber, a young man must gratify a drunken admirer. Mardrus/Mathers gets the right tone:

The old woman came up to him and said, 'Now you must run after the dear young lady and catch her. It is her custom, when heated by dance and wine, to undress naked and not to give herself to her lover until she has been able to examine his bare limbs, his rampant *zabb*, and the agility of his running. You must follow her from room to room, with your *zabb* in the ascendant, until you catch her. That is the only way she will be mounted.'

Lyons has

'Now,' said the old woman, 'you have achieved your goal. There will be no more blows and there is only one thing left. It is a habit of my mistress that, when she is drunk, she will not let anyone have her until she has stripped off her clothes, including her harem trousers, and is entirely naked. Then she will tell you to remove your own clothes and to start running, while she runs in front of you as though she was trying to escape from you. You must follow her from place to place, until you have an erection, and she will then let you take her.'

I don't want to seem sex-obsessed, no, no, not I, but in a mediaeval fairy tale, albeit for grown-ups, men do not have erections or even hard-ons; they have rampant (or even rampaging) *zabbs*. And to continue the theme, inevitable in this saga, in the story of a Prince 'Semi-Petrified' for Lyons, 'Ensorcelled' for Burton, a lover lamenting the unpunctuality of his mistress, says, according to Lyons, 'I will never again keep company with you or join my body to yours' but according to Burton, shouts 'nor will I glue my body to your body, and strum and belly-bump.' Which threat carries the more weight? Lyons mentions a ruined city 'echoing to the screech of owls and the cawing of crows'; fine enough, but for Burton it is a place where 'raven should croak and howlet hoot.' Divine. Unfortunately Burton also says things like 'verily this is a matter whereanent silence cannot be kept.' Verily, 'twas time for a new translation.

Yet the English reader may not be so badly served by the now-unfashionable Mardrus-Mathers version. Mathers is championed by the poet Tony Harrison, and Mardrus's admirers have included Gide, Proust, Borges, and James Joyce. As even their sternest critics admit, Mardrus and Mathers come closest to conveying the experience of a mediaeval Cairo storyteller, albeit at the cost of strict fidelity. Mardrus also dispenses with minor tales he finds dull, replacing them with others he likes better. A case in point is 'The Tale of the Sea Rose of the Girl of China,' remarkable for its transsexual subplot. Scholars universally accept the claim made by Mardrus's enemy, Victor

Chauvin, that Mardrus appropriated this tale from a Victorian source. But a little literary detective work on our part reveals that the source of this story is the Sanskrit *Mahabharata* which dates from more than a millennium before the earliest manuscript of the *Arabian Nights*. Who wins on pedigree?

Scholars object to Mardrus's adornment in passages such as the iconic first description of Scheherazade, where he adds an extra line of praise. Lyons here deletes a line which is considered by Haddawy, Burton and Payne, to be correct.

Two final quibbles with Lyons: the 'index' is an unalphabetised table of contents, provokingly placed at the back of the book, and page headers give the number rather than the name of the tale.

Despite these caveats, every aficionado will want to add Lyons to a rickety shelf which ideally will also contain Mardrus/Mathers, Haddawy, and the peerless *Arabian Nights Encyclopedia* by Ulrich Marzolph and Richard van Leeuwen, which is almost as much fun to dip into as the *Nights* themselves. Doughty Burton will serve to prop the whole thing up.